Charlemagne and his World

Charlemagne
and his World
by Friedrich Heer

B
C
c.1

Macmillan Publishing Co., Inc.
New York

Macmillan Publishing Co., Inc.
866 Third Avenue, New York, N.Y. 10022

Library of Congress Cataloging in Publication Data

Heer, Friedrich, 1916–
   Charlemagne and his world.

   Includes index.
   1. Charlemagne, 742–814. I. Title.
DC73.H35 1975   943'.01'0924 [B]   74–22219
ISBN 0–02–550450–9

First American Edition 1975

Printed in Great Britain

Frontispiece: Statue of Charlemagne at Müstair church.

Contents

Acknowledgements

Illustrations are reproduced by kind permission of the following:
A.C.L., Brussels 76–7; Alinari 66, 141, 145, 182, 242–3; Amiens Bibliothèque 197; Antivarisk-Topografiska Arkivet, Stockholm 174, 248, 252–3; Bibliothèque Municipale, Épernay 50, 51 top; Bibliothèque Municipale Valenciennes 186, 187; Bibliothèque Nationale 11, 17, 68–9, *82*, 122, 156, 158, 178, 179, 184–5, 199, 238, 245, *260*; Bibliothèque Royale, Brussels *84*; Bildarchiv Photo Marburg 19, 36–7, 42, 168, 173; Bildarchiv der Stadt Krefeld 33, 35, 40 top & left, 46; British Museum 235, 246; Bulloz 20, *28*, 45, 60–61; Caisse Nationale des Monuments Historiques, Paris 44, 90; Commune de Brescia 12–13; Douet d'Arcq, Paris 34; Dumbarton Oaks Collection, Washington 142–3; Paul Elek Ltd 101, 135, 164, 167; Foto Meyer 55; Françoise Foliot 15, 241, 251; Germanisches Nationalmuseum, Nuremberg *189*; Claus Hansmann 73, 118, 171; André Held 148; Kremsmünster, Austria *112*; Kunstgewerbemuseum Berlin 131; Kunsthistorisches Museum, Vienna 212; Laon Bibliothèque Municipale 194; Louvre *137*; Monza Cathedral Treasury 97; Anne Münchow 21, 31, *54*, 71, *81*, 104, *111*, 150, *163*, *190*, 200, 204, 208, 209, 210, *215*, *216*, 222–3; Museo Christiano 94; National Gallery 75; Nieder Österreich Landesmuseum 40 right & btm; Österreichische Nationalbibliothek 53, 176, 193, 257; Photo-Hachette 51 btm; Photographie Giraudon 25, 64, 93, *109*, *138*, 160–1, 240; Radio Times Hulton Picture Library 22; Rheinisches Landesmuseum, Bonn 58, 59, 72, 203; Royal Library Stockholm 110; Scala 26, 27, 56, 229, *230–1*, *258*, *259*; Schleswig-Holsteinisches Landesmuseum 120, 121; Service de Documentation Photographique 65, 220; Staatliche Museen zu Berlin 18; Stadtbildstelle, Aachen 8, 79; Stiftsbibliothek St Gallen 14, 48, 92, 177; Universitetets Oldsaksamling, Oslo 250; University Library, Leyden 86, 89; University Library, Utrecht 102, 126, 214.

Numbers in italics refer to colour illustrations.

Picture research by Sandra Bance.

I

Charles, King of the Franks

The name Charlemagne is a corruption of the Latin *Carolus Magnus* – Charles the Great. The title was given to Charles, king of the Franks, by the clerics of his entourage. It begins to appear in their letters and chronicles towards the latter part of his reign, when his rule extended throughout western Europe, from the North Sea to the Mediterranean, from the Ebro to the Danube. As Charlemagne he became, during the middle ages, a fabulous symbol of kingship and chivalry. More poems were written about him than any other king, except the somewhat less historical Arthur.

There can be no doubt of his claim to greatness. It is impossible to imagine what European history would have been like without his campaigns, his diplomacy and his imagination – he shaped its course for a thousand years. It is a mark of his historical importance that he is a national hero of both France and Germany; a unique achievement.

In fact, Charlemagne was neither a Frenchman nor a German. Nor, despite his revival of the Roman empire in the west and his Latin culture, was he a Roman. He was a Frank, and his history begins with theirs.

The Franks were a branch of the great Germanic tribes which in several centuries of migration spread all over Europe from their original home in the Danish peninsula, southern Sweden, Jutland and the Baltic coast. Descendants of the Germanic peoples form the bulk of the population in the Low Countries, Scandinavia and Britain, as well as in the German-speaking countries. At various times Germanic groups also ruled France, Spain, Italy, the North African littoral and even parts of Greece and the Holy Land.

Germanic expansion to the south and west was halted for a while after they came into contact with the Romans in the first century AD. Several of Caesar's campaigns were fought against the Germanic tribes, but the Romans soon gave up any serious thought of subduing them, and for two centuries were content to contain them beyond the Rhine and Danube frontiers. There was trade across the border, and the Romans took to recruiting many of their legionaries from the tribes of the Rhineland.

During the third century AD, conflict and pressure on the frontier of the

Opposite: Charlemagne with one of his sons and a scribe from Lupus of Fulda's *Leges Barborum*, a tenth-century copy of a Carolingian original. (Archivo Capitolare, Cod.0.1.2 f 154.)

empire were renewed. The Germanic peoples were being harassed in the rear by nomadic horsemen of Tartar stock moving in from the steppes, and the prosperity of the Roman empire was in decline, making it more difficult to finance the army and civil service. The army was no longer the well-drilled mobile body of citizens that it had been under the republic and the early empire, but had declined into a stationary frontier guard, growing cabbages and collecting customs dues. It was incapable of coping with the light cavalry tactics that the Germanic tribes had borrowed from the Tartars, and the barbarians were able to break through and devastate large areas of the empire, particularly in the western provinces.

Eventually they were held at bay. Extensive reforms of the army and government system followed, and oppressive civil measures were taken to finance them. The most important administrative reform was the founding of a 'new Rome' at Byzantium as the capital of an effectively separate eastern empire. For defence the Romans came to rely on 'federates', barbarian troops commanded by their own chieftains. This was partly owing to the difficulties of recruitment within the empire, and also because of the complete failure of the legions to adapt to the use of the horse in warfare. These measures propped up the empire until the end of the fourth century when under renewed pressure from the steppes the Germanic tribes began to move again.

It was at this time that the Franks first rose to prominence. One branch had managed to establish itself inside the frontier of the empire, in what is now Belgium, and had obtained grudging recognition from the Romans. Its war-bands served as Roman federates. After the sack of Rome in 410, when the western empire was abandoned by Byzantium and the outlying provinces left to their fate, the Franks continued to act as federates of the patricians and bishops of mixed Roman and Celtic stock who tried to organise local defence in the province of Gaul. In 451 Merovech, the king of one branch of the Franks, led his warriors to the aid of the Gallo-Romans when an attack by Attila the Hun – which in the end did not materialise – was feared.

In 481 Merovech's fifteen-year-old grandson Clovis succeeded his father, and immediately launched an attack on Gaul. He defeated the militias of the Gallo-Roman cities one by one, suppressed his rivals among the Franks and drove off other groups of Germans who tried to get a share of the plunder. By 496 he ruled the heartland of France, dominating the valleys of the Loire and the Seine from Orleans and Paris. His kingdom extended southwards to the borders of the Visigothic kingdom with its capital at Toulouse, and in the east it included the valleys of the Rhine and the Main. Some time after 493 he was baptised a Christian. His conversion was greeted enthusiastically by the defeated Gallo-Romans, and the fact that he had adopted Catholicism made him more acceptable in the south than the Visigoths, who were Arian heretics. With the help of the Burgundians he defeated the Visigoths and incorporated the lion's share of their kingdom into his own.

Clovis's conquests established the kingdom of the Franks, and his sons and

Two sides of a Merovingian coin probably from the reign of Clovis III (691–5). The coin is gold-plated, an example of the debased coinage of the late Merovingian kings. The obverse reads EBORINO MON – the name of the coiner; the reverse CHLOVODIO RIX.

grandsons completed his work. For convenience we shall call this kingdom France, although its boundaries were not those of the modern state. On Charlemagne's accession Brittany and the south-western districts, between the Garonne and the Pyrenees, were effectively independent; to compensate for this his kingdom included most of modern Belgium, much of Holland, and several provinces of central Germany – Hesse, Franconia and Thuringia. ('Franconia,' 'France' and 'Frank' all have the same etymology.) Several peripheral areas which at one time or another acknowledged Frankish rule, such as Bavaria, had again become independent. In the north-east and the east, along and beyond the Rhine, the inhabitants spoke an early form of German; in most of the country the movement of population had not been large enough to displace the *rustica romana lingua*, a colloquial Latin in the process of developing into old French, as the common tongue. Apart from a small ruling class of nobles, the south was hardly touched by Frankish settlers.

Clovis's successors, the Merovingian dynasty, elevated his grandfather Merovech to the dignity of a sea-god and claimed divine descent. They did not seem to find this piece of superstition incompatible with their newly-acquired Christianity. This is typical of the social history of the Merovingian kingdom, which is really the story of how the two civilisations, the Gallo-Roman and the Germanic, blended and fused. The Romanised element slowly lost its importance, partly for economic reasons, and by Charlemagne's time it is not even identifiable as a consciously separate section of the population. Urban life disappeared; classical Latin learning and even basic literacy were confined to a small group in the church. Some elements of Roman law were preserved, particularly in the common law of the church, but most of the population lived by a largely unwritten Germanic customary code. These customs were based on a tariff of compensation for wrongs done; they dealt in terms of disputes

between individuals rather than criminal offences to be suppressed by the power of the state. Deadly blood-feuds were still common, although the church encouraged the practice of accepting *wergeld*, money compensation, in its place.

The political history of the Merovingian period hardly deserves the adjective. It is a continual succession of murders, cruelty, deceit, treachery, usurpations, accusations of witchcraft, kidnappings of child rulers, war between brothers and disunity. Much of the trouble came from the Frankish custom of dividing an inheritance between all the heirs. The kings considered the kingdom their private property, and divided it between their sons in the same way. These divisions led to almost continuous civil war for two centuries, during which the kingdom was only twice united – and then briefly.

Gradually the peripheral areas conquered by Clovis's heirs fell away, and four main sub-kingdoms grew up within France. Neustria was ruled from

A fragment of Merovingian stonework, a peacock carved in a style similar to the Byzantine, from San Salvatore, Brescia.

An ox-cart, the traditional vehicle of the Merovingian kings, from a miniature in Folchard's Psalter of the ninth century. (Stiftsbibliothek St Gallen, Cod. 23 p. 12.)

Paris or Orleans, Austrasia from Cologne or Metz; Burgundy stretched from Alsace to Provence, and Aquitaine was all the region south of the Loire. The authority of the kings was steadily weakened and government passed into the hands of the nobles. In Austrasia, Neustria and Burgundy they ruled through an institution known as the palace; this had originally been the king's household but had developed into a permanent organ of government, which maintained continuity in an interregnum. In Austrasia and Neustria an official known as the mayor of the palace came to be paramount among the ruling nobles. Originally, the mayor of the palace had been a sort of royal authenticating officer, or chancellor; royal edicts were not valid unless confirmed by the mayor's signature. In a society which had an almost superstitious regard for correct form, it was not difficult to convert this key symbolic role into one of real power. The mayors became the king's deputies, almost prime ministers, and the leaders of the army; before long they were kings in all but name and legitimacy. The last Merovingians were their puppets, the *rois fainéants* (do-nothing kings). Einhard, a cleric who spent many years at Charlemagne's court, describes them contemptuously.

Nothing remained to the king, but to sit unshaven on his throne, satisfied with the mere name of king and playing the role of ruler, listening to ambassadors from all over the world and answering them with words he had been taught or ordered to speak as though by his own authority. ... Wherever he travelled he went in an ox-cart driven peasant-fashion by a cowherd.

Opposite: The semi-barbarous Latin of the Merovingian period written by Gregory of Tours in *Historia Francorum*, an early-eighth-century manuscript from Luxeuil in eastern France. The decoration consists only of zoomorphic initials. (Bibliothèque Nationale, Lat. 17655, f 41.)

Hoc faciente unum huius commemorat. XXIIII. Cum iam septimus
annus esset quod universa regio responsa dare haberet. & eo tempore pro eodem
ymagine pauculi & coniunctae fratris congregabantur & scandalizabantur quia respon-
sum sumer in queret. Dum commorat de sacra vehicula de aqua pauculum filium haberet theodobaldum nomine. cum sibi eam duxit uxorem. Qui in multos de tempora
haeret de functa illa adeam accipi ut sum tamen de eam multis non habuit qui
in Childebertus autem et Theodobertus commoventes
exercitum contra chlotacharium rex disponunt. Ille autem his auditis
cum parvis hominibus se agere non sustinet. In silva confugit & confidens in
Dei misericordia. Coram quo iple totam indi pietadem et verti fundit. Sed & chlotechilde
dirigit nuncios & audiens beatum Martinum sepulchrum ibi que noctione prosternitur &
totam noctem in vigilia. Qui sine ipse super bellum huius consurgeret. Cum quem in
ad modum cum exercitu uesser cum obsedendi et tantas illam dei et eludendi in pagensis
uis hi facto in locum deferendam regis ut eandem capta tenuerunt. ut domno impie
et cuncta subiecta. In impetu aquae huius grave imono duri uel ut lapidibus super eos descendere
ipsi quos super pars eorum grandine humum in facie prosternere & a lapidibus de coelis huc
grandine perterruntur? Nullum enim erat argumentum uel his gerere nisi parum cum annum.
Hoc magis me eadem hac ira ad quibus cessabatur in manus eius. Sed & quid erat eorum
ita de super uernat uel uix in unus si magis quam uel de parum ter foedis multae enim et erat per
se non fundi nuberit. Tunc illi a lapidibus uel de exanimati. & nimis prostrati perterriti etiam
habent ut ueniam petebantur dum quo vita contra pater genitorum eius eius uerba rebellandi.
Super chlotacharium uel rex nam quia uersa quid amplius gereret accedit dei eam ad eos quis
committit eorum et plaudens. Sed cum nullo ullis uel eo nullo loco reuersam. Huius dum
miseris nuncios ad eum pacem et concordiam petierunt. Quae agerem ut prospera sunt
regressi. Quod nullus ubi grate hanc prostrauerunt uigore beatum Martini reuersus uenit.
Post childebertus rex in Hispaniis abiit quum ingressus
cum chlotachario de sacra uirgine tam luctum infatum et exiit quae uallan uel rex
obsidit.

In fact Einhard's sneers about beards and ox-carts miss the point that these were the symbolic trappings of a kingship which had originally been semi-religious. The mayors carefully cultivated an atmosphere of superstitious reverence around the kings to bolster their own power.

Charlemagne was descended from Pepin of Landen, one of the first mayors who comes to our notice as wielding considerable personal power, and from Pepin's political crony, bishop Arnulf of Metz. Their line was known as the Arnulfings but from the date they acquired legitimate title to the throne, historians refer to them as the Carolingians, after Charlemagne himself.

Pepin of Landen was succeeded as mayor of the Austrasian palace by his son Grimoald, but a few more generations passed before the Arnulfings firmly established themselves as a ruling dynasty. During the disorder of the Merovingian period, the nobles had become too turbulent to be easily cowed. Grimoald overreached himself; he attempted to make his son king by getting his tame Merovingian lord to adopt the boy, then declared him king on the puppet's death. This was too much for the nobles. Grimoald was deposed and died in a Neustrian prison. The Arnulfings disappeared for a while from the political scene, until the Austrasians, frightened of the growing power and ambition of Ebroin, the mayor of Neustria, supported Pepin of Landen's grandson, Pepin of Heristal, in making himself mayor. Pepin of Heristal was probably implicated in the disappearance of the previous mayor and the murder of the reigning Merovingian. After Ebroin was murdered by a slave with a grudge, Pepin defeated the Neustrians in battle. He crushed Neustria as an independent state by confiscating the lands of the great Neustrian magnates and rewarding his own followers with them, and by putting forward his own candidate as mayor of the Neustrian palace. He then turned his attention to several successful campaigns on the long-neglected frontiers.

His legitimate sons died before him and on his death his achievements were nearly swept away in renewed civil strife. It seemed for a few months that the Neustrians would retrieve their independence and the Arnulfings would be swept away. Pepin's widow Plectrude attempted to rule as regent for her grandsons, but the Austrasian nobles had endured too many regencies and minorities during the Merovingian civil wars and would not tolerate another. Fortunately for the Arnulfing line, Pepin had sired a capable and energetic bastard, Charles, by an Austrasian noblewoman. Charles escaped from confinement, secretly collected an army in the Ardennes, rallied his countrymen, smashed the Neustrians in battle, and by his victory established his right to succeed his father.

When Charles seized power, France was in a state of virtual anarchy, and external enemies were pressing hard, particularly various heathen Germanic peoples on the eastern frontier and the Saracens from Spain. By ruthlessness to rebels and those who were reluctant to contribute to the cost of campaigns, Charles overcame these dangers. The crowning achievement of his rule was the defeat of the Saracens at the battle of Poitiers. This victory proved to be

Opposite: The Crucifixion illuminated in a Merovingian manuscript, the Sacramentary of Gellone. (Bibliothèque Nationale, Lat. 12048 f 143 v.) Figural decorations are rare in Merovingian illuminations. A sacramentary is the service book containing the bishop's part of the mass.

Two sides of a denier
from the reign of King
Pepin, father of
Charlemagne.

the high-water mark of the Saracen attempts to expand into Europe from their
Spanish base, and earned Charles his surname of Martel (the hammer).

On his death in 741, Martel divided the kingdom in the traditional Frankish
way between his two sons, Carloman, and yet another Pepin, surnamed the
Short. (Pepin the Short was Charlemagne's father.) The brothers got on well,
and continued Martel's vigorous campaigning policy, leading joint expeditions against their enemies. In their most important campaigns they subdued
Aquitaine and Bavaria and they also mounted punitive expeditions in
Germany. This cooperation continued until 747 when Carloman decided to
enter a monastery and Pepin took over his share of the kingdom.

The Arnulfings now ruled a united France and had managed to hand on
power through three successive generations. They were the hereditary rulers
of the most powerful Germanic kingdom in Europe. The only attributes of
kingship they did not possess were the title and legitimacy. For a few years at
the end of his reign Martel had ruled without a Merovingian king as figure-
head. In 751 Pepin took the final, momentous step in the consolidation of
Arnulfing power. At a ceremony in the great abbey of St Denis he was crowned
king by Boniface, the Anglo-Saxon bishop who was leading the missionary
effort in Saxony.

The Merovingians had been a royal clan rather than a family. Membership
of the clan was the necessary condition for succession to the throne, and the
nobles were theoretically free to elect as king any prince of the blood. The
ceremony in which they proclaimed their choice by raising the new king on
the shield shows the origins of the Merovingians as war leaders. Pepin could –
and did – have himself elevated on the shield but blood charisma is by definition not something one can acquire without being born to it. However if he
could find a greater charisma with which to authenticate the assumption of
the royal title, his sons could succeed him as legitimate kings.

The church solved the problem for him. In 750 Pepin sent a Frankish abbot
to Pope Zacharias to ask whether it was right that the title of king should be
held by the ineffectual Merovingians. Zacharias replied that the title should go
with the power and the responsibility. At Pepin's coronation he was anointed
with holy oil, which was actually reserved for the sacraments of baptism and
ordination. This implied divine sanction for Pepin's assumption of the royal
title, a claim which clearly pre-empted that of blood and had an obvious
symbolic value which mere papal approval did not. It evoked all the biblical
taboos about raising one's hand against the Lord's anointed.

In 754 Zacharias's successor, Pope Stephen III, crossed the Alps to meet
Pepin. On his arrival at the royal villa of Pontion, Pepin walked in front of the
pope leading his horse by the bridle, a gesture of exceptional respect. It echoes
the gesture attributed to the Emperor Constantine in the *Donation of Constantine*, a forgery concocted in the papal writing office at about the time of these
events. Throughout the middle ages it was widely accepted as genuine, and was
an imaginative piece of propaganda for two important papal claims. The

document describes Constantine's conversion by Pope Sylvester – a mis-attribution – and describes him – spuriously – giving the pope temporal authority over the whole of Italy and a looser general supervision of all the territories of the western empire. In token of the extent of this gift of power, Constantine is alleged to have done exactly as Pepin did. Whether Pepin's gesture inspired the forgery or vice versa we shall never be certain, but it undoubtedly gave currency to the ideas of the *Donation*: that the papacy was the legitimate heir to the Roman empire in the Italian peninsula, and that as primate of the church the pope had some sort of authority over all Christian kings.

Stephen also wanted Pepin's help against the Lombard kingdom of northern Italy, whose armies were pressing on the duchy of Rome, the small area of Italy that the pope did rule. At another great ceremony in St Denis he repeated Pepin's coronation, anointed his sons as kings as well, and conferred on all three the title of 'Patrician of the Romans', which implied a duty to protect the Holy See. Pepin soon led an expedition to Italy, defeated the pope's enemies, and handed over to him the keys of several cities he had forced the Lombards to give up. In this way two parallel Carolingian traditions of policy began: of close relations with the papacy, and readiness to intervene in Lombardy. Both were to be enormously important for Charlemagne.

Charlemagne's life is very well documented compared with those of other contemporary kings. This is largely due to his own efforts; he did a great deal

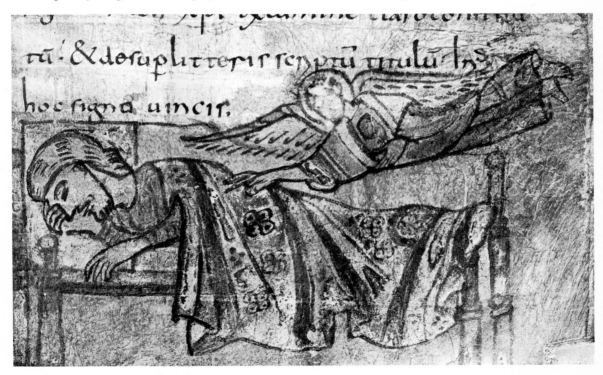

The dream of the Emperor Constantine from a ninth-century manuscript (Staatsbibliothek, Munich). Pepin's gesture of respect in leading the pope's horse may have inspired or been inspired by the forged *Donation of Constantine* made about the same time.

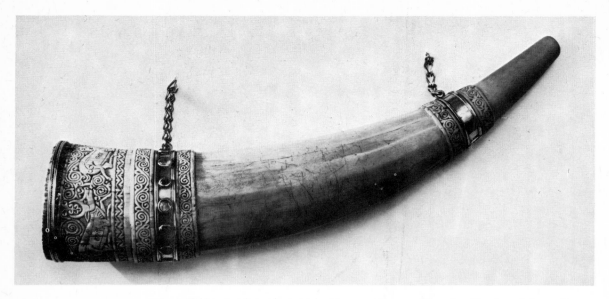

A beautiful hunting horn decorated with carved ivory and jewels, said to have belonged to Charlemagne. The king excelled at riding and hunting.

to encourage literacy in his dominions, and liked to have intelligent, literate men about him. This makes it all the more odd that the sources are reticent about his early years. His biographer, the cleric and courtier Einhard, disclaims all knowledge of his birth and infancy, although he was quite close to Charlemagne, and in a good position to make enquiries of the older men at court. It is probable that he knew the facts perfectly well, and was simply suppressing them; in all likelihood Charlemagne was born illegitimate.

As far as can be deduced, Pepin married Bertrada, Charles's mother, the daughter of a Frankish count, somewhere between 744 and 749. Charlemagne was probably born at least two years before the wedding and his brother Carloman a couple of years after it. Bastardy was not necessarily shameful for a Frank, and as Charlemagne's parents later married one would have expected Charlemagne to be treated as legitimate. However Carloman does seem to have been treated as *more* legitimate; he received the better portion of the kingdom on Pepin's death. The brothers disliked each other heartily.

Bertrada was famous for her piety and brought her sons up to be devout. Pepin had them trained to rule. In those days authority was so personal that to rule at all a king had to excel in all the skills that his vassals prized. These were first of all physical, the arts of the chase and of war. In his early years Charlemagne developed the strength in back and shoulders that enabled him to swing the long, heavy Frankish sword, or to impale a charging boar; and he acquired the skill in horsemanship that he needed to ride hundreds of miles every summer on campaign, hundreds more in the winter visiting different

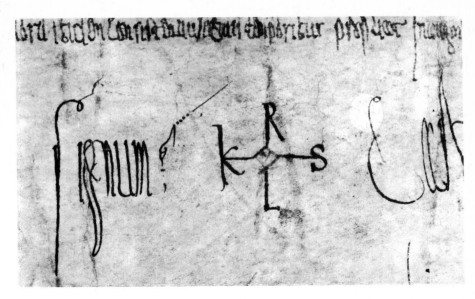

The monogram of Charlemagne from the document which appears on page 28. He only made the strokes in the centre as he could write very little.

parts of the empire, and to outride most of his courtiers every afternoon in the hunt.

The academic side of his education was not neglected either. The brothers' native tongue was the popular Latin, but Charles also knew German and spoke and read classical Latin, the language of administration and the church. As a mature man he learnt Greek and studied the Latin classics. He never learnt to write very well, although he had a tablet which he would often produce in an idle moment, to practise forming his letters. He knew enough arithmetic to reckon up accounts if necessary, which was as rare a skill as literacy, and he developed this interest in later life as well: astronomy came to fascinate him, and he would make involved calculations of the course of the stars.

Pepin also made sure that both brothers were thoroughly acquainted with the practical business of ruling. As soon as Charlemagne was old enough, he stood behind his father to hear him dispense justice. He fought in several of Pepin's wars in Aquitaine, and must have learnt something about diplomacy from the meetings between his father and Pope Stephen, at which he was certainly present. In 764 Pepin made both sons responsible for the administration of a group of counties.

There are a few portraits of Charlemagne which may be contemporary, although the famous equestrian statue in the Louvre is certainly not. None of the representations are meant to be naturalistic, but are more concerned with depicting the symbols of kingship. On his own seals, Charlemagne used cameos of various Roman emperors – the particular likeness was of no

importance. Consequently we have to rely on Einhard's description for an idea of Charlemagne's physical appearance.

Bodily Charles was well-built, strong and noble in height, measuring seven times his own foot. His head was round, his eye large and lively, his nose a little larger than the mean, his hair in his later years a brilliant white, his expression calm and cheerful, his bearing full of majesty, his tread firm, his carriage erect, his voice high, but not as powerful as his robust body would suggest. His clothes were Frankish; only very rarely and only in Rome did he dress in the Roman fashion. His constant companion was his long sword, with golden hilt and hangings.

Altogether he must have been an imposing figure. When the site of his grave was dug and his body exhumed, the archaeologists confirmed Einhard's estimate: Charlemagne had been 6 ft $3\frac{1}{2}$ in tall, which would have made him a good head taller than most Franks. The high voice was considered musical.

Charlemagne was moderate in eating and drinking. He liked to have a book read during meals, some 'diverting or instructive tale' or perhaps a work of theology such as St Augustine's *City of God*. The only time he would drink at all heavily was at the open-air meals that followed the hunt. Charlemagne got his exercise by riding, swimming and hunting and was particularly fond of the chase. He was also very fond of the court ladies, and it is said that only one unmarried woman at his court ever refused him. He had at least four legal wives; the difficulty over the exact number concerns whether he married the Frankish noblewoman who gave him his first son, Pepin (known as the Hunchback). Even if he did, he repudiated her fairly lightly to make a political marriage with Desideria, the daughter of the king of Lombardy, and did not return to her when he proceeded to repudiate Desideria in the following year. Pepin the Hunchback was well treated and often lived at court, but there was no chance of his being given any sort of authority; the Franks had a horror of physical deformity.

In the year he repudiated Desideria, Charlemagne married Hildegard, a daughter of the ducal house of the Alemans. She gave him his legitimate sons, Charles, Louis the Pious (whose twin, Lothar, died young) and Pepin. She died in 783, and the next year he married Fastrada, who was his queen until her death in 794; in the same year he married Liutgard, another Alemannian noblewoman. After her death in 800 he did not remarry, although he had four recognised mistresses, three of whom gave him children. Liutgard seems to have been his favourite wife, although Hildegard made more of an impression on his subjects and was widely mourned. Fastrada, according to gossip, was bad tempered.

Charlemagne always claimed it was his great affection for his daughters that stopped him letting them marry and leave the court. In fact it was probably his reluctance to start carving up his empire to provide dowries. There were not, in any case, many rulers left in Europe with whom it would have been worth making a diplomatic marriage: Charlemagne had conquered most of them.

Opposite: Charlemagne with a wife, from a manuscript written between 817 and 823 and preserved at the monastery of St Paul in Carinthia. The Emperor is portrayed in the simple Frankish costume which he preferred to wear.

There was talk of a Byzantine marriage and one of the princesses began to study Greek, but relations cooled and the match was called off. To make up for this Charlemagne encouraged his daughters in their affairs, which were notorious. He allowed one of them to set up house with her lover at Aix.

Pepin died in 768 at St Denis. In the Frankish tradition, his kingdom was divided between Charlemagne and Carloman. The partition followed no precedent. Carloman received a solid block of the central lands and most of the more important towns, including Paris and Orleans; Charlemagne had a great crescent of territory around Carloman's, including most of the rebellious or frontier districts. Pepin may have been indulging a preference for Carloman by this division; he may have wanted to ensure that Charlemagne, more experienced in battle, was given the lands that would be at risk; or he may in fact have been trying to lessen the risk of civil war by splitting all the important parts of the kingdom, such as Neustria, Austrasia and Aquitaine, between the two brothers to make it difficult for them to build up regional followings.

Civil war very nearly did break out in the year after Pepin's death, when the brothers went to put down a rebellion in Aquitaine. They quarrelled, and Carloman led his army home without striking a blow, leaving Charlemagne to subdue the rebels single-handed. Bertrada managed to persuade them to follow a common policy, which unfortunately was not a very constructive one. She imagined that it would be possible to be on good terms with the Lombards and the papacy simultaneously, and arranged the marriage with Desideria with this in mind. Events soon proved her wrong. The situation in Italy grew worse: Charlemagne supported the pope and Carloman the Lombards. Before an open breach could result, Carloman died. Charlemagne annexed Carloman's kingdom, repudiated Desideria, and prepared to honour the implications of his title of 'Patrician of the Romans'. The acquisition of Carloman's kingdom gave him a common frontier with the Lombards, from which he could launch the first of the major campaigns that dominated his reign. He never took Bertrada's advice on policy again.

Right: St Luke with his symbol, the ox, from the Gospel Book of Gundohinus. This book, completed by the scribe Gundohinus in 754, the third year of the reign of King Pepin, marked the beginning of Carolingian book painting. It was modelled on the art of northern Italy, and nothing like it had appeared before north of the Alps. (Bibliothèque Municipale, Autun, MS 3.)

Overleaf: Two frescoes which appear between the niches on the east wall of the oratory of San Benedetto, Malles, in the Italian Tyrol. On the left is a warrior nobleman, probably a donor to the monastery. On the right is a priestly figure bearing a model of a church. He may have been the donor abbot of the oratory but it has also been suggested that the figure represents St Benedict with a model of his monastery at Monte Cassino. The oratory dates from the early ninth century.

2
The Rule of the Nobles

All power in the Frankish kingdom was exercised by the king and the nobles. There were no other contenders for authority – no merchant class, no civil service, no standing army. The popular, collective institutions of the German-speaking part of the population had lost their vitality in the period of conquest and migration and the prolonged civil strife that followed. Even the church was not independent or international enough to have any real political weight.

The distribution of power between the monarchy and the nobility was complicated. Sometimes historians write as if the relationship of the two classes was one of constant opposition, a continuous struggle for supremacy, and there is a certain amount of truth in that. During the Merovingian disorders, the nobles seized every opportunity of limiting the royal power. Almost every peace settlement included legal or political concessions to them; they preserved separate palaces in Austrasia, Neustria and Burgundy even when a single king ruled France; and frequently they managed to keep as hereditary possessions the estates that the king gave them for a lifetime as the reward of office. It was not until Pepin of Heristal crushed the Neustrian magnates that France was united and the Arnulfings firmly established. Yet if we compare Pepin's career with that of his enemy Ebroin, the mayor of the Neustrian palace, the key element of Pepin's success soon becomes apparent. Ebroin wasted his strength in a struggle with the nobles; Pepin came to power and defeated Neustria with his nobles' support.

Theoretically the power of the Frankish kings – or under the later Merovingians that of the mayors of the palace who ruled in their name – was absolute. The Frankish monarchy has been neatly described as despotism tempered by religion and the fear of assassination. And in the sense that the king in his own right decided policy, decreed the law, did justice and made war or peace, it *was* absolute power. The concept of government being limited by law had disappeared with the Roman empire. A similar idea, that of the Christian empire, in which the duties of a ruler are prescribed by religion, became common in Charlemagne's reign. It affected his policy, but not his authority; with a nice combination of piety and political acumen, Charlemagne accepted the

Opposite: A document of 774 in which Charlemagne gives the forest of Kinsheim to the priory of Val de Liepure. Charlemagne's monogram can be seen in the centre above the last line.

idea but reserved to himself the responsibility of defining its precise theological implications!

In practice, the most important limit on royal despotism was that it could only be exercised through the agency of the nobles. Charlemagne, no less than his predecessors, depended on the high Frankish nobility to raise and lead his armies, to collect revenues, to maintain justice, to keep a semblance of order in the countryside and to provide most of the officers of his own household. The nobles had their independent power base in the ownership of land, but as a class their real strength lay in the monopoly they had established of the most powerful positions in the king's gift. The Frankish nobles were in fact a nobility of service. It was the king's service itself which conferred noble status (trebling a man's wergeld). The dynamic aspect of the power of the nobles, which allowed them to consolidate and strengthen the whole, was the authority they exercised in the king's name.

The annals and chronicles of the time show how closely the administration of the kingdom was identified with the nobility. The annual meeting of the nobles at court, which was where the king's edicts were promulgated, is referred to indifferently in contemporary records as the assembly or the 'full palace'. The same records reveal that Charlemagne's high officers came from a restricted group, which in its composition shows the continuity of Charlemagne's power with the original home of the Arnulfing dynasty in Austrasia. Of 110 men identified as having an important role in government under Charlemagne and his successor Louis the Pious, seventy were Austrasians: no less than fifty-two of these were related to the royal family. Carolingian France was ruled by a few dozen, mostly intermarried, great families.

Charlemagne's government machine was rudimentary; France cannot really be called a state at this period. It seems that even the concept of the state had been forgotten: the appropriate Latin term, *res publica*, does not occur in the contemporary documents. (Byzantium and the territories of the Caliph of Baghdad deserve the name, but the Franks knew those countries largely by repute.) The organ of central government was the palace, essentially the Merovingian institution but modified in some important respects by Charlemagne. The countryside was ruled through the system of counts and counties.

Charlemagne's palace was his court, not a building. During most of his reign it was itinerant, following him as he travelled through his empire. When he grew older, and his sons could act as his lieutenants, he tended to spend more time at the great palace (in the modern sense) that he had built himself at Aix. The palace mingled domestic and governmental functions – they were hardly distinguished – in an engaging way. Clerical dignitaries and the great nobles rubbed shoulders with court poets, royal mistresses and bastards, 'the hedge-warden, the houndsmen, the beaver-wardens . . . the porter and the paymaster', and rode beside them when the palace travelled from one royal villa to another.

Policy was made by Charlemagne, in council. There was a fixed list of

Opposite: A Byzantine cross designed to hang round the neck. It is said to have been Charlemagne's and comes from the Aachen Cathedral treasury.

members, who were both clerical and lay; they included officers and priests of the household as well as important men who were not resident at the palace, counts and other great vassals, bishops and abbots. Wherever he went, Charlemagne was accompanied by at least three of his councillors. Members attended a particular meeting strictly at Charlemagne's bidding, and the choice of councillors summoned would depend on proximity, special knowledge, and so on. Charlemagne always presided, and kept the council firmly under his control. It met when he called it, and discussed the subjects he put forward. However he was too intelligent not to realise the value of allowing criticism. Alcuin, the Anglo-Saxon cleric who was as close to Charlemagne as anyone at his court, consistently opposed him over several important matters, such as taking the title of emperor and the forcible conversions in Saxony, without losing Charlemagne's friendship or esteem. On the Saxon question Alcuin eventually saw his own views adopted.

The most detailed description that we have of the other departments of the palace and their functions comes from what is really a training manual for kings, written for one of Charlemagne's successors. The treatise was written seventy years after Charlemagne's death, and its author obviously saw Charlemagne's reign as a golden age; he sometimes exaggerates the degree of organisation in the palace in order to make propaganda for good administration. However the main outlines that it gives are confirmed by references in other documents, and we can distinguish several main groups of officers and their functions.

Charlemagne's palace did not have a flexible revenue in the way that a modern state does, but neither did it have any real recurring administrative expenses. There was no distinction between Charlemagne's personal income and public revenue, or between public and private expenditure. Taxation did not contribute a very great part of revenue, due to the decline in commerce and the shortage of coined money in circulation. Some of the old Roman tolls and customs duties were still collected, and there are references to the *cens*, a direct tax on land and goods. The proceeds of justice also came to the king. Offences against the royal *ban* (which translates as either 'word' or 'power') were punished by fines, which belonged entirely to the king, and he also received one third of any compensation paid to injured parties or their kin, and took over the estates of landholders dispossessed for treason or rebellion. Taxes and the tariff of wergeld were both calculated in terms of money, but payment was more often than not made in kind. The main royal income was from the king's own lands. Research has shown that these estates were very often identical with the Roman imperial estates in Gaul, and had been in the ruler's possession right through the Merovingian period. It has also shown that a great many of these estates ended up as the property of monasteries, a tendency that Charlemagne tried to reverse, although he too made a number of grants to religious houses. Several sources of income were connected with war: plunder, and tribute from defeated peoples; diplomatic presents, which were really bribes, and the annual 'gifts', really compulsory, from churches and landowners, which seem to have developed from the Frankish freemen's responsibility for supplying the army.

Unlike the Romans and the early Merovingians, Charlemagne did not pay money salaries. All the king's household servants were fed at his table, and their clothing was given them from his storehouses. The more important officers also had prebends, fixed claims on the produce of particular estates. Some nobles were also rewarded with a benefice, the life tenancy of a royal estate. Charlemagne's conquests brought him new estates which could be used for this purpose, thus avoiding the diminution in the royal lands that the Merovingians had often suffered from because of their inability to recover a benefice from the holder's kin on his death. Clerics in the king's service were often rewarded with an ecclesiastical living, another economy measure. There were no public costs; counts or palace officers requisitioned materials and

A ring found in the grave of a Frankish noble.

demanded labour services for public works like bridges, fortifications and the royal palaces. The army was raised and provisioned through a similar general obligation to serve or provide supplies. Government expenditure, then, was very limited; money was needed for diplomatic presents, to buy arms and horses for the household and to make gifts to servants, and for some of the expenses of the king's envoys, but for little else. Most of Charlemagne's expenditures were met from the royal estates.

Many of the people who carried out the administrative services of Charlemagne's palace were clerics, belonging to the body known as the king's chapel. The word 'chapel' had not yet come to refer to a building; in fact it is derived from one of the duties of the clerics of Charlemagne's court, which was to guard and venerate the royal collection of holy relics. These included the legendary cape (*capella*) of St Martin, the patron saint of the Franks, which he had cut in half to give to a beggar. Gradually the oratory in which it was lodged came to be known as the *capella*, and the clerics who had charge of it as *capellani* (chaplains). With this new meaning of a place of private prayer the word spread into general use.

The main duty of the clerics of the chapel was to attend to the religious needs of the king and his following. They celebrated the various divine offices every day, heard confessions, baptised children and administered the last rites. At the head of the chapel was a powerful official, who under Charlemagne's successors came to be known as the arch-chaplain or the arch-priest (the latter is a Byzantine term). As well as being responsible for a large group of clerics, he celebrated the more important divine services himself, said grace for Charlemagne at meals, dealt with the king's ecclesiastical business, heard church lawsuits and had general charge of the kingdom's religious affairs.

Under the earlier Merovingians there had been a staff of lay notaries at the palace, trained in Roman law and skilled in the protocols, the elaborate forms of words in which legal documents were drawn up. By the time of Charlemagne, the lay notaries had disappeared. Literacy and a good knowledge of Latin, the administrative language, were rare among laymen, and Charlemagne's writing officers were all clerics (this is the origin of the modern word clerk). A number of these were grouped into a department under an official known as the chancellor. He did not, however, head a true chancery, a central administrative secretariat. His competence to issue the king's documents was extremely limited, and his department did not build up any important archives. The chancellor's main function was to draw up and validate charters, solemn records of royal gifts of land.

His staff were probably used by Charlemagne to draw up royal documents, but the chancellor was not required to authenticate or issue them, and rarely filed a copy. These documents included letters of appointment or instruction, private correspondence, royal commands, and what were known as capitularies. The form of the capitularies clearly shows the limited value of the written word. Charlemagne was very much aware of the usefulness of writing in administration; he encouraged education and repeatedly enjoined his counts to have notaries about them capable of corresponding with the palace and explaining the king's written orders (the frequency of these injunctions shows that many counts did not comply). Nevertheless it was the spoken word that was of prime importance. The king's commands were oral; his word, his ban, was quite literally the law.

A written order was really a reminder of the oral command. Some of the capitularies were formal *precepts* (commands), properly validated in Charlemagne's name, a few others were more or less detailed minutes of royal decisions, but most simply listed Charlemagne's decrees point by point. In some examples that have survived, only the headings have been copied out; obviously this was considered sufficient to refresh the memories of the royal servants. The chancellor was supposed to receive a copy of each capitulary, but his collection was so inadequate that under the later Carolingians forgeries were often widely accepted.

Other 'government departments' were equally rudimentary. The chamberlain, a layman, had charge of the king's treasure: and it really was a treasure, in

A seal used by Charlemagne to ratify documents. It is not a representation of Charles himself but an antique design, probably of the head of Antoninus Pius or Commodus, set in a ring with the engraved inscription: XPE PROTEGE CAROLUM REG[H] FRANC[O]R[UM].

the sense of a hoard, and not a treasury. In his will, Charlemagne left most of the royal wealth to churches or to be sold for alms, and reserved very little for his successor. The chamberlain had two deputies, responsible for the plate and the 'liquid assets' respectively, and a few scribes to make inventories.

The duties of three other lay officers – the seneschal, the butler and the constable – show how little distinction there was between domestic and government functions. The butler provided the wine for the royal household, the seneschal the food, and the constable attended to the horses (his title derived from 'count of the stables'). However as these positions were the most important in the household, they were held by great magnates, who were Charlemagne's trusted advisers. The butler and the seneschal, through their role in provisioning, supervised the royal estates, and in wartime the constable was responsible for providing the army with remounts. These were much more important functions than dealing with the palace groceries, and in fact the holders of all three offices were often sent on diplomatic missions or given military commands.

The other important palace officer was the count of the palace. His title recalls that of the mayor of the palace, the office which had been the Arnulfings' route to power, but his responsibilities were much more limited. Charlemagne did not have anything like a chief minister, and governed himself, not through favourites. The count of the palace was Charlemagne's lieutenant only as president of the palace tribunal. This court conducted a great deal of business. It heard suits between or against members of the palace, cases involving great vassals and churchmen, and although it did not function as a court of appeal, individual Franks often brought their suits directly to the palace. The count had a small staff to draw up pleas and record decisions. Later in his reign, Charlemagne tried to limit the count's discretion by reserving to himself cases where both parties were 'men of power'. (He usually heard and decided such cases while he was dressing.)

Although life at court was rich, and there were plenty of opportunities for an able man to distinguish himself, the royal servants in the countryside, the counts, probably wielded more power. The territorial division into counties went back to the original Frankish conquest of Gaul. They varied considerably in size; in the south of France they were based on the dioceses, while in the more Germanic areas of the north and east they were much smaller. The precise number of counties is not certain, but at the height of the empire they probably numbered between two hundred and two hundred and fifty. The boundaries were not stable, and were often altered for convenience, a large county being split up or several smaller ones amalgamated.

In the territories for which he was responsible, the count was in all respects the emperor's deputy. His functions were extensive and well defined. The count presided over the tribunal, where he tried offenders, imposed sentence and collected the fines that resulted. He was responsible for enforcing the king's ban, and used the assemblies of freemen at the tribunal for publishing the royal

A bronze jug found in the grave of a Frankish noble.

The exercise of royal authority is shown in this scene from the life of David, where King Saul sends his messengers to seize him. The illustration occurs in the ninth-century Golden Psalter from the abbey of St Gall in north-eastern Switzerland.

precepts and capitularies. He collected tolls, taxes and the annual gifts, and after meeting local expenses and deducting a commission conveyed the remainder to the palace. If public works were necessary, it was the count who ordered their construction and impressed the men and materials required. In time of war the count levied and commanded the local contingent to the main army, and in peacetime used his retainers to maintain order, suppressing bandits and the like.

These were considerable powers, but the machinery for putting them into effect was just as inadequate on a local level as the offices of the palace were centrally. Since many counts did not even have a single notary at their disposal, there was no one in their following who could explain legal documents, cope with correspondence from the palace, draw up reports, record the decisions of the tribunal or cast up accounts. They probably depended on borrowing a scribe, when absolutely necessary, from the bishop or a monastery. They had some subordinates. In the western parts of the empire (modern France), there was often a permanent deputy, a viscount. In the larger counties, the counts often appointed agents, 'vicars' or 'hundredmen' to act for them. They had similar but more restricted powers in a smaller area. Their tribunals, for instance, were only competent to hear petty offences. Beyond these very few assistants the counts had to rely on their personal retainers.

The count spent some time every year at the palace to hand over the revenues from his district and to present his accounts. This was in addition to attending the annual assembly. Regular presence at court helped achieve some uniformity in practice, but the most important way of keeping an eye on the counts was Charlemagne's innovation of *missi dominici* (king's messengers). These were men of high standing, abbots, bishops or lay magnates, sent out each year in pairs – usually one layman and one cleric – to tour perhaps half-a-dozen counties in a region they knew and report on the situation there. The emperor might give them particular commands to deliver; they were competent to try lawsuits in their own names; they inquired into the conduct of the local tribunals, the behaviour of counts and the stewards of royal estates, and matters relating to religious worship. Charlemagne was particularly keen for them to check on whether the oaths of loyalty he required from his subjects were being administered and honoured. The missi were specifically charged to see that justice was given to the church, to widows and to orphans.

Their instructions were admirable, but many things limited the effectiveness of the missi. For a start, they had a very large area to cover, and often could not linger very long in a particular place. They set out in the spring of the year, and the tour was often cut short by a summons to the assembly or the army muster. In addition, most of the missi had their own duties to attend to. From the point of view of the ordinary inhabitants, their greatest drawback as a means of controlling an overweening royal vassal was that they came from the same class: many missi were themselves counts.

A count who was rebellious, corrupt or simply too independent could as a

Opposite : Bronze keys found in excavations of Frankish graves in North Germany.

Frankish ornamental work found in graves in Kottlach and Krefeld.
Top: The frame of a purse. *Left:* A sword hilt. *Right:* A plaque. *Above:* A brooch.

last resort be removed from office, which might involve the confiscation of his own estates as well as those which accompanied the office. Occasionally this happened; counts theoretically held power at the will of the emperor, who could revoke the appointment. There was no absolute right of hereditary succession. In practice, however, the difficulties of finding a replacement for a deposed count from the small group of noble families meant that counts were practically irremovable. They were only deposed for open rebellion. As a county was held for life, there was plenty of opportunity to acquire estates and put down roots in the area. Counts were usually succeeded by a close relative, if not actually by a son, which accentuated the tendency to treat their powers as theirs by right.

The rewards of office were considerable. Most important was the 'honour', a fixed endowment from the royal estates in the county. This might be swollen by the addition of benefices or a lay abbacy. In addition the count kept one third of the fines levied in his court, and another third of taxes. The total cut was large, and could easily be increased by corruption or dishonesty. It was easy for a count to retain more than the proper percentage of royal revenue, to exploit the fields of the honour too intensively, to summon freemen to unnecessary army musters or judicial sessions and levy the set fines from defaulters, or to exploit his legal position by accepting bribes or using the powers it gave him to oppress the tenants of his own lands. Churchmen in particular often reported popular resentment of the rapacity of counts, and the corruption of the missi sent to supervise them.

At the same time as they were making themselves indispensable to the Frankish kings, the nobles' dominance over other social classes was growing. When the first Frankish war-bands arrived in the territory of the Roman empire, their noble class was defined mainly by its military responsibilities – landowning does not seem to have been very important. All this changed with the distribution by Clovis of the huge estates of the Gallo-Roman patricians to his own retainers. The main function of these great *desmesnes* was to enable a very few men to live in idleness, abundance and the exercise of authority. A 'man of power' was known by the number of his retainers, his openhandedness, and the lavishness of his table. With the low agricultural outputs that prevailed (see chapter four) each noble family and its retainers needed vast tracts of land, and enormous manpower to cultivate it. The labour problem was partly solved by slavery, but in Charlemagne's reign the system of farming only a part of the desmesne lands directly, and letting out the rest in return for a share of the produce or for labour services, was already well developed. It was a crushing burden on the rural population. The surplus that might have financed improvements in production ended up as jewellery or armaments in the storehouses of the nobles. The close association between landed wealth and power and the fact that their authority was only prescribed by custom not defined by law allowed the nobles steadily to degrade the peasantry to a quasi-servile status.

3
The Peasants: Freemen,
Bondmen and Slaves

When the Franks swarmed across the frontier into Gaul, their society was already hierarchical. There were four classes: nobles, freemen, slaves and an intermediate class of bondmen or 'unfree'. The latter were not slaves, but they did not enjoy the full rights of a free man. The Gallo-Roman society which the Franks absorbed knew even more gradations of civil status: patricians, citizens, freemen who did not enjoy citizenship, freedmen (emancipated slaves), *coloni* (serfs, peasants bound to the soil) and slaves. The subtler of these distinctions disappeared with the decline of the Romanised element in France, but the status of the unfree Franks seems to have been assimilated to that of the even less free coloni.

There is no accurate information about precisely what was entailed by these differences in status. The monks who wrote the Carolingian chronicles and annals were not interested in the lives of ordinary folk, who only appear in documents which treat them as units of economic value: rent rolls, charters, and the inventories of estates. The Latin terminology in use is imprecise. The word *servus* is used for serfs as well as slaves, and for a long time this prevented romantically minded historians from realising that the Carolingian nobles did in fact possess large numbers of slaves.

'Free' and 'freeman' are also open to misinterpretation. They do not imply civil liberties in the modern sense. Every man, without exception, had a master: a freeman was someone whose relationship with his master was honourable. The freemen were sometimes referred to as the 'king's free', an expression that indicates they were full members of the community in a way that the serfs were not. In the old Germanic legal codes, freemen were not liable to the same humiliating physical punishments as bondmen. Freemen also served in the army, an honourable activity, and had an important part in the courts, where a panel of free 'doomsmen' both declared what they understood to be the customary laws and decided cases. However their standing in legal and military matters grew steadily less during the Carolingian period, as their economic status declined, and the expression 'poor freemen' became common under Charlemagne. A church council in the latter part of his reign complained:

Opposite: At the base of this ninth-century ivory cover to the Psalter of Charles the Bald is a scene with two shepherds: the poor shepherd on the left has only one animal, while the rich man on the right has a whole herd. In the top scene Nathan reproaches David and Bathsheba for the death of Uriah.

Detail of spearmen from the ninth-century Apocalypse of Saint-Amand (Bibliothèque Municipale, Cambrai MS 386). The military importance of the freemen who served in the army declined during the Carolingian period as cavalry became more important.

Opposite: In this ninth-century ivory book cover, infantry are portrayed with spears, helmets and rounded shields. The scene represents the meeting of Joab and Abner at the Pool of Gibeon.

'Because of various things which have happened the possessions of the poor have become much reduced: the possessions, that is, of those who are known as freemen but live under the dominion of the mighty. If our most gracious lord would have their legal position and the processes of the courts looked into, he would see that various circumstances have driven many to extremes of poverty.'

What is meant by a freeman who 'lives under the dominion of the mighty'? It refers not to a general vague supremacy of the rich and powerful, such as exists in any age or country, but to a very precise and even formal relationship, that of vassalage: in which a man of free or noble status 'commended himself' to a greater, by a special rite in which he placed his hands between those of his lord and swore an oath of fidelity. Most of Charlemagne's noble retainers were in this relationship to him, and we have seen the power, wealth, honour and prestige it brought them. For a free peasant, the effects of commendation were quite different. He kept his legal status, and could probably expect support

from his lord in hard times or a dispute, but he gave up a good deal of his liberty of action. He would be drawn into his lord's feuds and quarrels, and invariably became liable to labour service on the desmesne farm in the same way as a serf. It would not be such demeaning service as a serf owed, nor would it take up so much of his time, but it nevertheless blurred one of the essential distinctions between serf and freeman.

It was danger, privation and disorder which forced freemen to give up their independence; they weakened the bonds between the individual and the community and drew closer those between the rich and poor. Life for a peasant in the early middle ages was precarious. Even after a good year, hunger must have been widespread by the next harvest, and a wet summer, a cold spring, disease among the cattle or a fire in a barn meant disaster. The near anarchy of the Merovingian period added invading armies to the natural hazards from which the peasants suffered, and gave the nobles more exciting and lucrative occupations than putting down bandits.

In such exigencies, the Germanic tribesmen had been able to rely on the support of their kindred. Where the kindreds remained strong, such as in the original Germanic homeland in southern Scandinavia and north Germany, the nobles were correspondingly weak. On the Danish-German frontier, the nobles, until the thirteenth century, were merely peasants with military responsibilities. In contrast, the proud free settlers of Iceland, who had left Norway because they denied the right of Harold Fairhair to tax their ancestral lands, rapidly declined into absolute dependence on their lords; this can only be because they made the voyage as individuals, leaving most of their kindred behind. It was clearly the great migrations which weakened the effectiveness of the kindred.

An ornate helmet
from a Frankish grave.

Some of the institutions of kinship remained vigorous. In France, for example, the blood feud was by no means confined to the nobility, and there was a case in Namur as late as the fifteenth century when a killer was acquitted of murder on the grounds that he had killed in legitimate feud, the slain man's *cousins* having killed his father. The essential change, however, was that in Carolingian France it was no longer the kindred which held land, but the family. Kinsmen no longer combined to resist economic oppression. The potential strength of combinations among the rural population was recognised by Charlemagne and his successors, who issued many capitularies against 'gilds', the associations in which peasants joined together for mutual assistance similar to that which the kindreds had provided. The Carolingian monarchs were particularly opposed to oaths being taken to bind the gildsmen together; they felt this threatened the prestige of the loyalty oaths which Charlemagne demanded from all his subjects. Not only those gilds with directly unlawful aims were legislated against, but also those whose object was protection against robbery or violence. Only unions for mutual help in such emergencies as fires or shipwrecks were to be permitted, and even then without an oath. Offenders were threatened with nose-slitting, flogging and banishment.

Failing strong kindreds or gilds, the only way left for a peasant to obtain protection was to commend himself to a patron, giving up his land and receiving it back as a benefice. The immediate loss may not have seemed great, but the son of a man who became a vassal would feel it more; he would enter his inheritance only at the lord's pleasure. The nobles were always willing to accept a man's homage. It swelled the number of their retainers and the amount of labour they could call on to work the desmesne lands, thus augmenting their prestige and increasing the armed support they could call on in an emergency. Vassalage became so extensive that it even affected the church. No rural church was without its patron, who commanded the obedience of the priest and took a cut from the tithes. Churches were listed in the inventories of the great estates along with mills and bakehouses as particularly lucrative sources of income. It is no wonder that the church was unable to restrain the nobility.

Changing military techniques accelerated the decline of the freemen. Cavalry increased in importance under the Arnulfings, until during Charlemagne's reign it was the dominant arm. The early Franks had ridden to the battlefield, but they fought on foot, wielding their axes from behind a shield wall which reduced the need for body armour. A war-horse strong enough to carry an armoured man in a charge was expensive, and so were the armour and more sophisticated weapons of a cavalryman. The arms, horse and equipment might cost the equivalent of twenty cows, far more than the average peasant possessed (for comparison the annual Saxon tribute was five hundred cows). Only the owner of four times the notional peasant holding was supposed to find his own equipment for the army; freemen who held less were ordered by Charlemagne to co-operate in equipping one of their number. Increasingly military service and the honours that accompanied it were

ETSYRIAM SOBAL · ET CONVERTIT
IOAB · ET PERCVSSIT EDOM INVAL
LESALINARVM · XII MILIA ·

reserved for the wealthy. Many peasants probably did not mind the loss of the opportunity to get themselves killed; nevertheless they laboured under the additional burden of equipping their neighbours.

The synod quoted earlier was obviously uncomfortable that freemen should live in poverty. The contradiction was being resolved at the time of their complaint, but not by protecting the poor freemen. Civil status came to be replaced by economic standing as the yardstick of social position. The way in which land was held was the main determinant of economic standing. A freeman who was also a freeholder was much better off than one who had declined to being a tenant, who in other words held his land on essentially the same basis as a serf. In Charlemagne's time, the essential distinction at the level of village life was not that of free and unfree but between freeholders and servile tenants.

There were roughly two economic and legal classes of peasants; those who owned a plough and the team of horses or oxen to draw it, and the others – probably the majority – who relied on a hoe. The owners of the ploughs could cultivate more land, which helped them produce a small surplus which could be converted into money or livestock to help them over bad times. Their services were also more valuable to the desmesne, which put them in a better bargaining position with their lord. Generally they did their labour service as ploughmen or carters and were required to spend much less of their time on the desmesne lands than the peasants with servile holdings, who gave manual labour. In one example, the freeholders of St Germain des Prés owed five weeks service a year, while the serfs owed three days a week. Between the peasants and the lords there was a small class of modest farmers who kept their economic independence, although the nobles frequently forced these men to use their mills in order to tap their profits.

All these different relationships were directed towards the same end – providing enough manpower to cultivate the great desmesnes. The Roman patricians had had similar problems with their estates, but they also had a greater choice of solutions. Their most brutal system was to keep the entire estate in their own hands and use gangs of slaves, often chained together, to work it. Sharecropping combined with fixed term leases was also common, and persisted in northern Italy under the Lombards and Franks. Wage labour was rarely relied on as the mainstay of an estate, but as the chief purpose of Roman agriculture was to feed the towns, the large trade in foodstuffs made money rents feasible. It appears that many coloni, although forbidden to leave their land, paid money rent for it and disposed of their produce themselves. The absence of towns in Carolingian France meant that there was not enough trade in food to allow any widespread reliance on money rents. There was also little coinage in circulation, which made the employment of wage labourers difficult – although instances of hired labour on a small scale are known – as well as creating another obstacle to the use of rents.

Slavery simplified the problem. Christianity hindered the actual traffic in

Opposite: Mounted soldiers depicted in the ninth-century Golden Psalter from St Gall. Two of the horsemen wear tunics covered with metal scales. The short cloaks leave the right arm free. The helmets are simple, without a nose piece or the ear-guards shown in the helmet on page 46.

slaves to a certain extent, and probably restrained Frankish slave-owners from the grosser brutalities of their Roman counterparts, but the institution was too deeply rooted to be eliminated entirely. Breeding and prisoners of war kept the market supplied. Many slaves lived in the lord's hall or in a shed inside the stockade surrounding it, and were fed and clothed by him. These would have included the personal servants as well as agricultural labourers. Others were given a hut and a little land, and had a degree of freedom, although less than a serf. These hutted slaves provided nurseries for the children of slaves lodged by the lord. This slave population was in many cases supported by the profits of the monopolies that many lords established of such activities as milling. Any produce of their labour was therefore clear gain. However the concentration of agricultural work at certain times of the year made it difficult for landowners to rely entirely on domestic slaves. This difficulty was solved by directly farming only a part of the estate, the desmesne, and splitting up the rest into satellite holdings that were let out in return for labour.

Labour services were the main connection between the desmesne and the tenant holdings, but there were also various fixed dues, such as a few coins, some chickens, a sheep or a sucking-pig. These may have been private taxes, or payments for grazing or hunting rights, or derived from the obligation to provide supplies for the army. What is certain is that in the few cases where we have an idea of the sums and amounts involved, they were far too small to have made any real difference to the domestic economy of the lord. It is significant that these payments were made in an atmosphere of solemn ceremony. There was a strong ritual element, and some obligations were quite

Builders from the canon
tables of the Gospel Book of
Ebbo, early ninth century.
(Bibliothèque Municipale
Épernay, MS I f 13.)

A horse-drawn chariot from a ninth-century manuscript of *Psychomachia* by Prudentius,
a Christian poet of the fourth century. Like the oxen shown on page 14 the horses are still
harnessed with a collar, not a yoke, thus reducing their pulling power.

clearly symbolic, such as once a year beating the water of the ditch around the hall. It is hardly likely, as one commentator suggested, that this was intended to prevent the frogs disturbing the lord's rest. These dues were probably kept up simply as a ritual assertion of the landowner's supremacy.

Different sorts of labour service were exacted. Sometimes the work involved could be done at a man's leisure; a particular holding might have to supply a bundle of stakes for fencing or a few simple tools, or the women might be obliged to weave a certain amount of cloth. Other tasks were domestic – guarding the hall at night, spinning or washing alongside the women slaves. Most of the labour required, however, was agricultural. There might be a specific job, such as ploughing a set acreage every year, sowing it with the lord's seed and harvesting the corn, or erecting a fixed length of fencing. This was the kind of service performed by the more independent peasants. The serfs were usually obliged simply to work a certain number of days on the desmesne, often three a week. They did the manual jobs such as hoeing, reaping, thresh-ing, shearing and dipping the sheep. They were probably fed in the hall or refectory on the days they worked for the lord. Tasks known as nights could also be demanded: these were any jobs which meant that the peasant could not be sure of sleeping at home, such as driving a cart to a distant estate.

Historians have calculated that the amount of labour which could be called on was enormous; in practice the full theoretical obligations were rarely exacted. This left a certain amount of room for the peasants to attempt to reduce their obligations, maintaining that service demanded was not customary and even going to law over it. It was generally the peasants who lost such cases. Gradually even the distinction between serfs and freeholders fell into disuse, and the differences between classes of peasants depended solely on the value of the labour they had the equipment to provide. A freeholder who fell on hard times and could no longer keep a plough team would sink rapidly to the level of a serf, and spend half his time breaking his back in the desmesne fields to keep his lord in idle plenty.

Right: Some of the many labours of the peasants shown in a Carolingian illustration of the twelve months. (Österreichisches Nationalbibliothek, Cod. 1 f 90v.)

Overleaf left: This talisman has long been called Charlemagne's and was believed to have been found when Otto III opened the Emperor's tomb *c.* 1000. However, its workmanship suggests it may have been made in the second half of the ninth century. The talisman is in the form of a phial, designed to hold a relic, which would have been worn round the neck. It is now in the treasury of Rheims Cathedral.

Overleaf right: This reliquary of St Stephen, believed to have contained earth soaked in the martyr's blood, was made in the early ninth century in the style of Charlemagne's palace school. The side shown is covered in pearls and precious stones interspersed with small trefoil-shaped ornaments inspired by Merovingian motifs. The pattern of the stones forms a Lorraine cross. The reliquary stands a foot high.

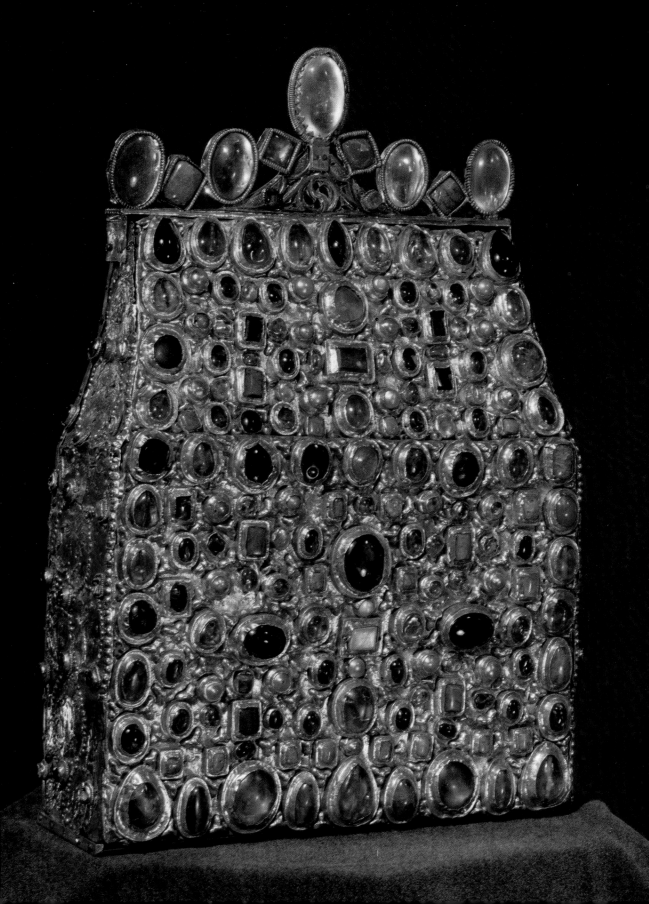

4
The Land, Rural Life and Agriculture

In the early middle ages the rural way of life was almost universal in Europe, and France was no exception. The few towns that had survived on Roman sites now rarely exceeded two or three hundred acres in extent, and even that reduced area was not densely occupied. There was even less trace of real urban life. Commerce was small in volume, and limited to luxuries; apart from smiths there were very few artisans. Most of the inhabitants of the towns earned their living from fields and gardens outside the walls. The bishops generally lived in the towns and administered their dioceses from there; the towns were also the locations of the counts' tribunals. It was only as permanent sites for this sort of public function that the towns kept any importance. In the parts of the empire that had never been occupied by the Romans there were no urban settlements at all.

France was still mainly wooded. Thick forest, untouched by axe or plough, alternated with brushwood, the occasional natural clearing, and undrained swamps. In the low-lying lands and the river valleys there were small areas of fields clustering around small villages: islands of cultivation and settlement in the waste. With the tools and techniques available, forest clearing was not practicable and it was difficult to work the heavier clay soils which required deep ploughing and elaborate drainage systems. The area of arable land was not significantly extended until the great forest clearings of the thirteenth century. Agriculture was confined to light soils with good natural drainage, and in such areas continuous cultivation helped anchor the village to its site. Points of settlement were fixed; the peasantry was stable and rooted in its environment.

The villages were collections of simple houses, all built on the same basic pattern. The framework of heavy timbers was thatched with straw and the gaps between beams were filled with a mixture of straw and clay to make the walls. There was only one storey, but the ends were sometimes partitioned off to make separate rooms; smoke escaped through a hole in the roof and the floors were of trampled earth. The church and the lord's hall were more elaborate, but not usually of stone: only the greatest nobles and the wealthiest

Opposite: The gateway into the now-destroyed abbey of St Nazarius, Lorsch, near Worms. The design follows that of public monuments in the late Roman Empire and may have been erected as a celebratory arch to welcome Charlemagne when he rode in to consecrate the monastery in 774. The upper storey is decorated with flat pilasters, triangular gables and small windows above the keystones of the lower arches. The brightly coloured stones are arranged in a carpet-like pattern. The roof is of a later date.

ecclesiastical houses could afford masonry. The lord usually occupied a complex of buildings, protected by a wooden stockade and perhaps a ditch. His own house, hall, chambers, kitchens and store rooms, was built facing inwards around an open courtyard, in a modification of the classic Roman villa pattern. If he were wealthy it might achieve two storeys and a colonnade or two. The palisade also enclosed a stable, barns, silos, workshops, the slave quarters and possibly the mill.

Methods of cultivation and the complicated legal status of village land, as well as the shortage of suitable soils, also favoured permanent settlement. The land encircling the village was composed of three zones, each used in a different way. The immediate vicinity of the cottages was typified by an intensive garden cultivation. Immediately adjacent was the arable, where the cattle were grazed when it was not under the plough. Beyond that again were the wastes, which were the source of game and the pasture for the herds of pigs.

Each cottage had attached to it a small area of land. The house and its dependent patch were both surrounded by a hedge or a palisade of stakes. In English the whole enclosure is known as a toft. Food stocks and implements were kept inside it, and livestock were brought in at night. The fence protected the sleeping peasants and their meagre possessions against marauders; the obligations of communal service and the exactions of lords stopped at the threshold. Occupation of a toft meant membership of the village community, and brought with it a share in the collective use of the surrounding fields. Newcomers to the village lived beyond the tofts, and did not gain common rights until they were accepted into the community.

In the tofts the soil was exceptionally fertile. It was manured and enriched by human and animal waste, and because of its closeness to the cottage could be repeatedly dug over. The more delicate plants, the 'herbs and roots', ancestors respectively of the modern cabbage and turnip, and even the vine, could be

grown in this rich soil, protected from the worst of the weather by the enclosure. The vegetables were a staple of the daily diet.

The arable was much larger in extent, less intensively cultivated and much less fertile. Most of it was given over to the cereal crop, which was the really important one. After the harvest it was used for grazing, but neither domestic animals nor the plough teams covered the fields closely enough to dung them thickly. Fodder was not systematically grown, and what little hay was harvested could not provide for all the animals, many of which were slaughtered in the autumn. The small amount of stable manure was kept for the tofts, so the ploughland had to lie fallow periodically or it became exhausted.

The cattle grazed in the wasteland on the edge of the woods as well as in the fallow fields. Wastes and woods were an indispensable source of supplements to the village economy. In their natural state the varied vegetation of the woods provided not only pasture but, the habitat of all sorts of wild life which could supplement the peasant diet – game birds, fish in the streams and marshes, rabbits, wild boar, deer, and bees, whose honey was the only available sweetener. The peasant was probably as skilled with the hunting spear, the bow and the net and stick used for catching rabbits as he was with the plough. The woods also supplied him with timber for building, stakes for his fences and fuel. Above all, they maintained the herds of pigs, whose bacon was the only meat most peasants ate at all regularly – scrawny black animals with pointed snouts, sharp tusks and long thin legs that feasted on acorns and beechmast. The forests were not entirely benign, however. They also provided cover for wolves and bandits.

Agricultural technology was primitive. The most elaborate machine in use was the water mill; adopting this Roman device was the main technical improvement the Franks had made in agriculture since the forest days. Building a water mill was expensive and required varied skills: a stream had to be

Overleaf: A reconstruction of the style of villa owned by a prosperous Carolingian landowner. The complex includes farm buildings and is protected by a stockade. The lord's own chambers are built around the courtyard.

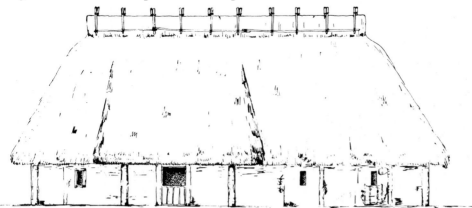

Above: A reconstruction of a house at Gladbach, projected from the excavated foundations.
Left: A model of a Frankish settlement based on excavations of a seventh-century site at Gladbach in West Germany

59

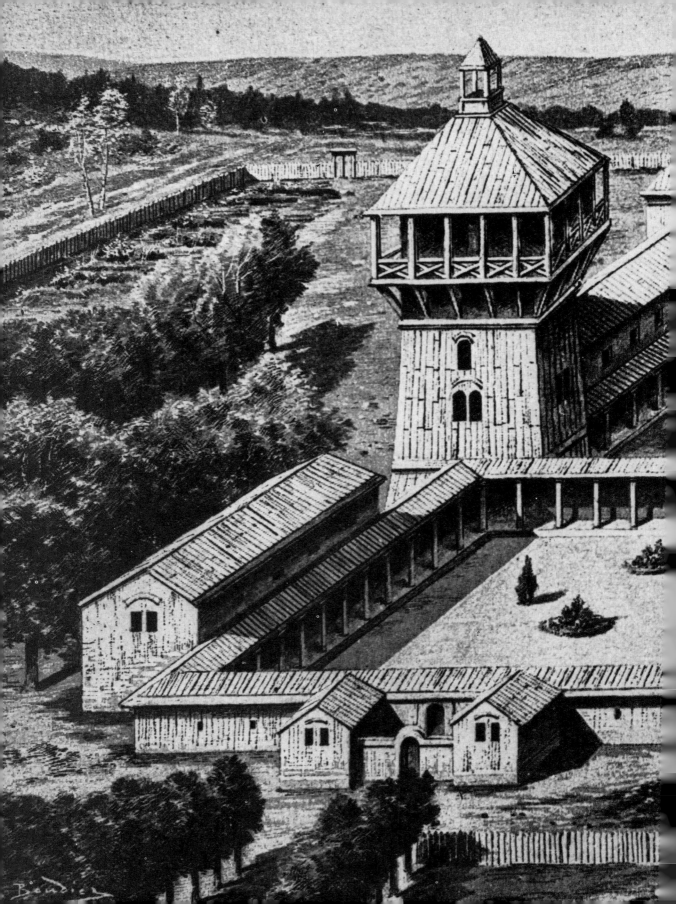

dammed to make the race; millstones had to be hewn, transported and set in place; the driving machinery required regular maintenance besides demanding highly skilled carpentry and the services of a smith for its construction. The mills were far beyond the means of even a fairly prosperous peasant, but on the great estates they were not uncommon. Good stewards, particularly the monastic ones, knew how useful they could be. They saved the labour that would otherwise be spent in the tedious, arduous task of grinding the corn in a hand quern. There was a considerable profit to be made from grinding the grain of the peasants, who also appreciated the saving of labour; the profits were such that a lord or an abbey often resisted the construction of a rival mill.

There were two types of plough in use, a primitive one called the *araire* and the more efficient and elaborate *charrue*. The araire was essentially three long wooden struts, joined at one end and held apart by crosspieces at the other. The two upper lengths were the handles and the lower one, perhaps tipped with iron, the share. The ploughman held it up, and kept the point of the share in the ground against the forward pull of the team. It was light, easy to handle, and did not require particularly powerful animals to draw it. In southern lands the team was often a donkey and a cow yoked together. Its disadvantage was that it broke only the surface of the ground, and shifted the soil without turning it. Consequently it was necessary to dig the fields deeply with a wooden spade at least every twelve years and often as many as every four. The amount of manual labour thus needed to supplement the draught animals was considerable: digging perhaps twenty acres over by hand is a lot of work. For poor peasants, however, working light soils with a feeble team in the absence of skilled craftsmen, the araire was a useful tool.

The charrue was wheeled. Its name derives from the same root as 'cart' and

An eighth-century relief from San Saba, Rome, showing an animal, possibly a deer, grazing. The head of an antlered deer can be seen on the right.

'chariot'. It had a deep asymmetrical share to cut well into the ground and begin the furrow, and a mouldboard to turn the furrow over. (The coulter, the blade in front of the share which increases both the cutting power and the depth of the furrow, was not invented until much later.) It turned the soil deeply enough to aerate it and to incorporate the humus in the roots of last year's crop, the ashes of the stubble and the manure deposited by grazing beasts. Yields were improved and digging by hand became unnecessary. On the other hand, the charrue took more effort and skill to manage than the araire, and required a more powerful, better fed team to draw it. It was an expensive and fairly complicated tool, and could only be built by skilled artisans, while the average peasant could make himself an araire without too much trouble. Judging from the number of peasants summoned to work on the desmesne in the ploughing season, the charrue was fairly rare.

Many of the peasants did not even possess the less efficient araire, but had to break up the soil in their fields with spades and hoes. Their task was made harder by the fact that the tools they used were wooden. Even on great estates, most of the metal tools available were woodworking ones, hatchets, augers, gouges. These were the equipment of a small workshop where they were used to make and repair the wooden implements in general use. The only agricultural tools usually made of metal were the cutting blades for reaping and for felling trees. Even these were scarce; in the inventory of an estate large enough to have two hundred head of cattle, the sum of metal agricultural tools available was two scythes, two sickles and two iron-tipped spades. The ordinary peasant's sickle was probably a wooden haft set with flints. In view of this it is not surprising that the blacksmith ranked with the goldsmith, and had the same wergeld. These inadequate tools required a vast expenditure of manpower, and were quite inadequate for dealing with the waste.

The arable beyond the tofts was held in common. When the ploughing season came round, moveable barriers of stakes were put up to mark off the cornfields, and the herdsmen were forbidden to graze their cattle inside these fences. Each peasant in the village was allocated a number of strips within the fields, every toft carrying with it the right to an equal share. The notional peasant holding, including the potential share of the fallow, was reckoned to be a hundred or a hundred and twenty acres (the 'long hundred').

There were two ploughing seasons, in spring and autumn. The arable land was often divided into three, for the winter sown crop, the spring crop and the fallow. Bread grains, wheat, rye and often barley, were sown in winter; oats and the leguminous crops, peas, beans and vetches, in spring. Seed was scattered broadcast, another contribution to inefficiency. In the usual rotation, winter crops were grown one year, spring crops the next, and during the third the field was left fallow. Between harvest and ploughing the field was left for grazing. Thus at any given time one third of the agricultural land was producing cereals, one third vegetables and the rest nothing. There were many variations on this pattern. The lighter soils of the Midi were often left fallow every second year, and in other areas some land was only ever sown with spring crops, producing a harvest only once in three years. In better soils, spring crops might be sown more than once during the three year course.

Output was extremely low. A comparison of the quantities of grain stored on several estates after the harvest with the amount of seed used showed that the ratio of new crop to the grain sown to obtain it was never much higher than three to two, i.e. two thirds of the grain so laboriously obtained had to be kept for the next season's planting. Such low returns could very easily fall to nothing after a bad harvest. Despite the peasants' enormous toil, hunger was never far away.

Bread was the basis of their diet. Vegetables, herbs and roots, even meat, were only the *companaticum* – the accompaniment to bread. It was baked from oats as well as wheat, rye or barley, and all these grains were also used to make a coarse porridge or brewed into ale, which was as thick as a country soup – as much food as drink. The vegetables were eaten as soup. Meat was a luxury. The autumn slaughter of the beasts for which there was not enough fodder provided some meat, but the animals were generally underfed and lean from years of pulling at the plough. They were valued for their hides and as draught animals as much as for their carcasses. Even milk products do not seem to have been common, probably also due to underfeeding. Sheep and goats were kept for their wool and hens for the eggs which were often pickled and kept for winter. Eggs, beans and bacon were the main sources of protein.

Most of the peasant's needs were produced in the household. Sheep pro-

The poor and sick receiving food from a good lord; an illustration to Psalm 111 (CXII) from the Utrecht Psalter. 'Blessed is the man who feareth the Lord . . . Wealth and riches shall be in his house . . . He hath given to the poor; his righteousness endureth for ever . . .' The Utrecht Psalter was written at Hautvillers between 820 and 830 and is remarkable for the vivacity of the figures, the precision of the pen strokes and the depth of perspective.

vided the wool which the women spun and wove, cowhide furnished shoes, simple furniture and utensils could be carved from forest timber. Money was only needed for the dues or taxes which could not be paid in kind, or to buy essential metal tools such as a knife or hatchet. Small village markets, selling a little produce to travellers, monks or townsmen allowed the peasants to save the small sums needed. Some did quite well, and were able to accumulate enough to add to their holdings by purchase. Sales and bequests helped to concentrate freehold land in the hands of either the monasteries or the more prosperous class of peasants. Natural increase of population, which could not be relieved by colonisation of the waste, increased the pressure on the other village holdings. For fiscal purposes and to assess responsibility for military service, it was assumed that the individual holding was one 'manse' – a toft and the 'hide' of common land that went with it. The correspondence was rarely so neat. About a quarter of the village land was perhaps held by nobles, though very often more than one held land in the same village. Independent farmers and the wealthier peasants often held several manses, sometimes on different terms from different lords. A serf, for instance, might also hold freehold land and own slaves to work it; he would not long remain servile. The majority of the manses, however, were subdivided, and occupied by two or three families. Most of the peasants had barely enough land for subsistence. For them there was no escape from the cycle of excessive toil, oppressive systems of land-holding, poor breeds of livestock, primitive techniques and the wasting of the meagre surpluses of the good years in conspicuous aristocratic consumption.

A ninth-century paten (communion plate), known as Charles the Bald's. It is made of hard green stone with clouded patches to resemble plant-life and eight tiny goldfish. The stone is set in a golden jewelled frame.

65

5
The Carolingian Economy

The years of Charlemagne's reign are part of what used to be known as the 'dark ages'. Like the 'dark continent', the dark ages have recently become much better known, due particularly to archaeological discoveries and the use of this data in evaluating written sources. But historians did not use the phrase only to indicate their own lack of knowledge; it was intended to suggest the twilight into which European civilization had been plunged on the collapse of the Roman empire. In the traditional view, the economic life and social structures of the empire were destroyed at the same time as the power of the Roman state, and by the same force – the barbarian invasions of the fifth century.

There is no disputing the extent of the fifth-century military disasters, or the upheavals in political systems and social arrangements that followed. Roman power disappeared completely in the west, and in the east developed into something quite different, the Byzantine empire: Greek-speaking, ceremonious, inward-looking, increasingly oriental in manners and fanatical in religion. Yet as we have seen, even the social disruption was a much slower process than the immediate transfer of power. The movement of population in the Germanic kingdoms was rarely large enough to swamp the Roman (or Romanised) inhabitants, and the invaders did not have the governmental ability to dispense immediately with Roman skills and institutions. This is particularly true of Spain, Italy and the Midi. Roman money, weights and measures remained standard; Roman law was widely accepted, though it ceased to develop; Roman institutions such as the self-government of cities through their patrician magistrates, often survived hardly changed. A pure Latin was still written, laymen were versed in classical authors, and wrote poetry and philosophical treatises – on the whole indifferently, it must be admitted – in the classical manner. The continuity of Roman life was to a certain extent conscious, and not simply a matter of habit or convenience.

By the time of Charlemagne most of this Roman culture had disappeared Those elements which survived were assimilated by the Franks, or preserved in isolated pockets by the church. The political importance of the old Gallo-

Opposite: Two Roman legionaries from the base of a column from Mostra Augusta, Rome. Historians have long believed that when the military power of the Romans collapsed their culture was also lost, but discoveries such as that of the seventeenth-century drawing of the ninth-century Einhard's Arch (*overleaf*) prove that information on antique models had survived to Charlemagne's time.

This sketch shows both sides of Einhard's Arch, a reliquary in the form of a Roman triumphal arch, which was made of wood plated with chased silver. On the pediment was an inscription recording the donor's name; Einhard presented it to his abbey at Maastricht.

AD TROPAEVM AETER
NAE VICTORIAE SVSTI
NENDVM EINHARDVS
PECCATOR HVNC AR
CVM PONERE AC DEO
DEDICARE CVRAVIT

Roman ruling class inevitably declined when they became the subjects of the Franks. Their culture lost its power to innovate, and became nothing more than a conservative persistence in the habits of a nation that had been destroyed. Above all, their distinctive urban way of life dwindled almost to nothing, and the reason for that was economic. Trade and industry in the Carolingian period were minimal and neither required towns nor created the wealth that would support them.

Medieval economic history is a fairly new field. One of its earliest great controversies was over the date and nature of the collapse of the economic life of the Roman empire. It was once thought that the Roman 'money economy' was completely destroyed by the fifth-century invasions, and replaced by a 'food and services' or 'natural economy', in which exchange is effected through barter; the transition was seen as a sharp one. In the early decades of this century information was collected about a recession in the Roman economy *before* the successful invasions, and it was also suggested that the final decline did not come until the seventh century, and that the economy of the Merovingian period was almost as flourishing as that of the late empire. What has never been disputed is that the Carolingian economy was totally depressed; western Europe had sunk to a level of economic inactivity from which it did not begin to recover until the twelfth and thirteenth centuries. It is worth tracing the progress of this recession in some detail.

Roman economic life, particularly in the first and second centuries AD, was highly developed. Internal and international trade flourished, providing markets for a wide range of products, and creating sophisticated financial institutions. The wealth generated by this economic activity financed the army and civil service through taxation, and we have direct evidence that government spending stimulated production. Contracts for provisioning the army were lucrative, and many towns in frontier regions owed their existence to this commissary trade. The magnificent vineyards of the Rhine valley were originally laid down to produce wine to sell to the garrisons. Keynes would have been delighted to find such elegant confirmation of one of his theories.

Trade also financed a luxurious way of life in provinces like Italy that were no longer self-supporting in foodstuffs. The wealth of Egypt and Libya was largely founded on Italian demand for their corn. The iron that was mined in Spain, along with lead and gold, provided the raw materials for large scale production of arms and armour, which were exported to the east as well as being bought to equip the legions. Gaul gradually replaced Italy as the main manufacturing centre of the empire, producing particularly glass, pottery and bronzeware, all of fine quality. Gallic products have been found in large quantities in the Danube provinces, and beyond the frontier in Scandinavia, Russia and even Asia.

There were two main external markets: Asia, which was at least as civilised as Rome, and the barbarians across the Rhine and the Danube. Imports from Asia were mainly luxuries: goldsmiths' work, spices for flavouring, medicines and pickling the winter supplies of meat, incense, embroidered Persian silks, Armenian carpets, leather goods, and, especially coveted, prunes from Damascus. (In view of the Roman's gluttonous habits, these were probably very necessary.) These goods, being relatively light, came by camel caravan, probably changing hands several times between middlemen on the way. The names of the towns on the caravan routes read like a litany of all the romance one associates with the ancient east. Some of the traders began their journey in Tashkargan, where the Oxus rises in the Hindu Kush; this was the meeting-place of three cultures, Mediterranean, Indian and Chinese. They continued westward through Ctesiphon, Trebizond on the Black Sea, the fertile valleys of Armenia, between the headwaters of the Tigris and the Euphrates to Odessa, finally descending the Syrian coast to the ports of Antioch, Tyre and Gaza.

The outward trade was bulkier, and went by ship. Roman relations with Parthia, the empire which had a joint frontier with Rome in Asia Minor, were generally bad, and in any case carts were inefficient, and unsuitable for long journeys. It was in the hands of Alexandrian merchants, who bought in goods from all over the empire and shipped them down the Red Sea to Arabia and India. They utilised their bulk-carrying capacity to import cotton and possibly silk from the east, and set up factories in Alexandria to produce cloth. The Alexandrians exported primary products, such as corn and timber, and manu-factured such goods as linen, glass and metalware of all kinds. The composition of these exports suggests very clearly the nature of the Roman economy.

Trade across the Rhine and Danube frontiers did not require such heavy capital investment in transport, and involved fairly basic goods. Glass, pottery and cloth were exported, in exchange for slaves, horses and such produce of the forests as furs, hides and honey. Much of the business was in the hands of the flourishing Jewish trading communities which were established very early on at Cologne and Trier.

The heart of the Roman economic system was the sea-routes of the Mediterranean. By far the majority of the important commercial centres were either on the Mediterranean or had easy access to it. It was a Roman lake, completely encircled by the provinces of the empire, many of which had in-deed been acquired by naval expeditions. Wheeled transport, as mentioned earlier, was quite inadequate for bulk carriage; the magnificent system of paved highways had been built for the legions. Trade on any scale would have been unthinkable without extensive use of ships, and the sea was often the cheapest and quickest way to make a long journey for the individual traveller (like St Paul).

Massive quantities of coined money were used in Roman commerce. There were a large number of mints, turning out coins in gold, silver, brass and copper, usually located near the great mercantile cities such as Trier, Pavia and Antioch. Ever since Julius Caesar established the *solidus aureus* as the standard gold coin, and tied silver and copper coinage to it in fixed proportions, it had been possible to use Roman currency as a medium of exchange for the foreign

A silver denier with the head of Charlemagne minted at Frankfurt after 804. It is not a likeness of the Emperor, but copied from the style of Roman coins. Charlemagne introduced sound silver currency which became the official instrument of exchange.

Frankish pottery of the Carolingian period.

trade. When the balance of trade was favourable, the empire gained gold, but this was supplemented, or a deficit financed, by the output of mines. Spain was the province richest in gold and silver, as in most other ores. Mineral rights were the property of the emperor, and mines were often worked directly by the state; otherwise they were leased to individual merchants or to merchant *collegia* (gilds). The mines were productive; engineering and drainage were sophisticated, and slaves provided the bulk of the work force. Such sources of the precious metals made possible a stable, plentiful currency, which in turn allowed the state to meet most of its expenses and collect most of its revenues in coin. Both civil servants and soldiers received money salaries. Large sums of gold were still available to the eastern emperors in the fourth and fifth centuries. A treaty made with the Huns in 443 provides for them to be paid 6,000 lbs of gold immediately, and 2,100 lbs annually thereafter. The gold pound was reckoned to be worth seventy-two solidi, and as that coin was roughly the size and weight of the English sovereign, the sums involved are clearly very large.

Transactions were also frequently made on credit, and there were many bankers. There is particularly good evidence for this from Egypt, where the dry climate preserved the papyrus on which the bankers kept their accounts. These men accepted deposits, lent money out at interest, paid interest themselves on capital lodged with them, and carried out complicated financial transactions for their clients at a fee, by methods including simple transfer between accounts. The Roman treasury conducted a large and profitable banking business.

Frankish glassware of seventh-century workmanship.

Roman commerce and industry began to decline well before the collapse of the western empire. The first blow was the barbarian invasions of the third century. Archaeological finds have provided a very accurate picture of the damage done in the province of Gaul. The picture is of an almost complete collapse of trade and industry for half a century. Towns shrank in size; flourishing estates were abandoned; the gilds of merchants disappeared; prices rose by 1,000 per cent between the years 256 and 280; and industrial production ceased. Bronze, glass and pottery could no longer be sold profitably in other parts of the empire. After 276 the potteries of the Argonne region, which had been famous for high-quality Samian ware, ceased production, and the bronze-ware which had been sold in quantity to the Danube provinces was no longer found.

In the fourth century there was a partial revival, particularly in pottery and glass; the latter industry did so well that glass became cheaper than pottery and began to replace it in ordinary domestic use. Interestingly, this industrial revival is centred in the less Romanised north of Gaul, and the towns of the Midi lost their industrial pre-eminence. Part of the reason for this shift was the demand created by the vast amounts of money being spent to pay the troops defending the northern frontier, but it may also indicate that the empire's internal trade, shipped on the Mediterranean which was within easy reach of the Midi towns, had ceased to be profitable. The industrial centres of north Gaul may have been producing goods for export to the barbarians.

The revival came to an abrupt end with the next round of invasions, in 406 and 407. (This was of course the time of the sack of Rome and the withdrawal of the legions from Britain.) Manufacturing did not take place on any scale in Merovingian France. Goods were produced by small artisans and cottage industry, for local consumption. There is, however, evidence for the continuation of the Mediterranean trade, which was once thought to have been destroyed by Vandal pirates operating from the Germanic kingdom they had set up in North Africa. The Byzantine empire certainly managed to protect its own shipping and seaways, and as it held the provinces of Syria and Egypt until the Arab conquests of the seventh century, this involved maintaining control over the whole of the eastern Mediterranean. It may have been more dangerous than before for merchants to sail from Alexandria or Byzantium to Marseilles and Narbonne, but they certainly made the journey; it would hardly have been in the pirates' own interests to have eliminated commerce entirely.

Much of this trade was in the hands of Syrians who were generally the shippers, and the Greek and Jewish communities of the south coast ports. Syriac, Greek and Hebrew were all spoken there in the fifth and sixth centuries. Surviving records relating to royal storehouses reveal the kind of goods that were still being imported from the east: cinnamon, pepper, spices, oil, dates, figs and, revealingly, large quantities of papyrus. This was a writing material made only in Egypt, from river reeds, and at the height of the Roman empire had been very cheap. Parchment, the expensive alternative, lasted much longer and was used for particularly important texts, such as Virgil or the law codes. The Merovingians used papyrus for all their records and letters, and for most books. During the early Merovingian period, writing was still widely used in the administration, and the large quantities of papyrus necessary all had to be imported from Egypt. Apart from papyrus, the eastern trade was mainly in luxuries. The main exports were corn and slaves, often war captives brought from Britain.

Coined money circulated more widely than it was to do under Charlemagne. There is some evidence, though it is not conclusive, that the king's staff were paid in coin, and the Merovingians were certainly still able to pay out quite large sums from their treasury; the abbey of St Denis received an annual grant at one stage of two hundred solidi in gold, which would have been unthinkable under Charlemagne. Money continued to be struck – there was a mint in operation at Reims from at least the beginning of the sixth century – but there are significant differences between Merovingian and Roman currency. Merovingian coins imitated Roman models in design; Clovis's merely had a C before and after the Emperor Anastasius's name, under his profile. The coinage steadily declined in gold content, and with it sank the reputation of the currency. Many of the coins in circulation were struck in small local mints, from ingots or plate melted down as a convenient way of making payments. These coins were struck to mobilise assets, to pay, for example, the royal share of taxes collected by a bishop or magnate who enjoyed an 'immunity', the

Opposite: Detail from a painted wood panel *c.*1500 showing the Carolingian altarpiece and cross (now lost) in the abbey church of St Denis.

A piece of Byzantine textile from the Carolingian period depicting a charioteer driving four horses. Textiles were among the luxuries imported into the west from Byzantium.

right to collect taxes within his own lands. They often bore the name of whoever was responsible for having them minted, as a guarantee of value and sign of origin. Neither the local mints nor the treasury had the authority to maintain a money of account, like the Roman copper coins, whose face value was guaranteed by being tied to a stable solidus. The needs of local trade under the Merovingians had to be met by a weak silver currency. Even the solidus itself was no longer minted; it was replaced by coins worth half or a third of it, and the latter, the *triens*, became the standard gold coin. The solidus was, however, still used as an accounting unit. By contrast the value of the Byzantine gold coinage very nearly maintained that of its Roman predecessor.

In this use of coined money and the east-west trade – although both of these were relatively restricted – the Merovingian economy had some continuity with the Roman one, even if only as a postscript. The essential difference is the absence of manufacturing. It was the Arab conquests of the seventh century that caused the next recession, which marks the transition in economic life between antiquity and the middle ages. The Arabs, inspired by Islam, rapidly over-ran Syria, Egypt, the North African coast, and most of Spain; they gained a foothold in southern Italy and soon held Sicily as well. Thus the whole southern coast of the Mediterranean was in their hands. The Byzantines still managed to protect their own reduced seaways, but outside the Black Sea, the Aegean and the Adriatic, merchant ships were at the mercy of Saracen pirates. Sea trade in the western Mediterranean shrank to virtually nothing. Pilgrims setting off from France and England for the Holy Land travelled overland to Naples and took ship there. Papyrus suddenly and completely ceased to be imported, and disappeared from use soon after 670. Its place in legal documents, correspondence and manuscripts was taken by parchment. Spices, and the embroidered silken cloths from Persia, already luxuries, became even rarer under the Carolingians. Spices were imported by the sackful, not the shopload, and for the most part came overland from the Italian entrepots, Pavia, Venice, or Naples.

The gold coinage disappeared almost as suddenly. The Arabs and the Byzantines remained on a gold standard, while the Carolingian empire and nations in a similar position, such as England, used silver. Gold was kept in the form of plate and ornaments, and struck into coins only for exceptional needs; these coins did not pass into circulation. The Carolingian mints obtained their silver from mines on the central plateau of France, which remained in use throughout the middle ages, but even given these domestic sources, the metal was scarce; the silver coinage becomes progressively lighter and less intrinsically valuable, until the thirteenth century. The only coin was the silver penny, the *denier* (from the Latin *denarius*); the *sous* (solidus) survived only as a unit of account, reckoned as twelve silver pennies. This Carolingian standard spread all over western Europe, and the names of the units are the origin of the symbols for shillings and pence in the old English £ s d. It is clear from such documents as accounts rolls that as well as having a low metal content these coins were very scarce; it was usual for payments reckoned in silver shillings to be made in shillings 'in grain'.

The Carolingian economy was not, then, entirely a natural economy. Although currency was used only for marginal purposes (see chapter four) the idea of money as a standard measure of value was well established, and too useful to dispense with. Wergeld, sales of land and goods, and the payment of taxes were all usually computed in money terms. There are also a few examples of the use of a commodity with a stable value as a medium of exchange, such as bolts of a particular kind of cloth in Frisia. There is an example from the eleventh century, when the same economic conditions still applied, of a Norman man at arms quite unconnected with the spice trade, paying his rent in pepper.

The main use of coin was in the markets, of which there were two kinds. The small rural markets which grew up in Charlemagne's reign have already been mentioned. The volume of trade there was small, and consisted of the peasants' tiny surplus and the products of rural artisans such as cobblers or carpenters. Some of the better-managed estates — which means monastic ones – produced goods for sale, or at least were astute enough to collect enough of their dues in corn, flour or livestock to have a saleable surplus. This business was often handled by serfs, who may have sought direct customers, but probably more often sold their produce to a merchant.

During the Carolingian period there were professional merchants, but the term can be misleading. These men were not a wealthy elite of large traders and financiers, and did not conduct business on anything like a Roman or early Merovingian scale. They were more like packmen or peddlars. Most of their business was done at the second type of market, the annual fairs, where they bought up local surpluses, sold their spices or silks, sold wine to their Anglo-Saxon counterparts, and bought cloth from the Frisians and slaves from the Bavarians. Their capacity was limited by the complete absence of credit systems, the shortage of coin, and transport difficulties. Harnessing for carts remained primitive until the tenth century, and metal was too expensive to be used to protect parts that might wear. Small boats were useful but limited; they could be used to go down the Rhône to Marseille, for instance, but could not be brought back up loaded against the current. Packhorses were the norm.

Communities of merchants grew up, often opposite a castle or a fortified town. They were themselves unfortified. There was a settlement of slave merchants across the river from the cathedral city of Verdun on its heights, and another immediately beneath the walls of the castle of the Count of Flanders at Ghent. The fortification and the trading settlement became the twin poles of the later medieval town. As well as living in their own settlements, the merchants travelled in groups for mutual protection, each man owning a few pack animals. The monks acknowledged their toughness, but also accused them of being lecherous, drunken and given to feasting and telling dirty jokes.

Gilded jewellery in the style of a solidus of Louis the Pious.

Some of the conventions which became the market law of the later middle ages, such as the idea of the 'just price', were already in existence, and merchants were often very well informed about prices in overseas markets. To that extent they had their own ethics and expertise. Yet their economic importance was small and their political significance nil. We cannot really speak of a merchant class in the sense of an established social group; being a merchant was still an occupation. Some idea of the minute quantities of goods handled can be learned from a case in Barcelona, where a merchant bequeathed twenty bolts of cloth to the cathedral canons. This represented considerable wealth, and enabled the canons to re-establish their chapter. Nevertheless all the cloth could have been loaded on a couple of mules.

Politically, the importance of the Carolingian recession was that land was left as the only important form of wealth, which meant that the nobles were the only wealthy class. What organised manufacturing there was, such as the potteries in the hills between Bonn and Cologne, tended to be in their hands; they were the only people who could mobilise the necessary labour. This primary importance of landed wealth was a necessary condition for the development of feudalism.

Opposite: St Mark with his symbol, the lion, from the Gospel Book of Ada, a manuscript of the palace school produced at Aix *c.*800. The book is named after the lady, possibly a sister of Charlemagne, who is mentioned in a subsequent annotation as having commissioned the manuscript. (Municipal Library, Trier, Cod. 22 f 59v.)

Overleaf: Pages from two of the finest volumes decorated by artists of the palace school at the beginning of the ninth century.
Left: Canon tables from the Saint-Médard Gospel Book, made for Charlemagne at Aix but presented by Louis the Pious to the abbey of Saint-Médard at Soissons in 827. The spiral column in the canon table is a copy of an antique column still to be seen in St Peters in Rome. (Bibliothèque Nationale, Lat. 8850.)
Right: The opening of St Mark's Gospel from the Abbeville Gospels, written on purple vellum at the abbey of Saint-Riquier under the authority of Angilbert, a friend of Charlemagne's. (Abbeville Bibliothèque Municipale, MS 4.)

INCIPT EVANGELIUM
SECUNDUM MARCUM
INITIUM
EVANGELII IHU XPI
FILII DI SICUT SCP
TUM EST IN ESAIA
PROPHETA
ECCE MITTO ANGE
ANTE FACIEM TUAM
LUM MEUM QUI
PRAEPARABIT VI
AM TUAM

6
Permanent War

Charlemagne began his reign as king of part of France, and ended it as emperor of almost all Christian Europe outside the Byzantine empire. Apart from isolated events which passed off peacefully, such as succeeding to his brother Carloman's share of Pepin's kingdom, most of Charlemagne's acquisitions were warlike. His campaigns were the crucial events of his reign, making all his other achievements possible. His instrument of conquest was the Frankish army, or to be precise the Austrasian host. Although he often raised troops from other parts of the empire, it was the eastern Franks on whom Charlemagne especially relied.

Unfortunately, our information about the Carolingian army is very patchy. The clerics who compiled the contemporary records did not underestimate the importance of Charlemagne's campaigns, but they tended not to give much detail about the actual fighting. We do not know for certain how the Frankish army actually fought, which has to be pieced together from other evidence. The central problem is whether the Franks fought as cavalry, which in turn depends very much on what use they made of the stirrup.

The Romans never mastered the use of the horse in warfare. Under the republic, a legion consisted of five or six thousand men, of whom only fifty or so were mounted. They were used as scouts and messengers. Later, auxiliary cavalry were raised from non-Roman peoples within the empire, but they were not intended as line of battle troops. The barbarians who over-ran the western empire gained an important advantage from their use of the horse, but precisely what their tactics were we do not know. The Goths, who killed the Emperor Valens and destroyed a Roman army at the battle of Adrianople, seem to have fought on foot, using the horse simply for mobility, while the Huns certainly rode their horses into battle.

There were three stages in the development of mounted warfare. Homer described the first, chariots; one man drove while another shot arrows or hurled javelins. The battle was often finished on foot, in a series of single combats. With the introduction of bit and spur, riders could control their mounts more easily, and light cavalry tactics, which still depended on the use

Opposite: Christ with the four evangelists from the Xanten Gospels produced by the palace school at Aix *c.*800– 10. The apostles are draped in togas; two are writing and two are reading, the latter with their heads resting on their right arms in the classical attitude of meditation. Their symbols are placed on hillocks behind them. The figure of Christ seated on the globe of the world dominates the page. (Bibliothèque Royale de Belgique, MS 18723 f 17.)

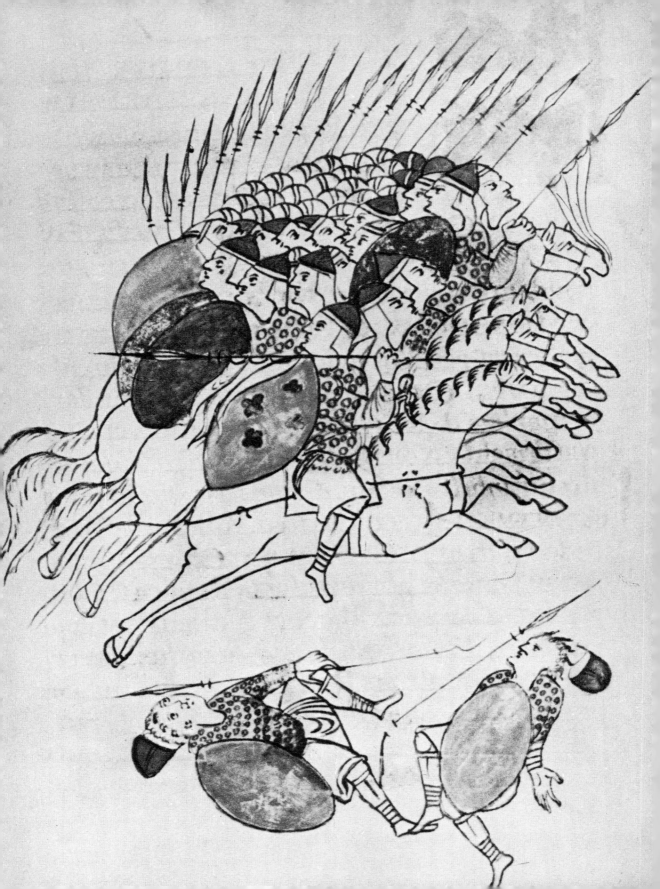

of missiles, replaced chariots. A body of horsemen could now charge to within range of the enemy, loose off their missiles, wheel more or less in formation and charge again. (These tactics, incidentally, are essentially those used very successfully by the Boers in South Africa.) At the climax of a battle, such troops might well have ridden into the enemy ranks and fought hand to hand. Their main advantage at that stage of the fighting would have been the extra height given by the horse.

The third stage was the transformation of cavalry tactics that came with the introduction of the iron stirrup, which gave the horseman a much more secure seat. Before stirrups were general, a rider could not couch his lance under his arm and let the combined weight of himself and his galloping horse deliver the blow; he would have been swept off over the horse's tail. Instead, he wielded a spear at the end of his arm, and used it as a stabbing weapon. Swordplay was also limited. Without stirrups, a powerful blow that missed its target might overbalance the rider, and topple him out of the saddle; and a horseman who cannot stand in his saddle to strike downwards on his blind side is very vulnerable to footsoldiers.

Stirrups were invented in the central Asian steppes, possibly as early as the third century AD; what is uncertain is the date of their introduction into Europe. The horsemen of the legions did not have them, and in fact did not even have a proper saddle. The word used in Roman documents for mounting a horse means 'jump'; by the tenth century, the word used is 'climb' which strongly suggests stirrups. They were certainly universal among the Norman knights at Hastings, but that still leaves us with a margin of seven hundred years.

Historians have written as if the archaeological discovery of one undoubtedly Frankish stirrup would prove that the Franks used the classic heavy cavalry tactics of the massed charge at full gallop. This is too simple. Stirrups went through several stages of evolution before the introduction of the iron device we know; earlier versions included a rigid hook, a loop of cloth hanging down on either side of the saddle, or a wooden ring suspended on a thong. (The cattle herders of north-eastern Brazil still use the latter, inserting only the big toe.) None of these would be adequate for heavy cavalry tactics, and besides it is likely that there would have been a time-lag between the introduction of the iron stirrup and its full military exploitation.

Under Clovis, the Franks fought on foot, using a barbed spear or a one-handed axe from behind a shield wall. It is possible that it was with these tactics that Charles Martel broke the Saracen light cavalry at the battle of Poitiers. However, beginning in the period of Martel's rule, the proportion of horsemen in the army increased steadily. By Charlemagne's time they were the overwhelming majority of the actual fighting men in the army. Of course, this is not necessarily conclusive; the horsemen may have been mounted infantry rather than cavalry. (There are some intriguing details in the campaign which ended in the Saracen defeat of Poitiers. The Saracens began by

Opposite: Mounted soldiers from the Book of Maccabees, an early tenth-century manuscript from St Gall. (University Library, Leyden, Cod. Perizoni 17).

attacking Duke Eudes of Aquitaine, and defeated him in two major battles. In both of these, Eudes had tried to hold them at a river crossing, the sort of place that only a general who relied on infantry or was heavily outnumbered would choose. The country around Poitiers, however, is open and rolling: classic cavalry terrain. This suggests that Martel was possibly already using cavalry, but that the innovation was too recent to have spread to Aquitaine.)

Equipment is much more conclusive. The infantryman carried a spear, a shield, a bow with twelve arrows and a spare string, and a *scramasax* (an old Germanic weapon, a short, heavy, single-edged sword not unlike a machete). He probably did not wear body-armour or a helmet. The horseman also had a spear, with a prominent cross-piece just behind the head, and a round shield; as well as the scramasax he wore a long sword. Frankish swords were famous throughout Europe for their temper and balance, and several capitularies forbade their export. He was protected by a thigh-length jerkin of thick leather, sewn with metal plates, and sometimes had a helmet.

The only possible function of the cross-piece on the spear is to stop the point impaling an enemy too deeply, so that the spear was difficult to remove, which was unlikely to happen with a weapon swung at arm's length. The bar only makes sense if the lance was meant to be couched under one arm and used in the charge. The long sword is also a typical cavalryman's weapon, suggesting that the rider had a firm seat and could swing it with all the power of his arm. The short corselet and round shield were not very well adapted to fighting on horseback, however; the corselet in particular would have left the rider's thighs exposed, which is where a horseman is particularly vulnerable to an upward blow from a man on foot. On balance, it seems almost certain that the Carolingian host fought on horseback and used heavy cavalry tactics, but that these tactics had not been in use long enough for suitable armour to be developed.

There was no standing army. Charlemagne had palace guards, but these were not organised as a military unit; they were not household troops like the Anglo-Saxon *huscarls*, the picked fighting men who died to the last man at Hastings rather than abandon the body of their king. In theory, every Frankish freeman was liable to serve unpaid in the army, providing his own equipment. The need for cavalry, requiring a good horse and expensive weapons which it was beyond the means of the growing numbers of poor freemen to provide, meant that this requirement had to be modified in practice. Only someone with four hides of land was required to equip himself: Those with less were supposed to join with their neighbours and equip one of their number for every four hides. As the hide was a notional unit, and rarely corresponded to actual holdings, it was effectively left up to the count to decide what military obligations people had. The counts were not slow in exploiting this for their own profit, and using the military obligation as a threat to extort bribes, which caused a great deal of resentment and contributed, late in Charlemagne's reign, to a widespread refusal in one year to attend the muster. To keep numbers up, Charles insisted that monasteries should provide their quota of

Opposite: The destruction of Jerusalem from the Book of Maccabees.

88

Soldiers guarding the tomb of Christ on a ninth-century ivory relief from the cathedral treasury at Nancy in north-east France.

horsemen from among their tenants. The numbers involved in Charlemagne's battles indicate that all those obliged to serve were very rarely called out; only particular provinces were summoned. Once issued, however, the summons was strictly enforced and there was a very heavy fine for failure to attend the muster.

The army gathered some time between March and May, depending on the weather or the distance of that year's objective. March had always been traditional, until Pepin summoned the army for his Italian campaign in May, to allow the snows to melt in the Alpine passes. The army usually remained in the field for three to six months, which meant that the soldiers often missed harvest and sometimes a planting as well. Campaigns rarely extended through the winter.

The counts were responsible for publishing the summons to the muster, levying the contingent from their own district and commanding it. Each of these *ad hoc* formations was divided into smaller units, which rode behind a triangular banner based on the standards of the Roman cohorts. The infantry were attached in small groups to these units. It is unlikely that this citizen army had the opportunity to practice complicated manoeuvres, which require long training to be carried out successfully. After the initial charge, the cavalry probably fought hand to hand as individuals. The infantry had specific tasks, such as battering down the gates of fortified places. As they only brought a dozen arrows with them, it is unlikely that archery was important in a pitched battle; the bows were probably for outpost duty. Although they fought on foot, the infantry generally rode to the battlefield.

Each soldier had to bring with him three months' supply of food, as well as armour, arms and tools. A large baggage train trundled along in the rear of the army, with wine, food, clothes and spare equipment drawn in two-wheeled carts, each manned by two soldiers who hung their weapons from the sides. Herds of cattle were driven along on the hoof. These supplies were requisitioned from landowners, and Charlemagne often wrote letters the year before a campaign detailing his needs. Indiscriminate plundering was forbidden, and the amount of forage the army was allowed to take on the march was strictly laid down. It was very unusual for later medieval armies to organise their supplies so efficiently, and they usually wasted a great deal of time in foraging and treated the peasants appallingly badly. Charlemagne's army moved fast, and he only allowed general looting as a punishment for rebellion. To loot a captured fortified place, and to strip the dead on the battlefield of anything valuable, were however a soldier's perquisites.

Probably half the army were army servants – wagon drivers, herdsmen, cooks, carpenters and so on. Many of these were armed: the drivers in particular were expected to defend the baggage train, and probably took their turn at guard duty. They brought their own farmcarts with them.

Charlemagne planned and organised his campaigns himself, in considerable detail, and often began the year before. He made a point of collecting detailed

information about the country he was going to invade – its geography, the people, their customs, the time of harvest and so on. He did not fight himself, but rode with the army and kept command. His strategy was unusual. Most of his major campaigns were begun with the army divided into two or more columns, and crossing the frontier at different points. Splitting one's forces is usually considered an elementary blunder, but it worked well for Charlemagne. He usually managed to create so much uncertainty about his intentions that his enemies kept retreating before him, enabling him to re-unite his forces at the critical moment. This was Charlemagne's preferred type of campaign, rapid manoeuvres followed by one decisive battle, but he was able to conduct sieges as well, or to adapt his strategy to deal with opponents who avoided set battles. The best evidence for his generalship and the military prowess of the Franks are his victories.

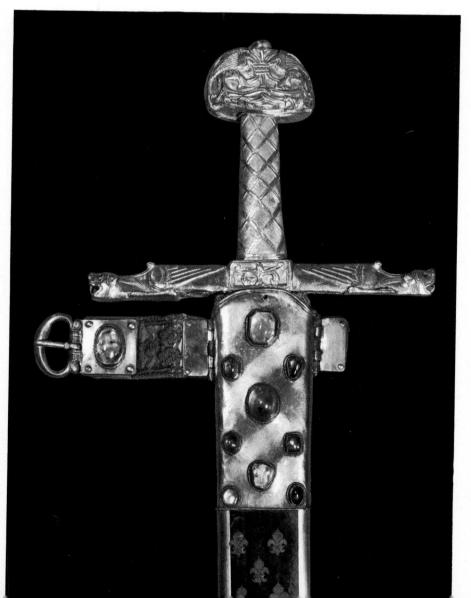

Opposite: Carolingian cavalry and footsoldiers portrayed in the ninth-century Golden Psalter of St Gall. (St Gall, Stifts-bibliothek, Cod. 22 p. 141.)

A sword of the Carolingian era, said to be Charlemagne's. It was forbidden to export Frankish swords which were the finest in Europe.

7
King of the Franks and Lombards

When Charlemagne became emperor, he took as one of his titles *pacificus* (the peaceful). It seems an odd description of a man who had conducted more campaigns than any European general since Caesar. In those times of almost constant warfare, however, a ruler brought his subjects peace only by the sword, by suppressing rebellion and defeating external enemies. Admittedly, Charlemagne's desire for peace is often difficult to distinguish from his aggrandising Arnulfing habits: to be pacified by Charlemagne, as the Saxons found, was an extraordinary painful process. To his contemporaries, the title meant peacemaker, in the sense not of conciliator but of a ruler strong enough to impose strong government. That this government was Christian justified aggressive measures.

During the forty-six years of Charlemagne's reign, fifty-three major campaigns were fought. Just under thirty were led by Charlemagne himself, and the rest, though commanded by his sons or magnates, were closely directed by him. To Charlemagne and his retainers, the summer campaign was the most important event of the year. Years when there were no hostilities were seen by the chroniclers as exceptional. Charlemagne's first campaign (see chapter one) was the successful suppression of the rebellion in Aquitaine in 769, when Carloman left his brother to keep the field alone. His second was against the Franks' traditional enemies, the Saxons, in 772. The army he took was small, and although it was successful, it was by no means decisive. Politically, however, it was important as the first major expedition since the kingdom had been re-united on Carloman's death. Its success undoubtedly increased Charlemagne's standing with the former vassals of his brother. He was preparing another Saxon expedition in 773 when events forced him to intervene in Italy, against the Lombards.

The Lombards invaded Italy in 568; there were not many of them, and they were accompanied by bands of Saxons and Bulgars. Some of the invading Lombards had fought in Italy before, as federates in the pay of the Byzantines. The sixth century saw a long struggle in Italy between the Ostrogothic kingdom, established when Rome fell, and the Byzantines who claimed the

Opposite: The Cross of Desiderius from the late eighth century, probably made in Italy. The gold is encrusted with precious stones and glass cabochons.

country. Narses, the seventy-four-year-old eunuch who was the Byzantine general, broke the Ostrogoths in 552, killing their king in battle and restoring Italy to the Roman empire, but only for sixteen years. Although the Lombards never quite succeeded in dislodging the Byzantines from the maritime-regions and the great ports, they over-ran most of Italy and held it – divided into a northern kingdom and several southern duchies – for two centuries. The remnants of the Latin senatorial class had come to an accommodation with the Ostrogothic kingdom, which was strongly influenced by Latin culture. The Lombards swept away the senators; their long, intermittent struggle with the Byzantines, their eventual conversion to Christianity and the continuing presence of Byzantine territory exposed them to Greek influence, reflected in art as well as administration.

The Byzantines maintained their interest in Italy. They continued to appoint officials and military commanders, and occasionally sent troops. Preoccupied with the eastern frontier, the emperor at Byzantium could never spare a large force, which made it difficult for the pope to play off Byzantine against Lombard to preserve the integrity of the duchy of Rome and the papal patrimony (the pope's estates outside the duchy). The popes were not reluctant to avoid the eastern emperor's claims to be the temporal overlord of Rome and, effectively, lay head of the church, but this involved them in seeking the protection of Pepin. The anti-Lombard party in Rome soon became of necessity pro-Frankish, and whether Pepin's sons would honour their commitment to protect the Holy See must have been their paramount concern for several years after Pepin's death; Bertrada's diplomatic meddling in Lombard alliances, and particularly the Lombard marriage she arranged for Charlemagne, threatened Roman interests.

The papacy's difficulties began in 767, the year before Pepin's death, when Pope Paul I died. The Lombard duke of Tuscany intimidated the electors, and forced them to elect his brother Constantine as pope. As Constantine was a layman, it was first necessary to push him rapidly through the seven clerical grades. This was strictly forbidden by the church, which insisted on intervals of several years between the various stages of holy orders, and made Constantine's ordination uncanonical. His hasty consecration as pope was therefore doubly uncanonical; it had been secured by force, and the candidate's assumption of clerical status was invalid.

Papal administration was in the hands of a *schola* of lay notaries, drawn from the nobility of the Rome region. Their power in Rome and their influence over the pope was considerable. Constantine's election outraged the notaries, who saw it as a threat to their own influence, and with the help of another Lombard faction, Christopher the primicery (head of the *schola*) deposed Constantine by force and had his eyes put out. (This piece of cruelty was an imitation of what was virtually standard practice at Byzantium.) Christopher then had a Roman priest consecrated as Stephen III. In 768 a Lateran council at which twelve Frankish bishops were present passed a canon restricting the

The iron crown of Lombardy forged, according to legend, from a nail of the true cross. Six gold plates set with enamels and jewels surround an iron hoop.

choice of candidates for the papacy to Roman priests and deacons – in other words, members of the papal household in full orders – and forbade laymen to take part in the election.

Desiderius, the king of the Lombards and Charlemagne's father-in-law, could hardly ignore the mutilation of the brother of one of his great vassals, however justified the deposition had been, and in any case resented independent behaviour from the Roman nobles. In 771, while the Frankish queen mother was actually in the city, Desiderius led an army to Rome, terrorised the pope, and had Christopher and his son murdered. He did not bother to depose Stephen, probably assuming he would be pliable after this aggressive demonstration; this may have been a missed opportunity. He did, however, publicly declare his intention of keeping the lands enumerated in the Donation of Pepin, which was an open insult to Carloman and Charlemagne and a breach of his solemn oath to their father. For Charlemagne, this spelt the end of Bertrada's policies, and he returned the insult by repudiating Desideria. Stephen III revealed his subservience to the Lombards by strenuously objecting to Charlemagne's subsequent marriage to Hildegard, but only succeeded in irritating the king and his advisers even further. Charlemagne was not yet strong enough to enforce the Donation, and it is not even clear that he wanted to. The death of Carloman in December 771, his succession to Carloman's lands, and preparations for the Saxon campaign of 772 were more than enough for Charlemagne to think about. With Carloman's death, however, Charlemagne now held the Franco-Lombard frontier.

In February 772, the acquiescent Stephen III died. He was succeeded by a deacon of the papal household called Hadrian, an excellent choice. By birth he was one of the Roman nobility; he had been trained as a notary and had served for a long time in the *schola*. This not only made him a tough lawyer and an experienced administrator, but meant that he was closely tied to the anti-Lombard laymen who had swept him to power as well as to the clerics of his household, and commanded the respect of both these important groups. He had an elevated notion of the importance of the Holy See, and severed the remaining formal relations with Byzantium; dating his letters by the year of his own pontificate instead of the year of the eastern emperor's reign, striking his own coins and appointing civil officers in Italy without seeking imperial approval.

Desiderius protested at Hadrian's election, but did not have time to prevent it – Stephen died on 1 February and Hadrian's election took place two days later. Believing that Hadrian could be intimidated in the same way as Stephen, Desiderius led his army into the former Byzantine exarchate, which Pepin had forced his predecessor Aistulf to surrender to the pope, right up to the walls of Ravenna. He demanded that Hadrian should crown Carloman's sons as kings of France, and when the pope refused Desiderius got his agent at the papal court, Paul Afiarta, to try to kidnap the pope and keep him prisoner till he agreed. Hadrian got wind of the plot, and expelled the pro-Lombard faction from Rome. Afiarta fled to Ravenna, where he was executed by Archbishop Leo. Desiderius blamed Hadrian for Afiarta's death, which is unlikely in view of the old quarrel between the ecclesiastical authorities of Rome and Ravenna, and used it as an excuse to march into Tuscany and threaten Rome.

Hadrian hastily sent envoys to France in January 773 to seek Charlemagne's help. It was an inconvenient moment, and Charles would have preferred a second Saxon campaign. He was not keen to operate with the Alps between his army and their bases while the Saxons were aroused by his expedition of the previous year, and offered Desiderius the large sum of 14,000 solidi in gold to restore the towns of the exarchate to Hadrian. Desiderius refused, marched on Rome and prepared to besiege the city. Hadrian had concentrated his troops there, and was preparing to resist. His most effective weapon turned out to be the excommunication he launched against anyone who should dare to attack the city walls. Unsure of the loyalty of his Catholic army when faced by the threat of eternal damnation, Desiderius withdrew.

Charlemagne now had several motives and excuses for intervention. He was patrician of the Romans, and his assistance had been requested by Hadrian, who was more seriously threatened than his predecessor had been when Pepin intervened. There was the insult of Desiderius' refusal to honour his oath to Pepin, and the added insult of his refusing the very generous offer of Frankish gold. An added danger, and possibly a serious one, was the danger of rebellion in France provoked by Desiderius in his role as protector of Carloman's sons. Several of Carloman's advisers were in Lombardy with the princes and their mother, but how Carloman's former vassals felt about Charlemagne is not known.

Charlemagne finally managed to persuade his nobles to support a Lombard war, and assembled an army at Geneva in May 773. He led the main body himself, directly south over the Mount Cenis pass. It took the Franks five days to reach the twelve-thousand-foot-high summit. His uncle Bernard led the other contingent by an easterly route over the Great St Bernard, which was then known as the Jupiters-Berg. The Lombards had earth works and a ditch at the southern end of the Mount Cenis, but did not fight. There is a legend that a minstrel showed a party of Franks an undefended track around the fortifications, whereupon the disconcerted Lombards abandoned their position; the minstrel was rewarded with all the land where his horn could be heard from the summit. It is possible that this legend was based on the success of Bernard's flanking movement. In any case, when the two armies met in the plain of the Po, they found the Lombard troops shut up in their walled towns, Desiderius holding Pavia and his son Adalgis in Verona with Carloman's widow and her sons. Verona was quickly stormed; Adalgis fled to Byzantium, and Charlemagne captured Carloman's family. He sent them back to France, and apparently treated them quite well; a Merovingian would have murdered them. Pavia was too strong to be stormed, and the Franks did not have siege engines, so they settled down to blockade the city and starve it into submission.

Without waiting for Pavia to fall, Charles went to Rome to keep the Easter feast. He did not wait for Hadrian's invitation, but went there as of right; the pope had annoyed him by trying to appoint a new duke to the duchy of Spoleto, which Charles considered part of the spoils of war. When the two men met, they took to each other and became close friends; on Hadrian's death, Charles wept for him as for a father. During this Easter visit, Charles supposedly made his own Donation. The document is quoted in the *Life of Hadrian* in the *Book of Popes*, and involved territories which were not in Charles's gift, such as the Byzantine territories of Venice and Istria, and others he never gave, such as the duchies of Spoleto and Benevento. It would have given the popes their consistent aim of temporal supremacy over all Italy. The version given in the *Book of Popes* is obviously spurious or exaggerated. As Charlemagne claimed that he now ruled Lombardy it was unnecessary for the pope to be given any more territories, and the *Donation of Pepin* was obsolete, as it had been made as a guarantee against the Lombards.

In June 774, Pavia fell, starving and suffering from an epidemic. Desiderius and his family were sent to French monasteries; the former king apparently found monastic life more to his liking than politics and war. Charlemagne restored the exarchate of Ravenna to the pope, and gave him the other cities promised in the *Donation of Pepin* but never surrendered. He claimed the Lombard kingdom himself, as the spoils of war, and meant to keep control of it. At first, however, he ruled with a light hand. He took over the royal estates, which like those in France had originally been the estates of the Roman treasury, confiscated a few other estates and granted them to Frankish churches, and appointed a number of Frankish counts, though not, at this stage, very many; he hoped to be able to rule Lombardy with a light hand. Archbishop Leo of Ravenna annoyed Hadrian by claiming ecclesiastical jurisdiction over all the former Lombard territories, including those now returned to the pope. To save trouble, Charlemagne diplomatically allowed the elderly archbishop's claim, assuming that the pope's counter-claim to appoint the archbishop would sort the matter out quite satisfactorily on Leo's death. From July 774, Charlemagne assumed a new and rather splendid title, used in full in the protocols to all his documents: *Carolus, gratia dei rex Francorum et Langobardorum atque patricius Romanorum* (Charles, by the grace of God king of the Franks and Lombards, and patrician of the Romans).

Italy was not subdued all at once. The Lombard dukes and the Byzantines resented Charlemagne's assumption of the crown, the latter out of pique. A famine in 775 caused popular discontent, and Hadrian warned Charlemagne that the Lombard duke of Friuli, at the head of the Adriatic, was conspiring with the dukes of Spoleto and Benevento and with Adalgis, who was to lead a borrowed army of Byzantines to support them. Charlemagne had to abandon a Saxon campaign to deal with the revolt, and arrived there in December, much later in the year than it was usual to remain in the field. The death of the Emperor Constantine v prevented Byzantine support, and the south did not rise. Charlemagne killed the duke of Friuli in battle, appointed his own man to replace him, and incorporated Friuli into his Lombard domains.

The Lombard dukedoms and the Greek districts in the south gave Charlemagne problems for longer. The duke of Benevento, Arichis, who was the son-in-law of Desiderius, refused to take an oath of loyalty to Charles. He called himself *princeps* (prince), dated his letters from the year of his 'reign', and claimed the lordship of all southern Italy. In the 770s he encroached on the papal patrimony in the south, just as Histluf and Desiderius had done in the north. The patrician of the Greek province of Sicily arrogated the titles of *basileus* (king) and imperial viceroy, and used the royal title on the mainland as well. He seized the town of Terracina from the pope, and although Hadrian's troops recaptured it in 778, they could not hold on to it.

Hadrian again wrote to Charlemagne, warning that the papal army stood to lose the whole plain of the Campagna between Naples and Rome. Charlemagne returned to Italy in 780, and his mere presence was enough to quieten the southerners. He kept Easter at Rome, and dealt with Hadrian's request for the implementation of the Donations. He refused to give the pope anything that would have diminished his own Lombard lands in the north, or any lands in the south that would have required a campaign. However as Hadrian's relations with Byzantium were improving, Charlemagne did restore the papal patrimony in the duchy of Naples.

At the same time Charlemagne managed to settle his quarrel with the Byzantines. His opportunity was the death of Leo IV in 780. Leo's widow

Opposite: Christ in Majesty on the altar of Ratchis, *c.*750, at the church of Santa Maria in Valle, Cividale del Fruili. Cividale was the capital of the first Lombard duchy in Italy.

LII PSALMUS DAUID

IDICAMEDSET EMITTELUCEMTUAMETUERI CONFITEBORTIBIIN

ISCERNECAUSAMMEAM TATEMTUAM IPSAMEDEDU THARADSDSMEUS

ECENTENONSCA ABHOMI XERUNTETADDUXERIN QUARETRISTISESA

SEINIQUOETDOLOSOERU MONTEMSCMTUU ETIN MEAETQUARECONT

ME TABERNACULATUA BASME

LATUESDSFORTITUDO EINTROIBOADALTAREDI SPERAINDOQNMA

EA QUAREMEREPPULIS ADDMQUILAETIFICAT CONFITEBORIIII

ETQUARETRISTISINCEDO IUUENTUTEMMEAM TAREUULTUSMEIEI

UMADELICITMEINIMICUS

Irene – who in fact probably murdered him, and had probably murdered her father-in-law as well – came to power as the viceroy for her young son. Relations improved all round. The Byzantine emperors had been iconoclasts, opposed to the veneration of images; this implied a view on the Trinity that was considered heretical in Rome. Irene belonged to the opposite party, and achieved a reconciliation with Hadrian. Charlemagne's daughter Rohtrud was even betrothed to the young Emperor Constantine, and began to study Greek.

The marriage did not come off, owing to Irene's growing ambition (she later deposed her son and had his eyes put out) but it seemed a good time for Charlemagne to consolidate French rule in Lombardy. Hadrian crowned Charlemagne's three-year-old son Pepin as king of Lombardy, thus vesturing a nominal independence. In practice, however, Pepin was viceroy rather than king even when he reached his majority (at fifteen). During his minority, the kingdom was administered by the vassals that Charlemagne left behind to bring up his young son while he returned to France. Charlemagne also appointed more Frankish counts.

Arichis made trouble again in 786, by seizing Amalfi from the Byzantine duke of Naples. In 787 Charlemagne came to Rome, invaded Benevento, and defeated Arichis. The duke took an oath of loyalty, gave hostages and promised tribute. Charlemagne could now give Hadrian the Beneventan patrimony. Irene used this intervention as a rather weak excuse to break off the engagement, but did nothing effective. Charlemagne promised Hadrian more territory to persuade him not to come to any arrangement with Irene, but to conciliate the Beneventans and prevent them making a Greek alliance either, he did not enforce the gift. When Arichis died in 787 his son was allowed to succeed. Adalgis finally turned up with his long-promised Greek army in 788. It seems that there had been Frankish provocation, possibly out of pique at not being invited to the anti-iconoclast council of Nicea, to which Hadrian had sent legates. Adalgis was easily defeated, and the Franks occupied Istria.

Hadrian ruled Rome and the patrimonies for another seven years; his relations with Charlemagne were close and friendly, but on large issues, such as foreign policy and the Donations, Hadrian gradually realised that he was quite powerless. Charles took his title of patrician seriously, and regarded himself as the temporal ruler of the duchy of Rome. He demanded oaths of loyalty from the pope's subjects, established a mint for his deniers at Rome, heard complaints against the papal government, and directed papal policy. Hadrian had invited a protector and received an overlord.

Opposite: At the bottom of this page from the Utrecht Psalter is a battle scene illustrating psalm 44 (XLIII). Above the fighting, surrounded by angels, the Psalmist invokes God's aid in the fight of his people: 'Arise for our help, and redeem us for thy mercies' sake.'

8
Wars of the Cross: the Saracens

After the death of the prophet Mohammed his followers, inspired by his teachings, began an astonishingly rapid series of campaigns. The Arabian tribes had always been warlike, but until their conversion to Islam spent their energies on fighting each other. United, they were more than a match for the Byzantine empire. By 640 they had taken Persia, Palestine, and Syria; Egypt and Libya had fallen by 650. They turned their attention for a while to Constantinople, which they threatened several times, and developed a fleet which enabled them to take Cyprus and Crete and pass the great stretch of waterless desert between Libya and Tunisia. The western parts of North Africa were much more difficult to subdue; most of the population were Berber tribesmen, as tough as the Arabs and used to the same terrain.

The deserts, which to other nations were impassable wastes, were the Arabs' natural habitat; the direction of their expansion and their style of campaigning depended on the desert. They used it to make surprise attacks, as a safe retreat, and for their communications. Their strategy was usually to found a town on the edge of the desert as a base, and make their incursions from it. The scarcely Romanised Berber tribes were equally familiar with the desert; it took over fifty years for the Arabs to establish a precarious supremacy over the whole Maghreb – modern Tunisia, Algeria, and Morocco – and another hundred to finally subdue the tribes.

It was partly to pacify the Berbers by involving them in a war of conquest that the Arabs invaded Spain. The Visigothic kingdom, weakened by treachery, collapsed after just one battle, at Jerez de la Frontera in 711. By 712 the Saracens had conquered the whole kingdom, except for the Christian kingdom of the Asturias in the north-west, on the shore of the Bay of Biscay, and adjoining Navarre, inhabited by some of the loose coalition of Basque tribes who also lived north of the Pyrenees, where their territory of Gascony extended nearly to the Garonne. The Arab and Berber tribes which conquered Spain remained distinct for a long time, and cunning rulers of adjacent territories, such as Duke Eudes of Aquitaine, Pepin the Short's contemporary, were able to exploit the divisions.

Opposite: The fall of the Saracen-held city of Pampelona to Charlemagne in his campaign of 778, from his tomb at Aachen erected in the early thirteenth century. The hand of God is shown smiting the walls of the city.

When Spain was firmly under their control, they began raiding north of the Pyrenees. At times their armies penetrated as far as the Loire and the Rhone; in many years it seemed that France might go the way of Spain. The defeat of the Saracen army by Charles Martel at Poitiers in 732 checked these raids in strength, and prevented them turning into an invasion, but raids continued; the last serious incursion was defeated by Pepin near Narbonne in 759.

Nominally, Spain and the Maghreb were ruled from Qairawan, on the edge of the Sahara, but conditions in Spain were so different that the sub-ruler there, the emir of Cordova, enjoyed almost complete discretion. This independence became total in 756. A dispute arose over the nature of the succession to Mohammed as caliph (leader of Islam) who now ruled from the more convenient administrative centre of Baghdad, not the old holy city of Medina. In 750 the Ommayyad dynasty was overthrown by the Abbassids, descendents of Mohammed's uncle. (Their brand of Islam became less austere and aggressive, and they were great patrons of learning). One Ommayyad, Abd ar-Rahman, escaped the massacre of his dynasty in Baghdad after the coup and made his way to Spain, where he became emir. Later he elevated the country to the dignity of a caliphate, in rivalry to the Abbassid caliph of Baghdad.

Between 770 and 777 Abd ar-Rahman had to deal with frequent rebellions fomented by Abbassid agents. Not all the leading Saracens who had accepted his rule at first were loyal to him. In 768, the caliph of Baghdad sent envoys to Pepin with presents, and a Frankish embassy apparently spent three years in the east. The caliph may have been trying to make an alliance, but using infidel support against fellow Muslims would hardly have been popular with the faithful; it is more likely that the caliph wanted to secure Pepin's neutrality, and to persuade him not to try to take advantage of an Abbassid invasion of Spain. Pepin died just after his envoys returned, before any agreement could be made, so we do not know what its provisions might have been. However, Charlemagne could maintain that the negotiations showed that Pepin recognised the Abbassids, which made the Ommayyad Abd ar-Rahman the usurper.

In 777 the Abbassid governor of Barcelona, Suleiman, led an embassy to Paderborn, where Charlemagne was holding a particularly grand assembly to impress the Saxons. The presence of a Saracen embassy probably delighted Charlemagne, as it would prove to the Saxons the extent of his fame. Suleiman, who had been involved in the negotiations with Pepin, declared that he would rather make a pact with the infidel than live under Ommayyad rule. Suleiman promised to turn over the cities he held to Charlemagne, and use his own followers to capture the great fortress of Saragossa and turn that over too; he promised that an Abbassid army from the Maghreb would move simultaneously against Abd ar-Rahman; declared that Charlemagne's reputation for invincibility would rally all the Spanish Christians to his support; and finally, promised to submit to Charles with all his followers after the eventual victory. Charlemagne was to be ceded all of Spain up to the River Ebro.

Charles allowed himself to be persuaded. What his motives were is not clear; the campaign is not treated very fully in contemporary sources. The dissensions in Spain, following the humiliating victories of Charles Martel and Pepin the Short, had weakened the Saracens, and the Pyrenees were a very useful frontier. At the Mediterranean coast, however, the Eastern Pyrenees were much less of an obstacle; the road into Septimania and Aquitaine from Saragossa and the outposts of Huesca and Barcelona was much easier. Possibly Charlemagne was afraid that Abd ar-Rahman might be tempted to lead a raid on France to boost his prestige among the Abbassid dissidents in Spain; certainly he was quite sincerely convinced that it was his duty, as a Christian ruler, to extend Christendom by the sword, and the Christians of Spain, living under heathen rule, aroused his sympathy. It is likely, however, that Charlemagne's recent military successes had gone to his head. He imagined that he had finally subjugated and Christianised the Saxons (he was wrong on both counts) who had been the enemies of Franks ever since Clovis's time; he probably thought he could subdue the other traditional enemies, the Saracens, just as easily. The fact remains that Charlemagne's Spanish war, unlike all his others, was completely unprovoked.

Charlemagne did not underestimate the fighting qualities of the Saracens, despite Suleiman's grandiose assertions, nor the harshness of the Spanish climate. He celebrated Easter at his villa of Thionville, and leaving his wife there, travelled to Aquitaine where the army was to muster. In an attempt to avoid the worst heat of the Spanish summer, the annual assembly was dispensed with in 778 and the army mustered early in March. After Easter, Charles set off. He had raised the largest army he had used till then, and only on two later occasions did he use a larger one. As well as his own Austrasians, and the Septimanians and Aquitainians, who could quite reasonably expect to be involved, he summoned the Lombards, the Burgundians, and the Bavarians. The latter, whose duke Tassilo had thrown off the Frankish allegiance which Pepin had imposed on them, were probably attracted by the prospect of booty.

One division of the host took an eastern route, through the pass of Puigerda, north of Barcelona. Charles himself led the main force through the Pyrenean gorges into Navarre, possibly over the pass of Roncesvalles. The two divisions were to rendezvous outside Pampelona; it was essentially the same strategy that had worked so successfully against the Lombards. The route that Charlemagne took was harder and more dangerous; Navarre itself was difficult enough country, even without having to cross the Pyrenees, and the Basques of the region fought Asturians, Franks, Saracens and each other with admirable impartiality. On this occasion, however, they left the Franks alone.

Arriving at Pampelona, Charlemagne found it held against him, although it was a Christian city, and had to take the place by storm. He had obviously miscalculated about the Spanish Christians; although many were discontented with Saracen rule, others were quite content. The Muslims were on the whole much more tolerant of other religions than the Christians were, particularly of

Judaism and Christianity whose adherents they regarded as fellow 'people of the Book' because all three religions accepted the Old Testament. After their conquests they tolerated the practice of different faiths, and did not discriminate against those who sincerely held to their old beliefs; only scoffers and lapsed converts to Islam were treated severely. Abd ar-Rahman, moreover, had been very careful to leave the Navarrese alone.

At Pampelona, Charlemagne accepted the submission of a number of local Saracen chiefs. He heard that Suleiman had captured Saragossa, and was writing to surrender it to the Franks, but after leading the united army there, found it held against him by a different chief entirely. The walls were too strong for Charlemagne to storm, and he could not spare the time for a full siege; it was July, the army's three months supply of provisions was running low, and Abd ar-Rahman was gathering an army and waiting for Charlemagne to make a wrong move. All Charlemagne had to show were the cities of Barcelona, Auesca and Gerona, delivered up to him by Suleiman's underlings. He could not afford to press on beyond the Ebro to engage Abd ar-Rahman while Saragossa held, and could not leave isolated garrisons in the towns while the countryside was insecure. On the whole he was disappointed in the Abbasid help that Suleiman had promised. The North African army arrived, but Suleiman quarrelled with its leaders, who sulked and refused to move; Suleiman himself, who seems to have been trying to play both ends against the middle, did not join Charles, and most of the lesser chiefs were wisely waiting on events. Charles withdrew to Pampelona, abandoning Barcelona, Gerona and Auesca. It is possible that he had met Abd ar-Rahman and been defeated, but the sources are so reticent we cannot tell. He decided against trying to hold Pampelona as an outpost through the winter, with the Pyrenees between a garrison and reinforcements; instead, he razed the walls and led his army back towards France, apparently in something of a hurry.

The Basques of Navarre, either to retaliate for Charlemagne's treatment of Pampelona or simply for plunder, prepared an ambush as Charlemagne's army climbed back over the pass of Roncesvalles, three thousand feet high. They let the main body pass, and fell on the rearguard and the baggage train in its charge. The Basques had the advantage of surprise and the ground, the Franks were hampered on the narrow road by the ox-carts and packhorses of the baggage, and the ensuing debacle was one of the worst blows that Charlemagne's armies ever suffered. It is not even mentioned in the Royal Annals, and for shame the whole of the Spanish campaign was omitted, but everyone knew what had happened. A later chronicler who mentions the

Right: An ornate water jug presented to Charlemagne by Heroun al-Raschid.

Overleaf: The advances made by the palace school of manuscript painting can be seen in the contrast between these two illustrations of St Matthew: on the left from the Codex Aureus produced in Canterbury *c.*750 and on the right from the Abbeville Gospels *c.*800. The earlier saint is a stiff, austere figure in contrast with the graceful, mobile Carolingian model.

LIBER GENERATIONIS IHVXPI FILII
DAVID FILII ABRAHAM

battle does not bother to list the leading men who died with the rearguard; 'all men,' he wrote, 'know their names'. In the only contemporary source to mention it, the annals of a monastery, the entry is pathetically stark: 'in this year the Lord Charles went to Spain, where he suffered a great disaster'.

Einhard's *Life* gives the only nearly contemporary account which is at all circumstantial.

As Charles's army was moving forward, strung out in a long thin column because of the narrowness of the road, the Basques stormed down from the heights. They had been lying in ambush, for which the thickly wooded terrain was very suitable. They threw the baggage train of the rearguard into the abyss, and the troops who were covering the main body. Then they began to fight and killed everyone to the last man. They plundered the baggage and disappeared with extraordinary speed as night began to fall. The Basques were able to take advantage of their light armour and the lie of the land, while the Franks were impeded by their heavier equipment and their lower position on the mountainside. Many died in this battle, including the seneschal Eggihard, Anselm the Count Palatine and Roland, the governor of the Breton March. The Franks were unable to take immediate vengeance, for after the attack the enemy scattered so widely that no one knew in what corner of the earth to look for them.

There is a possible clue in Einhard's account to the reason for the extent of the disaster. The Romans had developed quite elaborate column formations, using vanguard, rearguard and flanking troops to protect the main body and the baggage train. The essence of these dispositions, along with other information on Roman military techniques, was known to the Franks from Vegetius' *Definitions*, which combined the functions of a Greek glossary and encyclopedia, and it is likely that they adopted some Roman practices. Einhard's phrase 'the troops covering the main body' clearly refers to what in Roman practice was the rearguard, and what he describes as the rearguard is the baggage train. It is possible that Einhard, who was not after all a soldier, is simply being careless; but if he is right, the army crossed Roncesvalles with the baggage train *behind* the rearguard, a formation which was perfectly acceptable for advancing into open country with the enemy ahead, but madness in retreat, especially through a narrow defile where manoeuvre is restricted. If the rearguard had been in a position to protect the baggage train, the outcome might have been different.

Einhard's mention of the governor of Breton March is the only historical reference to Roland, the legendary medieval hero. Roland became the hero of the *Chanson de Roland*, an epic written in Old French in the eleventh century, drawing on an earlier, oral tradition of improvisations in a strict form on a known theme. In the intervening centuries, the disaster had been completely transformed. The opening lines calmly state that Charlemagne had spent seven years in Spain and conquered the country 'as far as the sea'. Elsewhere in the poem we learn that Charlemagne was two hundred years old. The attack on the rearguard is carried out by the Saracens, which turns the ambush into an

Opposite: This splendid chalice is named after Tassilo, the duke of Bavaria who tried unsuccessfully to preserve his independence from Charlemagne. The chalice may have been made in Salzburg *c.*777 or even in Northumbria, since the Northumbrian influence is strong. It is decorated with images of Christ and the saints and is the only chalice bearing figures that can be found before the twelfth century. The duke presented it to Kremsmünster where it still remains.

episode in the wars between Crescent and Cross. The Franks are sacrificed to the Saracens by the treachery of a completely invented Judas, Ganelon; he feels that Roland and Charlemagne have undervalued and insulted him. (The scene in which he taunts the Saracens and provokes them into rejecting Charlemagne's peace overtures and planning the ambush is particularly well done). Roland and his chosen warrior companions, the Ten Peers, are at the centre of the story, and with one of them, Oliver, his relationship is reminiscent of David and Jonathan or Achilles and Patroclus. The sworn companions turn the poem into a celebration of the feudal ideas of knighthood; Roland in particular has the knightly qualities of bravery, loyalty and pride to excess. The disaster is partly due to his refusal to humiliate himself by blowing his marvellous horn, Olifant, to summon the Emperor back to help, until only he and Oliver are left alive. He dies by the side of Oliver, who survives him long enough to describe Roland's valour and staunchness. Oliver s death provokes a wonderful scene in which when the Emperor sighs, groans, sheds tears and faints, a hundred knights decorously imitate him in unison. The poem ends with a description of Charles's revenge on the traitor and the Saracens. After a trial by combat, Ganelin is torn apart by horses. An elementary blunder becomes a moral victory.

The poem is often crude, compared to the contemporary German heroic poems which had a much longer and more sophisticated tradition behind them, but it is vigorous, direct and vital. It is the simplest and earliest version of one of the favourite stories of the middle ages, and inspired a whole cycle of heroic poems dealing with Charlemagne's legendary deeds. Versions of the Roland myth were chanted at Hastings – before the poem we know was written down – and used by Pope Urban II to inspire the knights of France to join his crusade. Roland's sacrifice of the rearguard to his own pride was seen for centuries as the essence of knighthood.

In life, there was no immediate sequel. Charlemagne was prevented by events in Saxony from seeking revenge; Suleiman fought a rival for the leadership of the Abbassids, and the conspiracy came to nothing; Abd ar-Rahman was preoccupied with recapturing Saragossa and asserting some sort of authority over the Basques. The winter of 778–9 was one of famine in Charles's lands, partly caused by the absence of so many on campaign during the harvest.

After the disaster, Frankish authority in Aquitaine had to be strengthened. Charlemagne wanted to be sure that the Basques and Saracens would not be able to take advantage of the defeat, but he was also conscious that Roncesvalles had cost him considerable prestige. Aquitaine had often achieved *de facto* independence under the Merovingians, and its ruler, the young Count William of Toulouse, was able and popular. Charlemagne established nine new Frankish courts, settled Frankish vassals in the countryside, and appointed Franks to bishoprics and abbacies. In 781 he repeated the Lombard solution, by giving the Aquitainians Louis, his year-old son, as king. To be a separate kingdom, although it was ruled by Charlemagne's viceroys, assuaged Aquitainian pride and their feelings of racial distinctness and cultural superiority. The new kingdom included Septimania and (in theory) Gascony, as well as Aquitaine proper.

The infant king's advisers had considerable trouble with the security of their south-western frontier. The Basque tribes fought each other and were negotiating with the Saracens (revealing that despite Roncesvalles they knew that Charlemagne was the stronger party, the greater threat to their independence). In 790, the Basque chieftain Adelric captured Chorso, the duke of Toulouse. Charlemagne could not ignore this disrespect of his ban, and summoned Adelric to the assembly, held that year at Worms; unfortunately, the summons so incensed the Basques that Count William, Chorso's son, was forced to mount an expedition to quell the ensuing disorder. The Franks did not attempt another full-scale invasion of Saracen territory. Instead, small bodies crossed the mountains to seize and hold easily-defended towns; by 790 they loosely held a zone that extended three hundred miles down the Mediterranean coast from the eastern Pyrenees.

In 788 Abd ar-Rahman, the founder of the Ommayyad emirate at Cordova, died and was succeeded by his son Hisham, who was young, capable and pious. Hisham preached a jihad in 791, and had collected a great force by 793 which he led into Aquitaine. The Saracens sacked the suburbs outside the walls of Narbonne, and defeated Count William before Carcassonne. They carried off many captives and a great deal of loot, and decorated the walls of the great mosque at Cordova with the richest of the spoils.

The Franks still did not attempt to exact vengeance; instead, Charlemagne formally constituted the Spanish March in 795. 'March' to the Franks meant a defensive frontier zone, and signalled that Charlemagne did not intend to extend his conquests in that direction, and had decided to consolidate a defensive zone to protect the territories behind. Other examples are the Breton and Saxon marches, intended to keep out the Celts and Slavs respectively. The Spanish March was part of the kingdom of Aquitaine, but executive control was in the hands of Count William, as 'count of the March of Toulouse', a politically astute move.

King Louis and Count William developed the tactics that the Franks had used before Hisham's offensive, and in 796 the tide turned. A Frankish raiding force crossed the Pyrenees, achieved its objectives and returned safely. The Franks captured and garrisoned a number of fortresses beyond the Pyrenees, courts were established, Christian refugees from Saracen territory settled in the March as they had done earlier in Septimania. The March was defended by a roving band of renegade Muslims and refugee Christians. Hisham died in 801, and the new emir, al-Hakam, quarrelled with his uncle and the governors of a number of northern towns. Discontented Saracen chiefs crossed the mountains and met Charles and Louis several times at Aix and Heristal. Frankish power was now close enough to the little Christian enclave of the Asturias to be useful to King Alfonso, who sent several embassies and pressed for an alliance. Count

William took advantage of the divisions following Hisham's death to capture Barcelona and, using ships collected in Italian ports, the Balearics. There were frequent campaigns, from 809 to 813 a campaign every year, ending in the conquest of Navarre. By the end of Charlemagne's reign, the March was firmly established. It later became the Margravate of Barcelona, which with the Asturias was the base for the eventual *reconquista*.

The only serious difficulties that Charlemagne had with the Saracens after 799 were connected with their slave-raids in the Mediterranean. War fleets from Spain and North Africa often attacked the coasts of Italy and Aquitaine, carrying off captives. The Saracens sought to use the Balearics, Corsica and Sardinia as sources of timber for ship-building, targets for slave-raiding, and bases for raids further afield. Charlemagne did not attempt to suppress the raiders at source, but he fought them for the islands, whose Christian populations did not gain very much from the Emperor's interventions. His efforts did, however, succeed in their primary objective of protecting the coasts of the mainland.

Around the turn of the century, when his power was at its height, Charlemagne succeeded in establishing good relations directly with the Abbassid caliph of Baghdad, Heroun al-Rashid, who became legendary as the caliph of the *Thousand and One Nights*. Two Frankish nobles, Sigismund and Lantfrid, left in 797 with Isaac, a Jewish traveller and linguist. Isaac returned in 801, without his two companions who had died on the long and arduous journey, but accompanied by ambassadors from the caliph. Their presents to the Emperor astonished the Frankish court; gems, fine plate of pure gold, rich embroidered ceremonial robes, delicately carved chessmen in ivory, water clocks with refined mechanisms and rare animals, including a white elephant. The elephant became Charlemagne's pet, and such a favourite at court that its name, Abul Abbas, has even come down to us. Charlemagne was so attached to it that he took it on all his campaigns, and was heartbroken when it died in the winter of 811 in Saxony. What other animal than an elephant could possibly have been Charlemagne's pet?

A piece of oriental textile from the Aachen treasury, patterned with elephants. Charlemagne was greatly attached to his pet elephant, Abul Abbas, presented to him by Heroun al-Raschid.

9
Wars of the Cross: the Eastern Frontier

Charlemagne's conquest of the Saxons was the hardest, fiercest and most protracted of his wars. Eighteen full-scale campaigns spread over thirty-three years, much incidental fighting and the harshest settlement that Charlemagne ever imposed on a conquered nation were required before they were subjugated. The war was also the most important for the future shape of Europe: it began the process of giving political unity to the German-speaking lands.

Einhard's words give a good idea of the passions aroused:

No other war was fought by the Frankish people with such perseverance, bitterness and effort, for the Saxons were like most of the Germanic peoples, wild, idolatrous and hostile to our religion, and they did not regard it as dishonourable to profane and break the laws of God and man.

Ethnically the Saxons were very close to the Franks, and their language and customs resembled Frankish ones at the time of the invasion of Gaul. They grew corn and raised cattle and horses; the sale of horses was their chief trade. They lived under a customary law, without a king or any form of central government; their social organisation was based on the four grades of nobles, freemen, bondmen and slaves, and on a highly structured kinship system. Decisions were made collectively; popular assemblies, folkmoots, made peace or war and the law was handed down by juries of doomsmen.

The Saxons inhabited the regions of Germany now known as Holstein, Hanover, Brunswick and Westphalia, from the North Sea and the Heligoland Bight southwards to the Harz mountains, from the river Ems in the west to the Elbe and the Eider in the east, at the root of the Danish peninsula. They were divided into four main nations: the Westphalians along the valley of the Ems; the Angarians along the valley of the Weser; the Eastphalians between the Harz and the Elbe; and the North Albingians, reckoned a Saxon people although they generally held aloof from the other branches and their wars, who lived between the Elbe and the Eider. The ill-defined frontiers marched with those of Frisia, Denmark, France and various Slav tribes.

On the southern frontier were the old-established Frankish districts of Hesse,

Opposite: An eighth-century picture stone from Gotland depicts Odin riding to Valhalla and greeted by Freya with a drinking horn. Below is a Viking ship. The religion of the Saxons was related to the Scandinavian cults of Odin and Thor.

A Saxon cross and (*right*) a warrior's hammer, both found in a grave.

Franconia and Thuringia. Hessians and Franconians were divisions of the Austrasian sub-kingdom, and as such particularly loyal to Charlemagne. The Thuringians were a distinct group, but fairly well assimilated into France. Frisia as far as the river Ems (roughly modern Holland) was Christian, and with its conversion had fallen under Frankish rule. Between the Ems and the Weser the Frisians were pagan, and owed allegiance to neither the Franks nor the Saxons.

Saxon religion was closely related to the Scandinavian cults of Odin and Thor, though perhaps rather less sophisticated. There were many sacred springs, groves and woods, as well as wooden enclosures – which may have doubled as fortresses – containing tree-shaped cult objects in wood or stone. They cremated their dead, practised augury, sacrificed animals and in times of stress men as well. Human sacrificial victims were hung. This was a ritual death, not then in use as a punishment, and was connected with a myth about Odin the All-Seeing, who was supposed to have obtained the magic of the runes after an ordeal by hanging. It is a myth of redemption and resurrection, not unlike the central theme of Christianity: the two traditions are in fact identified in an early Christian Anglo-Saxon poem, *The Dream of the Cross*. Saxon religion was firmly established; priests enjoyed a recognised status in the community, and were endowed with twice the usual holding of land. Many of their rituals were linked with fertility, which in an agricultural community guaranteed their status.

The Anglo-Saxon bishop Boniface had begun the missionary work in Saxony with the support of the Arnulfings, who obviously hoped that conversion would help bring peace, even without an extension of Frankish rule. Boniface's disciple Sturm, a Bavarian noble, founded a Benedictine monastery

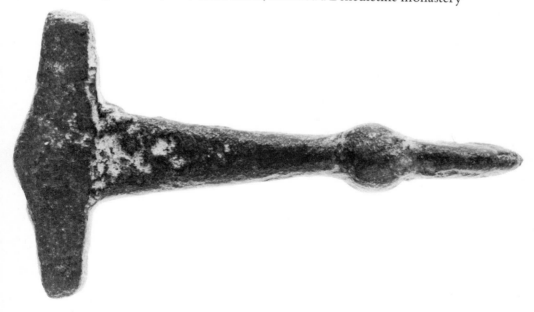

IMAGO HOMINIS

at Fulda on the edge of pagan territory in 744, as a seminary for missionaries; the abbey of St Martin at Utrecht, in Christian Frisia, did a similar job. The missionaries included Franks, Frisians, Bavarians, Anglo-Saxons and native Saxons, and were active all through Charles's wars. It was gradually becoming more difficult to persuade the Saxons to accept baptism; they looked at the Frisian example and decided that the traditional paganism and political independence went together.

Since the time of Clovis, the Saxons had remained outside the Frankish sphere of influence, despite attempts to incorporate their territory into France. Clovis had imposed an annual tribute of five hundred cows, but the Saxons had taken advantage of the internal disorders of Merovingian France to avoid paying it whenever they could. Charles Martel and his sons fought no less than ten campaigns against them, and eventually Pepin restored the tribute in the form of three hundred horses. These campaigns did not result in the permanent occupation of Saxon territory; they were punitive expeditions, consisting of massacres, looting, and the taking of captives rather than pitched battles. On Pepin's death, the Saxons again ceased to pay tribute.

At the assembly held in Worms in 772, Charlemagne announced his intention of making war on the Saxons. His justifications were the breach of the oath to Pepin and for good measure the expulsion of a number of missionaries and the destruction of their churches. Charles always took treaties made with his father very seriously, as the case of Desiderius shows, and made it a point of honour to uphold them. He also saw it as his Christian duty to bring the pagans under his rule so that they could be led to the true faith, and there is no reason whatsoever to suppose he was insincere in this sense of mission. However, as the Saxon wars dragged on, leaving little booty to be had and sapping the fighting spirit of the Frankish army, elements of personal pride and obstinacy appear in Charlemagne's conduct of the war, and his fervent piety begins to resemble bigotry.

Charlemagne took only a small army with him into Saxony in 772, perhaps no more than a thousand fighting men. He did not intend to begin a permanent conquest. The Franks were almost unopposed; used to fighting in small bands and relying on surprise attacks and ambushes, the Saxons did not concentrate against the invaders. Charlemagne marched through Westphalia, captured the stockade of Eresburg and held it for the defence of Hesse. He then proceeded to the source of the Lippe, where the holiest of the Saxon groves stood. Its cult object represented Irminsul, the universe tree (identical with the Norse Yggdrasil). He spent three days destroying the Irminsul totem and the enclosure, and despoiled the treasure house and distributed the treasure to his men. To get an idea of the sacrilege involved, one should imagine Harun al-Rashid stabling his horses in the nave of the church of the Holy Sepulchre in Jerusalem, installing his harem in the chancel, and eating his dinner off the high altar.

Nevertheless, the Saxons were still not ready to tackle the Franks. After Charlemagne had burnt a number of Saxon settlements, they gave him twelve

Opposite: A page from the Echternach Evangeliary *c.*730, which appears to have been at least partly illuminated by one of the British missionaries to the area, for the style is strongly Anglo-Saxon.

Utrec
Do

Quentovic

AIX-LA-CHA

AUSTR

Amiens

Rouen
Corbie △ Noyon   Laon   Ee

Soissons
St Denis △   Rheims

NEUSTRIA

Paris   *Hautvilliers*   V

Chalons

Lorra

Quimper   **Brittany**

Rennes

Le Mans

**Brittanic
March**

Orleans   Sens

△

Loire   *Germigny-des-Pres*

Nantes   Tours   Auxerre

Langres

· *St Philibert-de-Grandlieu* △

Bourges

Besancor

Poitiers

Chalon

L. Genev

· Saintes

BURGUN

Bordeaux   AQUITAINE

Lyons

Garonne

Vienne

St Didier △   Valence

Rhone

GASCONY   · Toulouse   Avignon   PROVEN

Pamplona   Navarre   *Gellone* △   **Septimania**   Arles   Aix-en-Pro

Narbonne   Marseilles

Spanish March

Gerona

Barcelona

Charlemagne's Empire

░░░ Extensions to the Empire made by 814 AD

☐ Kingdom of the Franks in 771 AD when the death of
    Carloman united the territories under Charlemagne

△ Abbeys, priories and convents

Saxon March

Hamburg

SAXONY

Weser

Corvey △

● Paderborn

ogne

Fulda △

Elbe

Oder

BOHEMIANS

SLAVONIC TRIBES

inz

● Frankfurt

● Worms

ch △

Swabia

Nordgau

Strasbourg

Ratisbon ● △ *St. Emmeram*

Danube

Bavaria

NNIA

● Augsburg

L. Constance

stance ●

Inn

Kremsmunster △

Pannonia

Tisa

Gall △

Salzburg ●

CARINTHIA

AVARS

L. Como

Friuli

LOMBARDY

Cividale △

an ●

Verona ●

March of Friuli

● Aquileia

ria ●

Drava

● Cremona

io △

● Modena

Bologna ●

SERBS

● Ravenna

● Pisa

Miles

0   100   200

● Spoleto

0   100   200   300

Kilometres

● Rome

ITALY

△ *Monte Cassino*

PICCATORVM · CARNIS   RISURRECTIONEM   UITAMAITERNAM · AMIN

INCIPITFIDESCATHO   LICAM
CIICUGUEUULT   UNAESTDIUINITASAE   SIMILITEROMNIPOTENS
SALUUSISSEANTEOMNIA   QUALISGLORIACOAET   PATER · OMNIPOTENSEI

A meeting of a church council from the Utrecht Psalter (f 90v).

hostages as a pledge that their raids on France would cease. Charlemagne was back in Heristal in time for the autumn hunting and the birth of Charles, his first legitimate son. The Saxons waited until the next year to retaliate, when Charlemagne was involved in Italy. The Westphalians raided Frisia, while the Angarians attacked Hesse, desecrating and looting Boniface's church at Fritzlar. In 774 Charlemagne sent punitive bands across Saxony, looting and burning in their turn, and began to prepare for a full-scale campaign the following year. Conquest was now his aim. At a council of bishops and magnates in January 775, he denounced the Saxons as perfidious, pagan treaty-breakers, and declared he would conquer and convert them.

Charlemagne summoned a full host for that year, and took monks with the army as missionaries. Crossing the Rhine in the spring, he defeated a Saxon army on the Weser, captured the stockade of Sigiburg and built a church there, rebuilt the Eresburg and left garrisons in both forts. He took oaths of fidelity from many Saxon leaders, and left an occupied and quiet country behind him.

Saxon war-bands sacked the two stockades in 776, while Charlemagne was dealing with the duke of Friuli. Charlemagne returned in high summer, put down the revolt, rebuilt Eresburg and Sigiburg and added another strongpoint which he called Karlsburg. This time he imported masons and had them built in stone; fortresses rather than stockades. They were to be the strongpoints of the Saxon March, a broad belt of territory to the north of Hesse and Thuringia which now seemed reasonably secure. Charlemagne appointed a Frankish governor, and left him a large discretion and plenty of troops.

At this point, Charlemagne hoped to bring the Saxon wars to an end. The establishment of a march indicates as much; now that a supposedly secure defensive zone protected the Frankish lands of central Germany and the missionary centres of Fulda, Fritzlar and Hersfeld, further conquest was thought to be unnecessary. In 777, he summoned the Saxons to a great assembly at Paderborn. Most of the leaders decided it was wise to attend, as he had a large Frankish army with him. They were further impressed by the arrival of a Saracen embassy from Spain. Crowds of Saxons accepted baptism – Abbot Sturm administered the sacrament in a nearby river – and took oaths of allegiance. There were no disturbances that spring or summer. On his return to France, preoccupied with Suleiman's promises and with plans for the Spanish war, Charlemagne seems to have anticipated no further trouble from Saxony.

It was a miscalculation. The Saxons held an oath as sacred as the Franks, but they may have considered that their oaths to Charlemagne were given under duress, and therefore were not binding. The Christianity of most of the more recently baptised Saxons was nominal, and they did not fear eternal damnation as a consequence of perjury. Charlemagne's vengeance was the only penalty they had to be afraid of, and he would have to catch them first. Widukind, a Westphalian noble who had been active in the earlier fighting, and was deeply committed to the old pagan ways, incited many of the Saxons to throw off their oaths and join him in revolt. Their raiding parties created havoc throughout the Frankish lands, and penetrated as far as the Rhine. Charlemagne, involved in the campaign which ended so ignominiously at Roncesvalles, was unable to retaliate in strength. He sent a small contingent to chase the raiders back into Saxony, which was unfortunately surprised and nearly annihilated at a river crossing. It was a bad year for ambushes.

Charlemagne spent 778 and 779 in Saxony, and wintered at Worms. The Saxons avoided a battle, and Charlemagne burnt and plundered farms, homesteads and halls from the Ems to the Elbe, reaching the border with the Slavs. Many Saxons were baptised at the point of the sword; against the advice of his churchmen, Charlemagne seems to have relied on the sacrament itself, rather than on the teaching of the Gospels, to Christianise the country. After wintering in Italy, Charlemagne held another magnificent assembly in the spring of 782, on the lines of that in 777, and this time received embassies from the king of Denmark and the khan of the nomadic Avars. He divided Saxony into counties, appointed Saxons as well as Franks as counts, and arranged for the defence of the Saxon Slav frontier; for which purpose the chamberlain, Adalgis, a count called Worad and the constable, Geilo, raised a force of Austrasians and Saxons.

When Charlemagne returned to France, Widukind may already have been back in Germany. He had taken refuge in neighbouring Denmark, and had obviously lost none of his appeal. On his reappearance in Saxony, he began swiftly and secretly collecting an army, which was ready soon after the assembly dispersed. Before Widukind declared himself, however, bands of

Slavs began to disturb the eastern frontier of Saxony. Adalgis, Geilo and Worad led their newly raised mixed force off to deal with them. On the march, they obviously realised that something was up; Charlemagne's cousin, Thierry, was summoned with reinforcements. When they finally stumbled on Widukind, they did not try to effect a junction with Thierry. Instead they tried to keep the glory for themselves, and pursued the Saxon army into the wooded Süntel hills, near modern Minden. Their troops were almost wiped out in the ambush that ensued. Thierry came up just in time to rescue a few survivors from the Saxon pursuit, but Adalgis, Geilo and four counts were among the dead.

Widukind was calling for the overthrow of Frankish suzerainty, the destruction of the missionaries and their churches, and a return to the old gods. The completeness of the victory in the Süntel probably convinced many of the Saxons of the correctness of his theological views. His followers marched through the district between the mouths of the Elbe and the Weser, burning churches, cruelly punishing Christian converts, driving out the Frankish counts, killing any priests or bishops who did not flee, and setting up the idols again. The combination of religion and politics was giving the war a nationalist tinge, most unusual in those days of local, hierarchical loyalties. A similar revolt and reversion to paganism broke out in the Christianised parts of Frisia.

Charlemagne, according to the chroniclers, 'raged'. His conciliatory, persuasive behaviour at the assembly had been in vain, and he took it personally. He was more than ever determined to crush Saxon independence, and abandoned any ideas he might have formed of doing it gradually. Although it was late in the campaigning season, he swiftly collected a large army, and led it into Eastphalia. Widukind's army, perhaps contented with the booty they had taken from the Franks who fell in the Süntel, or frightened by Charlemagne's supposed invincibility (they had never defeated a force led by him in person) or simply by the numbers of his troops, melted away. Widukind slipped off back to Denmark. Charlemagne summoned all the nobles of the region, and demanded the surrender of every man who had fought at Süntel. His fury must have cowed the Saxon leaders, for they gave up to him several thousand of the rebels – their own countrymen. At Verden, on a single day, Charlemagne had 4,500 of them beheaded.

The massacre shocked contemporaries. Legalistically, Charlemagne could point to the broken Saxon oaths, which according to the laws of both nations deserved the death penalty, but there is no indication that he gave the rebels any form of hearing or saw the slaughter as an execution. Morally, by the ideas of the times, he had a perfect right to avenge the annihilation of the frontier force. Neither defence justified the way he succumbed to his bloodlust, and many of his courtiers lamented that a ruler who had subdued whole kingdoms could not master his own brutal rage. Verden was a reversion to a barbarian type.

In the same year Charlemagne imposed direct Frankish rule throughout

Saxony, and made harsh and repressive changes in the law which in effect imposed martial law and reduced the Saxons to second class citizens. These measures were contained in a capitulary promulgated as the *capitualtio de partibus saxoiniae*. The Saxons were entirely subjected to Frankish counts; they were forbidden to hold their folkmoots, and the administration of justice was transferred from the doomsmen to the counts. The death penalty was introduced – and as far as we know applied – for a great many offences. Some of these were political, such as refusing to take the oath of loyalty to Charlemagne, or breaking it once taken. Others were religious, ranging from offences one might agree were serious, such as murdering a priest, deacon or bishop, or performing human sacrifice, to the relatively trivial: stealing from a church, breaking the Lenten fast, or cremating the dead in the pagan way instead of burying them.

The point of these measures is revealed by the imposition of the death penalty for refusing baptism; Christianity was to be imposed wholesale and by force, which involved destroying the whole apparatus of the pagan cult. Pagan priests were expropriated in favour of the church; their holdings went to their Christian successors, whose income was supplemented by a tithe of all produce. Along with the land, parish priests acquired some odder responsibilities, such as keeping the boar for the village; one wonders whether they realised what that particular obligation signified. The capitulary was bitterly resented in Saxony, and was criticised by Charlemagne's clerical advisers and the missionary leaders, despite their hatred of the worship of 'devils'. Boniface had complained about the poverty of the missionaries, as it often made it more difficult for them to gain the respect of the Saxons if they had simultaneously to beg their own bread. His successors did not think that the affluence that resulted from Charlemagne's decree was necessary, nor, in view of the disruption it caused in Saxon society and the burden it laid on the peasants, did they think it was desirable. Alcuin, who was firmly opposed to forcible conversions in any case, put the point neatly in a letter.

If only Christ's gentle yoke and his light burden had been preached to these people with as much zeal as tithe has been demanded! What, did Christ's apostles go into all the world levying tithe and asking presents? Certainly, to give tithe is a good practice; but it is better that tithe should be lost than their faith.

One effect of the harsh penalties intended to protect the church was to make Christianity appear even more bloodthirsty than the old pagan rites, which only rarely demanded men's lives.

The Saxons continued to be rebellious, but were no longer capable of putting an army in the field. The king and his eldest son Charles led their columns throughout Saxony in 783 and 784, terrorising the inhabitants, and pulling down their fortifications and sacred places. In the winter of 784 Charlemagne did not disband his army, but continued to send out raiding parties. He kept Christmas at the Eresburg, bringing his family there, strengthening the castle and building a church. He meant the Saxons to see that he would keep his court there among them whenever he wished.

In the spring of 785, Widukind and his lieutenant Abbio were located in their Danish retreat by Charlemagne's messengers, sent to summon them back to Germany to make their submission. Widukind, who was clearly a fine military leader, realised that although the Saxons were still capable of what we would call guerilla actions, they could no longer gather an army capable of ousting the Franks. Perhaps to indicate to his countrymen how useless further resistance was, and thus to avoid further bloodshed, Widukind agreed to submit. Charlemagne gave hostages for their safe-conduct, and Widukind and Abbio came to Altigny with a Frankish escort, where they took an oath of loyalty and were both baptised. Charlemagne himself acted as godfather, and gave the christening presents. It is an indication of how far he had recovered his equanimity and his political judgement that he did not have them put to death or blinded, as his forebears would have done. The pope decreed three separate days of thanksgiving at the news.

Under the new dispensation, the Saxons were liable for military service, and did in fact take part in a campaign against the Slavs in 789. Nevertheless, ambushes and minor revolts continued and in 793 rebellion became general. It lasted until 797. There was a massacre of Franks near the mouth of the Weser, churches were burned and priests were killed. They were miserable years for the Saxons. Their country had already suffered harshly from over twenty years of warfare, and there were now two parties among the Saxons, Christians who had accepted Frankish rule, and the pagans who still hankered for independence. According to the fortunes of war one faction mistreated, murdered and dispossessed the other. Charlemagne and his son repeated their scorched earth campaigns every summer, but the king realised that something more was needed if the Saxons were ever to be finally pacified. He deported thousands of Saxons from the most intransigent districts and settled them in France, replacing them by colonies of loyal Franks; and confiscated many large estates for his own use, and used the revenues partly to maintain standing garrisons in fortified posts throughout the land.

These measures finally broke Saxon resistance, and Charlemagne was able to begin undoing the harm done by the fierce *capitulatio ad partibus saxonicae*. It was replaced by the much milder *capitulare saxonicum* in 797, which substituted heavy fines for most of the death penalties of the earlier capitulary and restored the old Saxon customary laws. Charles had a written code of these laws edited and copied to help his counts administer it. Saxony remained peaceful, and the Frankish army was only needed to conquer the North Albingians, who had not been involved in the earlier fighting. Charlemagne was probably afraid that the district might become a haven for Saxon dissidents, and subdued it in three campaigns, in 797, 802 and 804. He had learnt from his experiences in Saxony, and applied the same policy of mass deportations and colonisations straight away. The permanent military posts and the massive resettlements

The Enger reliquary *c.*780, one of the christening gifts given by Charlemagne to Widukind when the Saxon leader was baptised in 785. The reliquary is made of gold and chased silver gilt over an oak core. The figures are Christ between two angels and the Virgin between two apostles.

must have been a tremendous strain on the financial resources and rudimentary administration of France. That they were undertaken at all is an indication of the doggedness of the Saxon resistance as well as of Charlemagne's determination.

In just the same way as he was drawn into a full conquest of Saxony after the attempt to establish a march had failed, Charlemagne's expansion in this region involved him in yet more fighting. In one case he felt the need to protect his new territories by subduing a hostile nation on their borders and at the same time securing a more easily defensible frontier; in the other, his growing power gave him the opportunity of settling an old score.

The quarrel was with Duke Tassilo of Bavaria. The Bavarians were of the same stock as the Saxons and Franks; they were Christians, like the Franks, just as civilised and had been settled just as long (in the lands between the Brenner pass and the Danube). The Bavarian church was strong, wealthy and deeply involved in the missionary work in Saxony. Supposedly Bavaria was part of France; it had been subdued by Clovis's sons, and the duke made to take an oath of allegiance. The proximity of Bavaria to Lombardy, its remoteness from the Frankish heartland and the fact that the ducal family was proud and old-established, all encouraged Bavarian aspirations to independence.

The Arnulfings had maintained Frankish suzerainty, with a certain amount of trouble. Charlemagne's uncle Carloman had made Duke Odilo take an oath of loyalty and cede a province as compensation for trying to throw off Frankish allegiance. Odilo was succeeded in 748 by Tassilo, who was a grandson of Pepin on his mother's side. He took an oath of vassalage to Pepin in 757, and later marched as his vassal to Pavia. In 768, however, he married Liutgard, one of Desiderius' daughters, and from then on his policy was pro-Lombard. (He was probably making exactly the same political miscalculation as Bertrada did.) He ignored the Frankish vassalage, without provoking trouble by openly repudiating it, and simply acted as an independent ruler. Bavaria had not in fact been mentioned in Pepin's will. Tassilo kept a splendid court at Ratisbon, issued his own capitularies to counts he appointed without consulting Charlemagne, and sent his son to be baptised by the pope. By annexing Carinthia and its Slav population he showed the Bavarians that Charlemagne was not the only king around who could make aggression pay.

Under Charlemagne's successors, he probably would have been allowed to get away with it. Although Charlemagne did not press his claim to suzerainty for several years after his accession, he meant to have it recognised sooner or later. The Bavarian army, which did not use cavalry, was no match for the Franks, and if Charlemagne's Lombard and Italian policies succeeded, Bavaria would be almost surrounded by Charlemagne's territories. Charlemagne may have been restrained by his friends among the high Bavarian churchmen, but they also kept him well informed. One bishop was in fact removed from his see for being too friendly with the Frankish king.

In 781, Charles prepared to assert himself. He suspected Tassilo of plotting with the Lombards, and of hoping to exploit any disorder in Italy for his own ends. Hadrian was persuaded to join in a joint embassy to remind Tassilo of his oaths; the duke travelled to Worms under a safe-conduct, renewed his oaths and gave hostages. After the oath-taking, Charles was too preoccupied with continual repression in Saxony to enforce Tassilo's allegiance. The duke gave him no help in the Saxon wars, and in 785 one of Charlemagne's counts in Lombardy was killed in a frontier brawl. In 787, realising that Charlemagne would soon be in a position to deal with him, Tassilo sent clerics to Hadrian and asked him to mediate. Hadrian did not want to see war between France and Bavaria; both nations were Christian, both supported the church, and their rulers were related by blood. If Tassilo had given his ambassadors power to give assurances in his name, Hadrian might have achieved something, but he had not done so and it was probably deliberate. Eventually, his sly diplomacy ended in complete failure. Hadrian threatened Tassilo with excommunication and his duchy with an interdict if he continued to disregard his oaths to Charlemagne.

787 was the year that Charlemagne received the submission of Widukind in Saxony and Arichis in Benevento, leaving his hands free for a time. He summoned Tassilo to an assembly at Worms to explain his conduct; Tassilo refused, which gave Charlemagne just the excuse he needed. An invasion was swiftly prepared, in overwhelming force. Charlemagne led one army himself across the northern frontier, while a second marched in from the east and King Pepin led his own host of Lombards up from Italy. Many Bavarian nobles were pro-Frankish anyway, and defected to Charlemagne; others were horrified at being asked to fight under the threat of an interdict. Tassilo for once judged the situation correctly, and surrendered without a fight. Charlemagne treated him with the generosity he had shown Widukind and Arichis. He made Tassilo give up his duchy, took oaths of loyalty directly from the Bavarians and carried off Tassilo's eldest son as a hostage, but gave him back the duchy as a benefice and showered him with gifts.

Liutberg, however, had still not forgiven Charlemagne, who had repudiated her sister and overthrown her father. She persuaded Tassilo to rebel, and Charlemagne's Bavarian friends were soon warning him that Tassilo was intriguing again, this time with the Greeks in Italy and the wild Avar nomads to the east of his kingdom. Whether the reports were true or not, they were quite in character, and Charlemagne had had enough. Tassilo was brought before a court made up of nobles from all the kingdoms, at Worms, and accused of conspiracy, encouraging false oaths and for good measure of an almost forgotten act of *herisliz* – deserting Pepin on one of his Aquitaine expeditions. The nobles condemned him to death, but Charles spared his life; he and all his family were forced to take monastic vows. In 784, to silence Bavarian discontent, Tassilo was presented to an assembly at Worms in monastic habit to renounce all his dynasty's claims to the duchy. It is not known whether Tassilo settled down quite as happily in the cloister as Desiderius did.

Charlemagne had now perfected the techniques of assimilating new territories. No new duke was appointed, Tassilo's domains were taken over for the Frankish crown, Charlemagne's capitularies were enforced and Bavarian customary law was codified; in short, annexation. The command of the Bavarian host was given to the prefect of a march organised against the Avars.

The Avar ruling caste was of Tartar stock, related to the Huns and similar in habits. They had fled westward from the Turks in the sixth century, and had settled in Pannonia, where they lorded it over a subject population of Slav agriculturalists. From their new territories they attacked the Byzantines, who paid them tribute for a long time. This was the foundation of their legendary wealth. The Avars still lived by and largely on their horses, as the Huns had done. They were professional pillagers, and built up a vast horde from the loot of their swift, savage raids. The headquarters of the Avar khan and his deputy the *iugur* was a great fortress known as the ring, which was where the treasure was stored. A description of the ring as having nine concentric ramparts of wood and stone has often been taken as fanciful, but it may be that they had adapted an Iron Age hill fort like Maiden Castle.

Their frontier was ill-defined, and the Avars were always ready to intrigue with Charlemagne's enemies, which would have been cause enough for war. In 788 one Avar army invaded Friuli, and two others Bavaria. They were, however, rather too late if they were expecting local support; all the plots against Charlemagne had been crushed. The Avar armies were successfully repulsed. It was clear that Charlemagne would have to deal with them, and in 791 he prepared a massive counter-attack from Regensburg. He led his armies to the Danube, where they spent three days hearing litanies and masses *contra paganos* (against the heathen). Then they moved off; the Bavarian contingent was rowed down the river in barges, and a Frankish column marched along each bank, but at some distance from it. The three divisions coordinated their march by using couriers. Simultaneously, Pepin led the Lombards up from the south. The Avars fled before the Franks, and were saved only by an epidemic which killed nine-tenths of the Frankish horses. Both armies withdrew to their bases, Pepin's in particular laden with loot.

Charlemagne began preparing for another expedition the following year, and to make it easier to tranship provisions from the Rhine to the Danube he conceived the grandiose project of linking the two rivers with a canal. The scheme was far beyond the modest engineering capacities of the Franks, and was abandoned after only two thousand feet had been dug. Remains of the work are still visible near Eichstätt, and to this day children still play in the Karlsgrab. Trouble in Spain and Benevento prevented the campaign; Pepin was given the job of forming a *cordon sanitaire* around the Avars to prevent them meddling in Saxony.

In 795 one section of the Avars submitted to Charlemagne and received baptism; Pepin led an expedition against the remainder. The decisive campaign took place in 796, when Eric, duke of Friuli, and the Slav chieftain Woynimir

'Karlsgrab' near Eichstätt, the fragment of the canal planned
by Charlemagne to link the Rhine and the Danube.

forced their way into the ring and seized a great deal of treasure. Charlemagne promptly used a lot of it to make impressive gifts to the pope, King Offa of Mercia and other European rulers. The khan and the iugur were killed in the same year in fighting between the tribes. There were risings in 797 and 803, but despite the deaths of Eric and other prominent Franks in ambushes, they were not really dangerous, and Charlemagne annexed the Avar lands as far as the natural frontier of the Danube, and organised this new territory as a new Bavarian march. Missionary work began among the Avars and their former Slav subjects, but without the forcible conversions that had caused so much trouble and suffering in Germany. Charlemagne had realised that it made good political sense to accept the arguments that Alcuin and others, for spiritual reasons, advanced in favour of peaceful evangelism. Colonies of Alemans were introduced from Germany, on the model of the Frankish colonies in the Saxon lands. Unfortunately for both Slavs and settlers, Charlemagne's descendants could not hold the district, and the Magyars conquered it. They were no better as overlords than the Avars, and caused just as much trouble to their neighbours.

When Charlemagne led his bloodless invasion of Bavaria, an Irish poet wrote some celebratory verses which treat him as a traditional barbarian king: a ring-giver, leader of the war-band, an upholder of oaths and settler of disputes. The writer may, of course, have been influenced more by the conventions of Irish poetry than by actuality, but it has been suggested that this is really how contemporaries saw Charlemagne until 800. If he had died before then, perhaps we should see him in the same way, distinguished from other Germanic kings only by his ambitions and aggressiveness.

Right: The only surviving example of Carolingian sculpture in the round is this bronze statue, 9 in. high, from the Louvre. The details of dress, moustache, fleur de lys on crown, and the shape of the sword indicate that the statue represents a Carolingian Emperor, probably Charlemagne but possibly Charles the Bald.

10
Pope and Emperor

At Christmas in the year 800, Charlemagne and his entourage were in Rome. The king took the opportunity of arranging for Charles, his eldest son and designated successor, to be anointed king by the pope. The ceremony was to be performed in the church of St Peter on Christmas day. Before the mass which was to precede the anointing, Charlemagne knelt in front of 'St Peter's confession', the shrine of the 'prince of the apostles', to pray. Pope Leo III approached, and as the king rose, crowned him with a diadem. Immediately the 'Roman people', in fact a number of noblemen, acclaimed him three times, shouting the prescribed formula: '*Carolo augusto, a Deo coronato, magno et pacifico imperatore romanorum, vita et victoria*' (to Charles, Augustus, crowned by God, great and peaceful emperor, life and victory). As they did so, the pope 'adored' Charlemagne in the Byzantine manner, prostrating himself and touching his forehead to the ground three times.

It was a momentous event. There had not been a Roman emperor in the west since the puppet Romulus Augustulus – the double diminutive is ironic – was deposed in 476 by his *magister militum*, the barbarian general in command of his army, who sent the imperial regalia to the Emperor Zeno at Constantinople without bothering to ask for them back for anyone else. It is a measure of Charlemagne's power and prestige that he should be the first western ruler for over three hundred years to measure up to the imperial dignity, and a measure of the real political importance of the event that while the circumstances surrounding it are well documented the motives of those involved are highly obscure. Some historians maintain that the coronation was a surprise move by the pope for motives of his own, others that he crowned Charlemagne on orders from the Franks, others again that it does not matter who was responsible, as the coronation was hardly more than a charade put on to satisfy the vanity of those responsible.

The immediate occasion of Charlemagne's presence in Rome in 800 was another crisis in the papacy, this time an internal one. On the day that Pope Hadrian died in 795, his successor Leo III was elected. Charlemagne was distressed by the hasty choice of pope, feeling that as patrician of the Romans

Opposite: One of the two angels in the apse mosaic of the church at Germigny-des-Prés built by Theodulf, one of Charlemagne's learned friends, c.806. It is the only complete mosaic surviving from the many which decorated churches in the time of Charlemagne. The two angels point to the Ark of the Covenant, as does the hand of God appearing from a rainbow between them.

he had a right to be consulted. After all, he had saved the papacy from the Lombards and had become effectively the overlord of the city of Rome and its environs. Nevertheless Charlemagne congratulated the pope on his election. The letter was not, however, merely the usual platitudes that a newly-elected pope might expect to receive. Charlemagne calmly instructed Leo on his duties, calling on him to live according to the canons, to reform the Italian church, and to root out simony (the crime and sin of selling or buying ecclesiastical offices) and heresy. He obviously saw himself as the pope's superior.

Leo meekly accepted Charlemagne's instructions, and sent him the banner of Rome and the keys of the confession of St Peter, symbolising Charlemagne's dual protectorship of the Holy See and the city, recognising that in the person of the king St Peter's had a lay patron in exactly the same way as any rural church in France. The gesture was probably supposed to placate Charlemagne over the failure to notify him of the election, and to bind him even more closely to the papacy and in particular to the present incumbent.

Leo III seems to have been a weak man, and far less astute politically than his predecessor Hadrian. He had been a priest of the papal household before his election, and had neither Hadrian's legal training nor his close links with the notaries and the nobility. The main opposition to him was a faction led by two of Hadrian's relatives who held high office in the secretariat of the Lateran, Paschalis the primicery and Campulus the notary paymaster. The notaries in general and the late pope's relatives in particular suffered a loss of influence with Leo's election; it may be that this was precisely why the election had been rushed, and that the priests and deacons of the household had put Leo forward to restore their own prestige. The nobles probably resented Leo's dependence on the Franks; they did not like the old imperial city being treated as a Frankish dominion. In addition, there were unpleasant rumours about the way Leo had secured his elevation; he was widely rumoured to have obtained it by simony.

On 25 April 799 Leo was ambushed by ruffians hired by Paschalis and Campulus, who pulled him off his horse, tried to put out his eyes and cut out his tongue, and dragged him to a cell in a monastery. (Interestingly, the particular mutilations they attempted are usually associated with the vicious intrigues of Byzantium.) He was rescued by two Frankish counts, and eventually taken to Paderborn, where his reception almost equalled that of Pope Stephen by Pepin. Alcuin and others had impressed on Charlemagne the necessity of maintaining the prestige of the papacy, whatever the shortcomings of the current holder of the office. Leo blessed a new altar, and added relics of St Stephen, the first martyr, to the royal oratory. His unhealed wounds shocked the court.

Back in Rome, Leo's enemies openly accused him of immorality, adultery and perjury. If they could sustain the charges, there would be good grounds for deposing Leo, which would have appeared to justify the attack retrospectively as a sort of unofficial deposition. It was not the first time that a pope's

Opposite: St Peter with Pope Leo III (*left*) and Charlemagne (*right*); an eighth-century mosaic removed to its present site in the Piazza San Giovanni in Laterano. St Peter gives the pallium, symbol of spiritual authority, to Leo, and the imperial banner, symbol of temporal power, to Charlemagne.

SCS PETRVS

DN LE O PP

CARVLO REGI

L

BEATE·PETRE·DONAS
VITA·LEON·PP·E·BICTO
RIA·CARVLO·REGI·DONAS

The mosaic over the Imperial door in Hagia Sophia, Constantinople, shows the Byzantine Emperor doing homage to Christ in the attitude of humility which the Pope adopted towards Charlemagne at his coronation. Subsequent popes thought this action demeaned the papal office and it was never repeated.

143

conduct had been less than edifying – a hundred years before one pope had in fact been declared a heretic – but people were not yet as cynical about the papacy as they were later to become, and the accusations caused a scandal throughout Christendom. For the prestige of the institution it was necessary to find some forum in which the charges could be examined, and the pope either clearly vindicated or canonically deposed. The difficulty was to do this without appearing to sit in judgement on the pope, who was not merely the vicar of Rome but the heir of the Fathers, the vicar (i.e. deputy) of the apostles, the prince of the church and the chosen of God.

Charles travelled to Rome in the autumn of 800, having been delayed on the way by the death of his queen, Liutgard, at Tours. He entered Rome on 24 November, and was welcomed by Leo on the steps of St Peter's. On 1 December, he presided over the opening session of an assembly of lay and clerical magnates, both Franks and Romans, who had been summoned to receive complaints against the pope. In effect, the assembly was a judicial inquiry. At the end of three weeks, Campulus and Paschalis were given an opportunity to state their case. Either the inquiry had not gone their way, or they suspected that Charlemagne had in any case decided to arrange matters in Leo's favour, for they declined. Then came the ingenious part of the proceedings. Having heard the evidence, Charlemagne did not proceed to deliver a judgement, but instead got Leo to take an oath of compurgation. This he did in St Peter's on 23 December. An oath of compurgation, a solemn declaration by an accused party of his innocence, was a quite normal Germanic legal procedure, but it was not normally combined with witnesses. The idea was to have the evidence aired, to vindicate Leo publicly, but then to let him *affirm* his innocence, so as a layman should not appear to sit in judgement on the vicar of Christ. Leo's words reveal the ambiguity of the arrangement.

In order to hear this case, the most clement and serene lord, King Charles, here present, has come to this city with his magnates and clergy: therefore I Leo, pontiff of the Holy Roman Church, without being judged or compelled by anyone, but by an act of spontaneous will, purify and purge myself in your presence, before God who knows my conscience, before his angels, before the blessed Peter ... in whose basilica we now stand, and I declare that I have not perpetrated or ordered to be perpetrated the criminal and sinful acts which have been charged against me.

Charles heard the case, and Leo quite without prompting chose to take his oath. It is a nice formula, but one wonders quite how many people were taken in by it. Whatever careful distinctions were made, the pope had obviously been kept on the throne by Charlemagne. There is not a great deal of difference between being pope at Charlemagne's will and being a Frankish vassal.

Charlemagne's first act after his coronation was to banish Leo's accusers, and one theory is that this was Leo's motive for crowning him. The argument depends on the legal fiction that it was the emperor at Byzantium who appointed the civil officials of Rome, and Paschalis and Campulus could not be

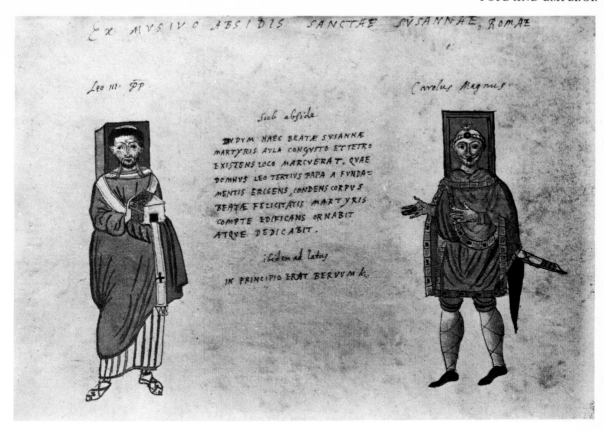

A drawing of a mosaic depicting Leo III and Charlemagne which once decorated San Susanna, Rome, but was later destroyed.

dealt with except by the emperor or his representative. This is a neat theory, and overlooks merely two facts: that since the pontificate of Gregory III (729–41) the pope had not even bothered to inform the emperor who his officials were, and that since taking the title of patrician the Frankish king had every right to act as chief magistrate in Rome. Another theory is that Leo was trying to show his gratitude. If so, the courtesy was not entirely appreciated by the Franks. 'It was at this time that he accepted the title of emperor and augustus. But at first he was so much opposed,' writes Einhard in his *Life*, 'that he affirmed that, even though it was an important feast day, he would not have entered the church that day if he had known in advance the plan of the pope.' It is unlikely that the coronation was entirely a surprise. Charlemagne may not have known that the pope intended to crown him on that particular occasion, but Leo must surely have been confident that Charlemagne was interested enough in the title, even if the timing did not suit him, not to publicly spurn the diadem that Leo offered.

Einhard's words fit this interpretation. What one cannot do is discount entirely his statement that Charlemagne was opposed to taking the title, which is what historians who want to argue that the coronation took place on Charlemagne's instructions must do. Einhard is usually accepted as a good source, and in the absence of direct evidence of what Charlemagne was thinking, there is no particular reason to suppose that Einhard is not largely correct on this point as well. What we are entitled to speculate about is whether Einhard is being entirely frank about why Charlemagne would not have gone to hear mass in St Peter's on Christmas day. To support his statement, the biographer mentions the difficulties with the Byzantines, who objected to Charles taking what they regarded as their title. (It is significant that in the account of the coronation in the *Book of the Popes*, the offending phrase, *imperator romanorum*, is modified to simple *imperator*, which suggests that the papal household realised that Leo may have been a little overenthusiastic.) There was indeed trouble with Byzantium, but this would not have been a deterrent. It was nearly two hundred years since the Byzantines had been able to enforce their point of view in Italy, and Charlemagne knew it.

Einhard may have been trying to suggest that Charlemagne did not seek the title in any way – other sources are careful to insist that he took it at the desire of church and people – or he may have been trying to cover up the fact that Leo had rather cleverly outwitted Charlemagne, and made a subtle piece of diplomatic propaganda. On 23 December, the supreme pontiff was in effect restored by the king of the Franks; on 25 December, the king of the Franks was created emperor by the pope. What the pope gave, it might be supposed, the pope could just as easily take away. Charlemagne had no independent claim to the title that the pope bestowed on him. The coronation obscured the humiliating oath, and made the events of December 800 look like the graciously reciprocal favours of two supreme rulers, one spiritual and one lay, confirming each other in power. It is reasonable to suppose that if Charlemagne had decided at leisure that he would have the imperial title, he would have brought the pope to Aix or St Denis, where Pepin had been crowned king by Stephen, to perform the ceremony.

Whatever his immediate reaction, Charlemagne began using the title in his protocols and on his seals. There was no change in the relatively simple court ceremonial at Aix, no attempt to imitate the elaborate rituals of Byzantium, but the title was useful in many ways. The political thinking of the court intelligentsia had already been moving in a direction which made the imperial dignity seem logical and even necessary. This new ideology is used by Alcuin in a famous letter written to Charlemagne in June 799. It reads like a reminder rather than an argument which is being presented for the first time.

Up to now three persons have been at the summit of the worldly hierarchy; first, the representative of apostolic serenity, vicar of the blessed Peter, prince of the apostles, whose seat he occupies. What has happened to the actual holder of that see you have taken care to make known to me. Second, there is the titular holder of the

imperial dignity, who exercises secular power in the second Rome [i.e. Byzantium].
Of the impious fashion in which the head of the empire has been deposed, not by
strangers but by his relatives and by his subjects, the news has spread everywhere.
Third, there is the royal dignity which our lord Jesus Christ has reserved for you so
that you might govern the Christian people. This one triumphs above the other two
dignities, eclipses them in wisdom and surpasses them. It is now you alone on whom
rest the churches of Christ, on you alone depends their safety, on you, the avenger of
sinners, guide to those who err, consoler of the afflicted and exalter of the good.

The remarks about the Byzantines are important. Eighth-century opinion
recognised that the emperor of Byzantium was in a strict sense the heir of
Augustus, but it was increasingly difficult to regard as Roman emperor a ruler
whose seat was not in Rome, whose culture was steadily becoming Greek
rather than Latin, and who could neither protect the papacy nor influence
events in the west. In 800, however, the imperial throne appeared to be
vacant. The Empress Irene, who was ruling as regent for her son Constantine VI,
appears to have become alarmed at his vigour and ability, and frightened that
he would soon want to rule himself. She and her followers deposed him in
797; his eyes were put out and he was left for dead in the same room in the
palace where he had been born. Irene, who had quite likely already poisoned
her husband and father-in-law, abandoned the pretence of a regency and
began to use the title *basileus* (king) and not *basilissa* (king's wife). Opinion in
the west was horrified, almost more by the idea of a woman emperor than by
the gruesome and callous way in which Irene had procured the murder of her
own son to retain power, and could not regard her as legitimate. It is wrong to
suggest that a new empire was founded in 800, or that the idea of separate
empires in east and west was being revived; in the eyes of contemporaries
Charlemagne's coronation ended a three-year hiatus in the imperial succession.

The extent of Charlemagne's conquests also justified his assumption of the
title. The idea of empire was firmly associated with rule over several kingdoms;
the Anglo-Saxon title *bretwalda* (overking) which represented a claim to rule
the whole of England, was generally translated emperor. But Alcuin and
Charlemagne saw this extensive rule in a particular way. A few years before
800, the term 'Christian people', which Alcuin uses in his letter, came into
vogue to describe the sum of different nations that Charlemagne ruled, and the
related term 'Christian empire' for the sum of his dominions.

The idea of the Christian empire is very precise. It originates in
Charlemagne's favourite book, St Augustine's *City of God*, the first theological
masterpiece. St Augustine had written the book to refute the suggestion that
the sack of Rome in 407 was due to the desertion of the old gods in favour of
Christianity. In it he argues that if the teachings of the Gospels and faith in
Christ entered the heart and mind of every inhabitant of a city, that state
would inevitably prosper, for a good Christian is by definition a good citizen.
When the word of God had spread to all the cities of the earth, the Christian
empire would have arrived. This was the end to which the historical process

tended, and it was the duty of every Christian ruler to do all he could to hasten its coming.

Charlemagne understood his responsibilities in these terms. The piety that Bertrada had inculcated was not something that he left outside the door of the council chamber. The duties of the Christian emperor were to extend the frontiers of Christendom, to maintain internal order (so that the peace of God might in time follow), to spread the faith among the heathen, to rule and protect the church and to protect it from heresy. Charlemagne had done all these things; his policy was always informed by the ideal they represent, and this is finally what distinguishes him from other rulers of his time. He had created the opportunity for the conversion of the Saxons and Avars, and had thrown back the Saracens; he had put down rebellion in the lands he inherited from Pepin, he had interested himself in church reform, called a council at which the Adoptionist heresy was condemned, and involved himself in the iconoclast controversy. In short, he was in every respect acting as Christian emperor before he became emperor in name. As in his father Pepin's case, the title followed the reality.

Charles and his advisers had been moving towards the idea, clearly revealed in Alcuin's letter, of the Frankish monarchy as the protectorate of Latin Christianity. It may not have been a coincidence that it was the day before Leo took the oath of compurgation that an embassy arrived from the patriarch of Jerusalem to present Charlemagne with the banner of the Holy City, the keys to the church of the Holy Sepulchre, the church of Calvary and of the Holy City itself. Certainly this recognition of Charlemagne's role could not have been more conveniently timed. The papacy, too, had been moving from the original idea of the king of the Franks as the military defender of the see and duchy of Rome to that of a protectorate of the whole of Christendom, but it tended understandably to see the emperor as the pope's agent. Nevertheless, both parties were agreed that the empire was apostolic. Despite the use of the title *augustus*, it was not the empire that Octavian founded that was being revived; it was that of Constantine, the emperor whom the medieval church so venerated that he was ranked as a thirteenth apostle. This is the elevated ideal that lay behind all the politicking and manoeuvering for position that took place in Rome in 800.

The cultural influence of Byzantium on Rome is seen in this mosaic c.820 in which the central figure, St Praxedes, is wearing Byzantine court dress. The mosaic is part of the apse in the church of San Prassede built by Pope Paschal I c.820. The Pope is on the left with a model of the church. St Paul presents St Praxedes to Christ.

II
The Carolingian Renaissance and Court Intelligentsia

Charlemagne's coronation did not make much practical difference to the mass of his subjects. It did stimulate a tendency to think of his realm as a unity, rather than as a patchwork of separate nations; there are more capitularies issued for the whole empire after 800 than there were before, and more councils of clerics and laymen drawn from all the different nations that Charlemagne ruled were held to discuss general questions. No attempt was made, however, to change the system of government or administration; there simply were not the resources. In practical matters, Charlemagne's new title simply formalised and strengthened existing relationships. The way the protectorate of the Holy See was exercised after 800 is a good example. The emperor was always careful to show great respect for Leo, and always consulted him on doctrine and the administration of the church, but expected to be obeyed in such matters as the disputes between Leo and King Pepin of Italy.

This dearth of visible effects has often been taken to mean that Charlemagne was not serious about the imperial title, and that the Carolingian Roman empire was hardly more than an elaborate charade. The first suggestion is fairly easily disposed of; Charlemagne fought a minor war with the Byzantines until 814 over his right to use the title, proof enough that he was serious about it. When the Byzantines got rid of Irene in 802 and elected the elderly courtier Nicephoras as emperor, the papal position that there was a vacancy in the Roman empire could hardly be sustained. The Byzantines at first refused to recognise Charlemagne's claim, and Nicephoras could not bring himself to salute Charlemagne as 'brother' in his letters, the protocol that one emperor could expect from another. During this dispute, Charlemagne's advisers recalled the old precedent of separate eastern and western empires, which they proceeded to apply to the current situation. The importance that Charlemagne attached to recognition is revealed by the fact that in order to obtain it he was prepared to restore to the Byzantines some territory at the head of the Adriatic that his troops had taken and could easily have held.

The objection that the Roman empire of the Carolingians does not really deserve the name has more weight. It was an empire without a comprehensive

Opposite: Charlemagne in the ceremonial dress of the Roman emperors, a ninth-century statue at St John's church, Müstair, founded by Charlemagne. The sculptor probably used a late antique model for the details of imperial dress in order to represent Charlemagne's ideal of a revived Roman Empire.

Before the Carolingian Renaissance important manuscripts were produced during revivals of art and learning in Ireland and Northumbria.
Opposite: St Matthew from the seventh-century Book of Durrow, illuminated at Iona where the Irish missionary St Columba founded a monastery. The framing decoration is derived from late antique borders. The body is made entirely of squares.
Left: St Matthew from the Lindisfarne Gospels *c.*700. The connection of the angel symbol to the saint by the halo is an innovation. The angel's trumpet represents the message of the gospel reaching out to the world.
Below: The opening of St Luke's Gospel from the eighth-century Irish gospels named after the monastery of St Gall in Switzerland (founded by an Irish monk) to which they were taken. St Luke is joined to his symbol, the ox, by a halo as in the Lindisfarne Gospels.

code of law or a standing army, without urban nerve centres, a professional administration or any developed economic life. It was not a state in the full sense of the term. Yet the idea of the Roman empire meant a great deal to the Franks, or at least to Charlemagne and his courtiers. The contexts in which the expression appears in contemporary sources are significant; the best known example is the seal struck in 803 which bore the inscription *renovatio romani imperii* (renewal of the Roman empire). Capitularies and similar documents are full of words like renewal, reform, regeneration, rebirth. The idea of a revived Roman empire was the key concept in the ideology of Charlemagne's government. It is in a way ironic that the term 'renaissance', rebirth, should have been applied by scholars to just one aspect of Carolingian society, for a rebirth was exactly what Charlemagne and his advisers intended to bring about throughout his empire.

'The Renaissance,' of course, is the name given to the revival of art, literature and classical learning which occurred in central and northern Italy in the fifteenth century. Originally, it was supposed to mark the end of the dark ages, but as we have seen (see p. 67) scholarship since the nineteenth century has steadily reduced the period which we can call 'dark'. It has now become common to speak of a twelfth-century renaissance, more limited in scope – it concerned philosophy, theology and jurisprudence rather than literature and art – and also in effect than that of the fifteenth century, but nevertheless important. The occurrence of other, earlier revivals of classical learning has also been established; the most important were in Visigothic Spain, Ireland and the Anglo-Saxon kingdom of Northumbria in the seventh century. The latter is particularly associated with the monks of Jarrow, the cathedral school of York, and the historical, theological and mathematical work of the Venerable Bede. Considerable evidence has also come to light of a survival of education in the classical syllabus in Italy. These intervals of light did not last for long; apart from a few original works and one or two fine manuscripts, their main importance was the contribution they made to the revival of learning in the Frankish empire, what is called the Carolingian Renaissance.

It has been aptly said, apropos of the rise of the middle classes, that there was no period of European history at which they were not rising. It sometimes seems, similarly, that no period of the middle ages was without its renaissance. To avoid the devaluation of the term, some historians have attempted to belittle the revival of learning under the Carolingians. They have pointed to the dearth of original work, to the narrowness and limited distribution of the education that Charlemagne and his successors tried to make available. In doing so, they have missed the point that despite Charlemagne's genuine interest in humanist learning, he was not concerned to promote learning or literacy for themselves. The intellectual revival under the Carolingians was a by-product of a definite and radical programme which aimed at nothing less than the total transformation of Frankish society.

In contemporary documents, the Franks are often compared to the Jews of the Old Testament, in their role as the chosen people of God. Charlemagne's ambitions for them were seen as a sign, a proof even, of particular divine favour; one pope referred to the Franks as 'the people who have acquired their salvation'. It was axiomatic at the time that baptism was more than a ceremony of church membership. Through the operation of divine grace represented by the holy oil, the sacrament of baptism called a new creature into being, transforming animal man into that higher, purer being, a Christian. This transformation was the pattern for the collective renewal of a whole nation which Charlemagne intended. The Frankish society into which he had been born, the instrument of his conquests, was governed by a mixture of Germanic and Gallo-Roman traditional usages. The absence of systematic principles made it possible to draw an analogy between a traditional society and the natural, unredeemed state of man; the traditional Frankish society was to be reformed by Christian principles in exactly the same way as the convert.

Pepin the Short's use of the title 'king by the grace of God' foreshadows this new attitude. There is no sign that Pepin was conscious of the political and theological implications of the phrase; for him it was probably no more than a political convenience. For Charlemagne, however, the idea of divinely sanctioned kingship expressed the king's central role in creating the Christian empire. Gradually the original need to legitimise the Merovingian's successors, which had inspired the expedient of creating a king with holy oil, was lost sight of, and the implications of having an anointed ruler became more prominent. The king could claim a power which no longer depended on concessions by his subjects, but on divine choice; this is revealed by the confidence with which Charlemagne multiplied the number of crimes which were treated as offences against the king's ban, rather than private disputes, which is the beginning of the modern concept of crime as a public matter. By another analogy, this time with the idea of wardship in Roman civil law in mind, the king was seen as *tutor regni* – the guardian of the kingdom. This reduced the nation to the status of a ward, in other words deprived it of all legal rights. The king, like the guardian, was bound to act in the interests of his ward the people, but he defined those interests himself. There was no possibility of a contractual relationship between ward and guardian, and hence none between people and king; it is the beginning of a systematic idea of royal absolutism.

Divine sanction also implied a close relationship between the king and the church, which was of course the only instrument by which the Franks could be transformed into the 'Christian people'. At first sight this relationship seems to put the king in the hands of his bishops, who are after all the guardians of dogma, and would have to define the principles of a Christian society. In fact Charlemagne was adept at manipulating the relationship, and used the concept of the *tutor regni* to do so. The responsibility of bringing about the Christian empire belonged to the guardian of the kingdom; the church, as the only public body available for the task, was to carry out his designs. Thus the king became in effect head of the church within his realm.

Before the realisation of Charlemagne's dream could be attempted, the Frankish church itself, the vehicle of the Latin Christianity which was to renew his people, had to be remodelled. The Carolingian renaissance, as an intellectual movement, was a by-product of church reform. A small group of men were at the heart of this complex of events; they evolved the theological and social ideas which Charlemagne adopted as his own, they were his agents for the reconstruction of the church, and they were themselves responsible for most of the important intellectual work of Charlemagne's reign. They were almost all clerics, and as the Roman techniques of administration were by Charlemagne's time an ecclesiastical monopoly, they were as important as councillors, ambassadors and imperial agents as in their more obvious roles as scholars, educators and ecclesiastical advisers.

Many of these men came from lands on the periphery of France. That Charlemagne was able to detect these reservoirs of talent and secure the services of many of their leading men was a considerable achievement, considering that he was himself barely able to write. The most prominent among the ecclesiastical courtiers was an Anglo-Saxon deacon named Alcuin. He was born in York in 735 of a noble family, brought up in the household of the archbishop of York, and educated in the cathedral school there. Alcuin's masters at York had been pupils of Bede; under them he studied the classics as well as the scriptures and the theology of the fathers of the church such as Augustine. He won praise for his learning, and seems to have achieved a certain prominence in the affairs of the ecclesiastical province of York and the kingdom of Northumbria, for when a new archbishop was elected in 780 it was Alcuin whom the king chose as head of the mission he sent to Rome to ask the pope for the new archbishop's insignia (this was the formal way in which the pope was informed of an election in the church and his confirmation sought). In 781 he met Charlemagne at Pavia, who invited him to come to France and take charge of a programme for training missionaries to Saxony, on the lines of those already operating at abbeys such as Fulda.

Anglo-Saxons had always been deeply involved in the mission to the Saxons, and had enjoyed the support of the Arnulfings since the time of Charles Martel. Their leaders, such as Boniface – who was seemingly instrumental in the coronation of Pepin, and performed the first ceremony with his own hands – had had plenty of opportunity to observe the calibre of the Frankish ruling family and their dedication to the cause of the church. The Arnulfings in turn were well aware of the capability, zeal and learning of the best products of the English church. It is not really surprising, then, that Charlemagne should have offered to take an Englishman into his service, or that Alcuin should have accepted. He first returned to Northumbria to complete his mission and set his affairs in order, and then joined Charlemagne in 782.

On his arrival at court he found that the King had changed his plans – Alcuin was to take charge of the palace school, and make it a rival to the cathedral school of York of which he had been master. There had been a palace

Opposite: A ninth-century illustration of the coronation of a Frankish king (said to be Pepin the Short). The hand of God holds the crown, indicating that kingship was thought of as divinely ordained. A churchman stands on each side of the king. (Bibliothèque Nationale Lat. 1141 f 2v.)

school at least since Pepin's time, and Charlemagne himself had acquired the rudiments of his literacy and Latin there. Some form of elementary education had of course been necessary for the notaries attached to the palace chapel, but it is doubtful whether Charlemagne would have come to rely so exclusively on clerical notaries if it had been normal for the young laymen of the palace to attend the school. It was exactly these young nobles, the sons of the Frankish ruling caste who would be his future counts and advisers and who had traditionally been brought up at the palace, that Charlemagne intended Alcuin to educate. Charlemagne's capitularies often reminded his counts that they should always have a notary with them; this deficiency would be remedied at source by educating the potential counts themselves. Furthermore, they were to have

Alcuin's handwriting is shown in the marginal annotations to a manuscript of the acts of the Council of Epheseus, made by him to guide his assistant. Alcuin was an Englishman from York cathedral school whom Charlemagne persuaded to take charge of the palace school at Aachen. (Bibliothèque Nationale, Lat. 1572, f 79.)

enough of a grounding in the liberal arts and the scriptures to appreciate the ideological aims of the court.

Alcuin was an excellent choice of subordinate for this task. He was not a great thinker, but he was prodigiously learned, had a disinterested love of learning and loved to teach. He was the senior tutor of the palace school, the household and Charlemagne himself. He wrote a number of textbooks, as well as a great deal of occasional and epistolary verse (Charlemagne's courtiers loved to write and receive their correspondence versified). He writes in conscious imitation of the classical Latin masters, and like the rest of the court had an almost naive regard for Ovid and Vergil, but his verses were not as lame as that might make them sound.

Written for his lost nightingale*

> Whoever stole you from that bush of broom,
>   I think he envied me my happiness,
> O little nightingale, for many a time
>   You lightened my sad heart from its distress,
>   And flooded my whole soul with melody.
>   And I would have the other birds all come,
>   And sing along with me thy threnody.
>
> So brown and dim that little body was,
>   But none could scorn thy singing. In that throat
> That tiny throat, what depth of harmony,
>   And all night long ringing thy changing note.
>   What marvel if the cherubim in heaven
> Continually do praise him, when to thee,
>   O small and happy, such a grace was given?

Alcuin's textbooks occasionally reveal more of his character than the neat, sincere but still conventional sentiments of poems like the one above. They are often cast in dialogue form, or use the more elementary method of questions and answers which the pupil had to learn by heart. (An educational technique which remained standard in many subjects until not long ago, and still survives in the Catholic catechism.)

What is life?	The joy of the blessed, the sorrow of the sad, a search for death.
What is death?	An inevitable happening, an uncertain pilgrimage, the tears of the living, the reason for making wills, the thief of man.
What is man?	The bondsman of death, a passing wayfarer, a guest sojourning on earth.
What is man like?	An apple on a tree.
What is his state?	That of a lantern in the wind.

The elegaic note of this extract is typically Anglo-Saxon, and is found in several of the surviving Anglo-Saxon lyrics. It seems that Alcuin was versed in his native culture as well as in the classics and the scriptures.

* Translated by Helen Waddell, Medieval Latin Lyrics, London 1929.

The apse mosaic of the oratory Theodulf built c.806 at his country residence at Germigny-des-Prés. (See colour illustration on page 138.) The Latin inscription reads: 'Heed the holy oracle and cherubim, consider the splendour of the Ark of God, and so doing, address your prayers to the Master of thunder and join with them the name of Theodulf.'

Alcuin became a prominent member of Charlemagne's council. He was one of the firmest supporters of the advance into Saxony, though as we have seen he disagreed fundamentally with Charlemagne over the policy of forced conversion. It was to Alcuin that Charlemagne turned for advice on his complicated relations with the papacy, and to guide the reforms of the Frankish church. Alcuin would also have contributed to the composition of the *Liber Caroli*, which sets out the official Frankish view on the iconoclast question and the pretensions of the Byzantine empire to adjudicate questions of dogma, but Theodulf the Goth, a deeper and more fluent theologian, has a better claim to its authorship.

Life at court for Alcuin was not without its less elevated satisfactions. Before giving his pious lectures, he would 'anoint his throat with wine and beer to improve his teaching and make his song more melodious'. There were also intense friendships, which may or may not have been actually homosexual. Certainly the way Alcuin expresses his tender feelings in letters to other men at court suggests that they were: 'If only, like Habakuk, I could be translated [to your presence]. How swiftly I would sink into your arms, how my eagerly pursed lips would kiss not only your eyes, ears and mouth, but also every single finger and toe, not once, but over and over again.' Feelings of this sort may have been the 'pigs of unchastity' that he confessed to have 'pastured in the fields of Gaul' and, with covetousness, singled out for mention when he wrote, in his retirement, and asked the pope to pray for the remission of his sins. In 794, at the age of sixty, the itinerant life of the court seems to have become too much for him. He did not, however, return to England; his beloved Charlemagne presented him to the holiest abbey in all France, that of St Martin of Tours. From a little hut in the garden he ruled the canons, and never ceased writing letters and poems. A constant stream of Irish and Anglo-Saxon visitors reminded him of his home. Despite these links with the court and his native land, Alcuin aged rapidly, became melancholy and as we have seen worried about his salvation. He died in 806 and was much lamented.

Several other scholars came to Charlemagne's court directly or indirectly as a result of the Italian journey on which he had recruited Alcuin; Peter of Pisa for instance, who like Alcuin never proceeded beyond the grade of deacon to full priest. Not a great deal is known about his career, except that he was fairly soon appointed head of the palace school, leaving Alcuin himself free for wider affairs. Peter was noted for his powers of debate, and his scholarship in the classical Latin authors. He was Charlemagne's tutor in his reading of the humanists, and taught him enough rhetoric to appreciate them.

Paulinus, another Italian, also shared in the teaching of literature at court. He was born in Friuli, of a Roman provincial family reconciled to the Lombard regime, and had been teaching in his native city before the Frankish conquest of the Lombards. In 787 Charlemagne sent him back to his native province as the Frankish agent. He was given estates in Lombardy and created patriarch of Aquileia, an important see; it was the mother church of Bavaria, and a Latin

Opposite: The top of a small portable altar from Adelhausen, probably the only surviving Carolingian example.

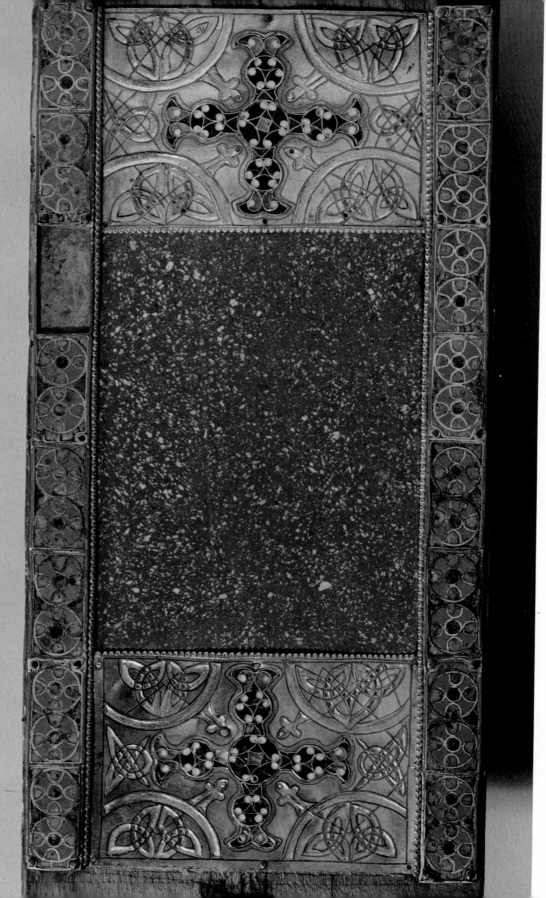

see bordering on the Greek obedience. Paulinus was an efficient, reforming bishop; he held synods, wrote a treatise on Adoptionism, and was often summoned to general councils of the Frankish church. In between attending to the king's business and that of the see of Aquileia, he found time to write a great deal of verse. He is the type of the learned Frankish churchman; simultaneously scholar, poet, theologian and man of affairs.

Paul the Deacon also came of a Friuli family. He was educated at the Lombard court of Pavia, and was for many years tutor to the household of Arichis, the Lombard duke of Benevento, before entering the Benedictine abbey of Monte Cassino, celebrated for its austerity and learning. Paul originally came to court to intercede for the family of his brother, who had been dispossessed and exiled for his part in the Lombard rebellion of 776. In a petition Paul described how the roof of his family home had fallen in, hips and brambles grew among the stones, and a great ash spread its branches among the ruins. His brother's wife begged for bread to feed her four children. Charlemagne did not restore Paul's brother's lands, but kept Paul himself at court; one assumes this enabled the deacon to look after his relatives. He spent nine years at the French court, teaching grammar (i.e. the pure Latin), composing occasional verses such as an epitaph for Charlemagne's daughter Adelaide, and homesick descriptions of his native Lombardy. This is how he remembered Lake Como: 'It is always spring on your luxuriant green shores. Olive groves in perpetual leaf surround you. Here and there a pomegranate shines red among the laurels. The scents of myrtles, peaches and lemons vie with one another. . . . Praised be the Trinity that made such wonders.' After his return to Monte Cassino, Paul wrote a history of Lombardy and another of the bishops of Metz, where it is probable he had spent some time.

This scholarly circle also included some Franks. The most prominent were Adalard and Angilbert, both members of the ruling nobility who had been brought up at court. Adalard took holy orders, Angilbert, although a layman, became an abbot. Adalard was the son of an illegitimate half-brother of Pepin the Short. While still very young he became count of the palace, but at the age of twenty took the tonsure at the monastery of Corbie in Picardy, from where he proceeded to Monte Cassino. Charlemagne brought him back to France to be abbot of Corbie, and in 774 sent him to Lombardy as one of the advisers to the infant King Pepin – in other words as a regent. After the death of Pepin in 810 he continued to act as Charlemagne's principal agent in Italian affairs.

Angilbert was young enough to be educated by Alcuin during his training as a notary. In 782 we find him in Lombardy, in charge of the notaries at Pepin's court; in 790 he was back in France, as abbot of St Riquier. His letter poems were greatly admired at court, and he earned the nickname Homer, possibly on account of a lost epic dealing with Charlemagne's conquest of Lombardy. While he was abbot, he was an important councillor, and was sent to confer with the newly elected Pope Leo in 795. He also fathered two

Opposite: The interior of San Salvatore, Brescia, which was part of a monastery founded in the eighth century and rebuilt in the first half of the ninth. The church is a basilica on a grand scale. A timber roof covers the nave and side aisles. Fluted columns, some of which, with their capitals, were taken over from classical monuments, support the arches of the nave arcading. Like many early churches, San Salvatore was designed with plenty of space for wall painting between the arcading and the upper windows. Some of these paintings have been uncovered at San Salvatore along with decorative stuccoes of particularly fine workmanship.

bastards by Charlemagne's daughter Berta, and lived openly with her at court.

Next in scholarly renown to Alcuin was Theodulf. He was a Goth, that is a Christian Spaniard, but had been educated at Narbonne in Septimania. He came to the palace aged about thirty-four, in 794, possibly as a result of some political trouble or religious persecution in his native Spain. He was wittier and livelier than Alcuin, who does not seem to have liked him, and a better poet; his hymn for Palm Sunday is still in the Latin liturgy. Unfortunately the fluency of his verse is lost in translation. He became bishop of Orleans, abbot of several houses, and travelled southern Aquitaine as a missus. It seems to have been Theodulf, rather than Alcuin, who was the court theologian, He defended the *filioque* ('... and the son ...') clause of the creed, which both the Adoptionists and one party at Byzantium found objectionable because it put Christ on the same level as the other two persons of the Trinity, in a treatise called *Concerning the Holy Ghost,* and is also the most likely author of the *Liber Caroli.* Among his other works was a manual on the ceremony of baptism. Historically the most interesting of his poems is *Against Judges,* where he described his experiences as a missus and attacked the corruption of Frankish judges and the harshness of the laws. He was a prominent member of the council, and witnessed Charlemagne's will, but under his son Louis the Pious became involved in a plot and spent the last seven years of his life in exile.

Alcuin hoped to make Charlemagne's court a new Athens (not that he knew a great deal about Greek literature or thought). This new Athens would be an improvement on the old, for in addition to the seven liberal arts it was blessed with the 'seven gifts' of the Holy Ghost. It is easy, in retrospect, to mock at the presumptuousness of comparing a semi-barbarian court with the Athens of Pericles or Plato, but the comparison is justified by the sheer delight that the Frankish court took in the things of the mind, despite their lack of originality. In imitation of a garbled story about Plato and his disciples, they formed themselves into an academy, over which Alcuin presided, a sort of debating society which gathered after dinner to discuss the humanities, hear poems and lectures, argue points of theology and test each other's wits with riddles. As well as the men that have been mentioned, other prominent ecclesiastics, palace officials, young clerics and nobles and some court ladies joined in. One of the most charming habits of the academy, that of giving nicknames, was brought from England by Alcuin. They often turned on a classical or scriptural allusion: for example Einhard, Charlemagne's biographer, who probably drew the plans for the palace at Aix and some of the great Frankish churches, was known as Bezaleel, after an obscure figure in Genesis who was a skilled craftsman. (To the court at large he was *Nardulus,* little dwarf, a pun on his name and short stature.) Alcuin himself was Flaccus (that is, Quintus Horatius Flaccus, the poet we know as Horace), Paulinus was Timothy, St Paul's disciple and colleague, Angilbert was Homer. Charlemagne himself was David, in a complex and rather sycophantic allusion to the Hebrew king's prowess in battle, his piety, the favour he had in God's eyes and his anointing at the hands of Samuel.

Opposite: Einhard's basilica, Steinbach, showing how the nave arches were filled in when the side-aisles were pulled down. The basilica was consecrated in 827 and was intended as the burial place of Einhard but later Seligenstadt (830–40) was chosen instead. In its original form the basilica had three aisles with a small apse and a transept with side chapels at the east end.

12

The Frankish Church

It is difficult to reconcile Charlemagne's mistresses and massacres with the idea that he was sincerely a Christian. But in the eighth century for many men Christianity was a public and social matter, not the deeply personal concern it has become since the Reformation. Charlemagne may have been a sinner, but no contemporary would have assumed that this invalidated his beliefs. What he did for the church was for them sufficient proof of piety. Nor would contemporaries have been uneasy that Charlemagne was using the church for political ends (for example in the subjugation of Saxony). The concept of the 'Christian people' meant that the aims of church and king were hardly distinguished. It is in this context that Charlemagne's attempts to reform the Frankish church must be seen.

In the eighth century, the institutional structure of the church was diffuse and localised, centred on individual dioceses and monasteries. The process by which the church in the Latin west was to become centralised under the pope had scarcely begun. The pope did not appoint bishops or even archbishops, but merely confirmed them; there were no seminaries through which the training of the clergy could be standardised, for future priests were trained in the households of individual bishops; and there were no unified monastic orders, only a number of specific ways of monastic life which independent monasteries followed with varying degrees of strictness. As if to make up for this rudimentary organisation, the church was usually understood in metaphysical terms, rather than as an institution: it was the body of Christ, in which he lived and worked still.

This conception seems to have been already formed by 313, when the church became a legal body and emerged from the catacombs. It was soon elaborated by theologians, who developed a theory of the four 'marks' of the church; it was 'one, holy, catholic and apostolic'. The oneness of the church had begun to be less obvious by the eighth century, but there were still no separate sects within it. Even the quarrel between Rome and Byzantium had not yet openly moved on from questions of precedence and ritual to substantial matters of doctrine. The church included all Christians (defined, of course, to exclude

Opposite: The westwork of the abbey church of Corvey (Corbeia nova). Corvey was founded in 822 by monks from Corbie in Picardy who named it after their old home. The westwork was built between 873 and 885 and is the only survivor of the many imposing blocks with vaulted storeys which were erected at the west end of the naves of Carolingian churches. On the ground floor is a groin-vaulted entrance passage with a square tower on either side. The two-storeyed tribune on the upper floor has been raised since the church was built and a third tower has been removed.

heretics). That the church was explicitly said to be holy might seem to be tautologous, but it was not: its holiness was contained in the moral ideal which distinguished it from superficially similar religions which also preached salvation, such as the mystery cults of Greece and the near east. This holiness was obviously prominent in the minds of Charlemagne's circle. Its catholicism indicated that it expressed a final truth, revealed once for all in the gospels; the apostolic quality meant that this truth had been handed down in a direct line of succession from Christ's disciples.

In the early days of the church, before a canon of scripture had been agreed on, this oral tradition guaranteed the faith. It was preserved by the bishops, whose legitimacy was therefore very important, and a careful memory was kept in each diocese of the episcopal succession. The *Book of the Popes* and Paul the Deacon's history of the bishops of Metz are in this tradition. The diocese, partly because of this primitive role of the bishop, was still the basic unit of church organisation in the eighth century. It was a territorial jurisdiction, based on the old Roman units of local government. A bishop was much more important in the early church than he is now; for a long time it was only the bishop who could give the sacraments or celebrate mass, and his priests had a role rather like that of the catechists in the nineteenth-century African missions, teaching and assisting in services but under very close control. The western church during the invasions evolved a system of training clergy based on the dioceses. At an early age, boys who appeared to have a vocation for the priesthood received the tonsure of 'ecclesiastical adoption' at the hands of the bishop in a ceremony modelled on that of Roman adoption, and were brought up in the bishop's 'family'. He was responsible for their training, and when they had passed through the grades of the 'clerical militia' – doorkeeper, exorcist, lector, acolyte, sub-deacon and deacon – would ordain them as priests. A priest's right to offer the holy mysteries was seen as coming directly from the bishop, who continued to employ him after ordination, either among the cathedral clergy or in the rest of the diocese. The sense of identity among the clergy of each see was strengthened by their responsibility of electing a new bishop on the death of his predecessor, from among their own number (although this was a right that kings were keen to usurp, and Charlemagne was no exception).

On a higher level, the independence of the diocese was paralleled by that of the great patriarchates. Originally there were four of these, Antioch, Alexandria, Jerusalem and Rome. Seleukia-Ctesiphon in Parthia was elevated to the status of a patriarchate with the missionary efforts beyond the Roman frontier, and Constantinople (Byzantium) was added when the imperial capital removed there. There were variations of practice between the different patriarchates, each with their dependent provinces or groups of dioceses under an archbishop or metropolitan, but the faith was supposedly kept pure by ecumenical councils attended by legates from the whole church. All the patriarchates were self-governing, and recognised no common authority other

Opposite: An eighth-century Irish bishop's crook made of walrus bone. Irish missionaries had been responsible for setting up many of the great monasteries in Europe, including Luxeuil, Bobbio and St Gall.

than the canons of the ecumenical councils. The eastern ones began very early to use the vernacular for scripture as well as the liturgy, a move that was not necessary in the west where Latin was widely understood long after the fall of the Roman empire. Partly because of the use of the vernacular the eastern churches were more susceptible to heresy, and the danger was compounded by the flight of heretics, particularly Nestorians and Monophysites, beyond the frontier of the eastern empire. The patriarchate of Seleukia-Ctesiphon seems to have become Nestorian before it was overwhelmed in the expansion of Islam. It was in response to this danger, as well as because of the aggrandising tendencies of Rome, that the western church was so keen to retain Latin as the medium of worship, and not out of any desire to monopolise the truth. Charlemagne recognised the desirability of, for example, making the scriptures available in German, but his advisers were also aware of how easily heresy could infiltrate a fragmented church. The dilemma was never satisfactorily resolved.

Monasticism and the regular clergy were not as clearly distinguished as they became in the high middle ages. Bishops were frequently recruited from abbeys, and monks often served churches in parishes where there was no priest. The careers of Alcuin and Paul the Deacon show how natural it was to pass between abbey and cathedral, or even court. The loose, primitive monasticism of the Mediterranean basin and Ireland had reached Gaul before the Merovingian period, planted by monks from Ireland. The monastic life had its origin in the Egyptian model of the solitary, contemplative, ascetic life; the Roman tradition of the family brought such men together, and the Christian virtue of compassion involved them in the sufferings of the people outside the community, especially during the period of the invasions. There were a number of different ways of monastic life, codified in treatises known as 'rules'. The rule of St Columba, the Irish missionary to Gaul, emphasised the original asceticism, while that of St Benedict laid its stress on 'perpetual praise' (continuous divine service, often with two choirs) and on scholarship.

The growth of Charlemagne's empire made the better-travelled ecclesiastics aware of the variations in practice within it, and the ideological programme of Charlemagne's court highlighted the need to make the clerical order more effective. Tremendous efforts had been put into missionary work in Saxony, yet France itself remained imperfectly evangelised. This was particularly true of the north-east, the more Germanic part, where, as in Saxony, Christ could be accepted without necessarily disturbing the old Germanic pantheon. The Germans saw their gods as guides and protectors, much more human in scale than the Christian God. The relationship with an individual god was like that between comrades; a young man might honour Thor, the god of war, and in his maturity turn to Odin, god of wisdom. Christ could easily be fitted into this scheme of things, making conversion easy but, without regular preaching and teaching, superficial at best.

The persistence of superstition and pagan beliefs and practices is shown in detail by capitularies of Charlemagne's aimed at suppressing such

Opposite: St Michael's chapel, Fulda, is the only remainder of the great abbey founded in 744 as part of the mission to the Saxons. The chapel was built in 820–22 by Abbot Eigel. It has a circular centre made by eight columns joined by arches.

A bronze image of Thor, the most powerful of pagan gods, clasping his hammer; the figure was found in North Europe.

un-Christian survivals. A capitulary of 742 re-enacts an edict of Carloman's (the uncle, not the brother):

We have decreed that each bishop, according to the canons, shall take heed in his diocese, the count who is the patron of the church in that area helping him, that the people of God do no pagan rites, but cast away and scorn all evil and heathen deeds: profane offerings for the dead, casting lots and divination, amulets, auguries, incantations and sacrifices, which fools perform near the churches with pagan ritual in the name of the holy martyrs and the saints of God.

There are more prohibitions in other capitularies, and the *General Admonition* of 789, a digest of canon law, sums them up. Its prohibitions include witchcraft, weather magic, sacrifices to Woden and Thor, fortune telling, pagan vows and charms, and dancing, leaping and singing by women on Christian festivals. It is a pretty comprehensive list, and one of its most interesting features is the special mention of the celebration of pagan rites at Christian festivals and shrines. It is clear that although the population might be nominally Christian, it was a long way from being so in its detailed beliefs and way of life.

Part of the reason for this was the low level of clerical education. Many priests were almost completely ignorant of scripture, could not read and did not even know enough Latin to understand the masses they mumbled. Boniface was shocked to find a Bavarian priest repeating the words of the baptism ceremony that he had learnt by rote, and by a series of grammatical errors baptising an infant 'in the name of the fatherland, the daughter and the Holy Ghost'. It was not always easy for a bishop to educate the young clerics in his family properly, when he had so much else to do; the problem was made worse by the habit that the nobles acquired, when they realised how lucrative tithes could be, of insisting on having their own serfs ordained to serve the churches of which they were patrons. Such men might learn to offer the semblance of a mass, but were quite incapable of preaching, and to make matters worse were in effect merely tenants of their own churches. Owing to the emphasis on the diocese and the tendency of bishops to keep their best clerics with them, many villages were without either church or priest.

Monastery schools were often better than cathedral ones. They did not have to find a benefice for the master, as he lived as one of the monks, so it was easier to find a good teacher to take charge of the school. They were really intended, however, for the young postulants, and did not make much contribution to the education of the clerical order as a whole. Monastic life was by no means perfect, either; the existence of a number of different rules led to confusion. The Columban rule had never been quite so clearly defined as the Benedictine, and its preference for austerity over learning often led to mere ignorance. Houses which were Benedictine in name had often let the original strictness of the rule decay, and others were really houses of canons, where the members of the community kept their own property and a good deal of their independence. Canons and cathedral clergy in particular were often attacked for loose and uncanonical living: hunting, making war, keeping mistresses and holding

The principal nave of Saint Philibert-de-Grandlieu, built 856–9; it is one of the few ninth-century churches to survive almost intact. Massively built of alternate stone and brick, it has three naves and three apses on different levels, chapels and a crypt.

drunken 'love feasts' where pagan and immoral songs were chorused.

The first steps in Charlemagne's programme were obvious: the better education of the clergy themselves, and a stricter observance of the canons in monasteries, parishes and cathedral chapters. In 774, Charlemagne obtained a collection of canons from Hadrian, and at about the same time he secured, either through Hadrian or direct from Monte Cassino, a good edition of the Benedictine rule. The collection of canons supplied the basis for much of his subsequent legislation about religious matters, and as many abbeys as possible were persuaded to adopt the Benedictine rule or to conform to it more strictly. In this impulse to make ecclesiastical practice conform to that of Rome, Charlemagne had been anticipated by Pepin, who after his meetings with Stephen had tried to make Frankish priests abandon the regional variations that had crept into the order of service. Charlemagne went much further, however, and produced a mass of legislation on religious topics. Provision for the education of the clergy featured prominently. Other matters dealt with include

Above: Wall paintings from the oratory of San Benedetto, Malles, possibly representing St Benedict giving his rule to his monks.

Right: A page of the Rule of St Benedict (*c.*480–547), early ninth century. His rule for monastic life is still used by the various branches of the Benedictine order.

Sunday observance, the duties of priests, parishioners and godparents, the dating of Easter and the contents of sermons. Doctrine is hardly mentioned.

A capitulary of 787 states Charlemagne's educational policy succinctly:

In every bishop's see, and in every monastery, instruction shall be given in the psalms, musical notation, chant, the computation of the years and seasons and in grammar; and all books in use shall be carefully corrected.

This was in addition to the minimum knowledge that the priest was supposed to have in a directly professional capacity, which is stated in another capitulary. A priest was to know the Lord's Prayer, the Creed, the rites of exorcism, the Book of Penances, the calendar of the church's year, the texts for Sundays and holy days, and 'Roman singing' – the office as it was given in Rome. Such modest demands show that the further injunction that a priest should also be able to read and understand the gospels was probably a counsel of perfection. The frequency with which similar decrees were issued by Charlemagne's

IN NOMINE DOMINI NOSTRI SPIRITU
XPI INCIPIT REGULE
PATRIS EM... BENEDICTI

Obsculta o fili praecepta magistri
et inclina aurem cordis tui &
admonitionem pii patris libenter excipe
& efficaciter comple ut ad eum per
obedientiae laborem redeas a quo per
inobedientiae desidiam recesseras;
Ad te ergo nunc mihi sermo dirigitur·
quisquis abrenuntians propriis uolunta
tibus· dno xpo uero regi mili taturus
oboedientiae fortissima atque prae cla
ra arma sumis; In primis ut quid quid
agendum inchoas bonum ab eo perficiam

successors show that he was not entirely successful; the base from which the programme began, the small scholar class within the clergy, was far too small for a rapid advance to be made.

Attention was also paid to the organisation of the parish clergy. Charlemagne insisted that bishops should supervise the rural clergy of their diocese properly, through rural deans and archdeacons. There was a new insistence on parish organisation: every subject had to belong to a parish, and was forbidden, except in unusual circumstances, to take part in another priest's services; attempts were made to define parish boundaries, and, to ease the manpower problem, to lay down a minimum distance from an existing church within which a new one could not be built. This concern for the parish reveals that the direction of the Carolingian renaissance was towards ordinary people, for

Ivory covers of the Drogo Sacramentary, written when Drogo was archbishop of Metz (826–55).

whom the parish priest was the main contact with Christian life and Christian law. Charlemagne was clear that the duty of the parish priest to preach was at least as important as celebrating divine service. In the *General Admonition*, bishops were reminded that preaching was essential if the Christian people were to understand the gospels, and were commanded, if there was a shortage of parish priests, to send the cathedral clergy out into the countryside to preach.

Sermons were the only medium through which moral and religious instruction could reach an illiterate population, and to have a rural clergy capable of preaching intelligently and intelligibly was the ultimate aim of Charlemagne's efforts in education. The sermons were of course in the vernacular, and not many have survived from the eighth century. The few ninth-century sermons that have been preserved indicate that although they were not at all original,

there is already simple, clear expression using such devices as allegory to emphasise meaning. A slow process of working over the basic tenets of Christianity, distilling them into striking and easily accessible formulae, had begun. It was a tradition which contributed a great deal to the literature which eventually emerged in the vernacular in the twelfth century.

The subject matter of sermons was carefully laid down in the *General Admonition* and added to in capitularies. The people were to be instructed in the obvious cardinal points of the Christian faith, such as the Trinity, the incarnation and the resurrection, and on the more important biblical themes, but the stress laid on teaching the Christian virtues is significant. The topics enumerated include chastity, humility, modesty, charity, liberality, compassion, moderation in eating and drinking, and abstinence from everyday activities and marital sex on Sunday. This insistence on the social and moral side of Christianity is part of the same spirit which led to an increasingly moral element in the capitularies on criminal matters. More and more offences against the king's ban were created not because they were a threat to the public good, but because they were considered wrong – *morally* wrong. What we are dealing with is clearly a serious attempt to change the moral outlook and way of life of a whole society, and a touching faith in the ability of the king's ban and the gospels to achieve this end.

Right: Scenes from the Passion surround the Crucifixion in an ivory book binding from the palace school, early ninth-century. Left side; top to bottom: The Ascension, the piercing of Christ's side, the betrayal, the Last Supper. Right side; top to bottom: Pentecost, the soldiers offer Christ vinegar on a sponge, the holy women at the tomb, the incredulity of Thomas. Top centre: the sun and the moon. Bottom centre: the soldiers divide Christ's garments.

13
Education and Literacy

Classical learning, and the knowledge of literary Latin that was the key to it, never quite died out in France, even during the most violent invasions. A small scholar class among the clergy kept it alive. Nevertheless, between approximately 450 and 750 the position of learning and even literacy was precarious. Their survival was threatened by a shortage of books, by the absence of schools, the absence of patrons, the instability of the times and the rapid evolution of spoken Latin away from the classical norm as it began turning into French, which meant that learning to read and write involved learning a foreign language. Gregory of Tours (538–94), the well-read bishop whose *History of the Franks* (see page 15) is the chief source for the Merovingian period, writes a clumsy Latin style full of grammatical blunders, and frequently apologises at length for his own lapses. Gregory was the foremost French writer of his time; that he did not feel at home in the language he wrote in suggests that the number of people who were at all fluent in Latin – the administrative, religious and literary language – must have been very small. Realistically, Charlemagne's first objective had to be to promote the spread of a competence in written Latin among the clergy. No schemes of social reform could succeed if the mass of the clergy were illiterate and ignorant.

The semi-apologetic tone of an undated capitulary of Charlemagne's shows that the court were aware of widespread doubts about the *usefulness* of learning, an attitude which is still familiar but always gains strength in times of general hardship.

It has seemed to us and to our faithful councillors that it would be of great profit and sovereign utility that the bishoprics and monasteries of which Christ has deigned to entrust us the government should not be content with a regular and devout life, but should undertake the task of teaching those who have received from God the capacity to learn. . . . Doubtless good works are better than great knowledge, but without knowledge it is impossible to do good.

The answer to the philistines was a religious one.

Under the Roman empire, public schools were provided, and the salaries of the *rhetors* who taught in them were paid by the state, to ensure a flow of

Opposite: A liturgical fan of the ninth century, made possibly at Tours *c.*875. On the handle are ivory reliefs depicting scenes from Virgil's *Eclogues.*

Two illustrations from a ninth-century copy of the comedies of the Roman poet Terence (*c*.190–159 BC). (Bibliothèque Nationale, Lat.7899 f 125 & f 37.)
Above: Characters from *The Eunuch*. *Right*: Masks on the frontispiece.

educated recruits into the civil service. These schools disappeared in the fifth century, but individual *rhetors* still taught for a while in areas where the Roman way of life was strong, giving lessons in the old syllabus for a fee. Except in the south and in Burgundy, these teachers did not survive for long under the Merovingians: there was soon no education for laymen, except for those very few nobles like Charlemagne who received some instruction, primarily intended for clerics, at the palace school. As we have seen, the education received even by most clerics was rudimentary. A priest who knew more Latin than would suffice to read the lessons in church was a rare man.

Alcuin seems to have used the palace school and the discussions of the academy to evolve a more ambitious syllabus of clerical education, which would at the same time be simple enough to be disseminated widely. He would have liked to revive the old Roman syllabus of the seven liberal arts as the basic curriculum, but realised that this would be aiming too high. He seems to have originated the division of the seven arts which became standard in the later middle ages, separating off the four mathematical subjects, arithmetic, geometry, astronomy and music, into the *quadrivium*, and making the literary *trivium* of grammar, rhetoric and dialectic into the basic course. Alcuin wrote textbooks for the *trivium*, but made very little original contribution to the

Illustrations of Pride (*above*) and Avarice (*right*) from a ninth-century copy of *Psychomachia*, the allegorical poem by the Christian poet Prudentius (348–*c.*415) whose work was a popular inspiration for medieval artists. (Bibliothèque Municipale, Valenciennes, Ms 412 f 12v.)

a forti pirator;

belloptes
Tantrage multabellicosas sps̄
insanensis...
cordis semensis incerte;

·I· superati crudeles· fortutu captauauerant.

Illum feroces fortereges coeperant
habitantes in i peccatricib; ciuitatib;
thammorantem criminosis urbibus.
urbes i incolebat r alienus
dome & gomorre quas fouebat aduena .·
u mens abrahe i dignitatis
ollens honore patruelis gloriae;

quadrivium. (The only people in Charlemagne's empire who knew much about medicine and architecture, which although classified as mechanical arts were often associated with the liberal ones, were Italians and Byzantines. The doctor at court in fact called himself by a Greek title, *archiatros* – literally, arch-doctor.)

The textbooks in use were either classical or based fairly closely on classical models. Grammar, as a subject, meant the study of the classical Latin language; the basic exercise was construing Latin texts according to the systems of the classical grammarians Priscian and Donatus. Alcuin was particularly keen that instruction in grammar should not stop at the point where the pupil could parse accurately, but should continue through formal exercises in prose and verse composition, so that future clerics would be able to write fluent and accurate Latin. Rhetoric, the art of persuasion, originated in Athens when the democracy was at its prime, and every citizen expected to argue his own case before the courts and to participate in the debates of the assembly. Under the Roman autocracy the emphasis on political argument very soon vanished, leaving rhetoric concerned with the questions of literary style and legal pleading – rather an odd combination. The Carolingian textbooks still placed a great deal of emphasis on the use of rhetoric in law, but this is probably merely in imitation of the Roman originals; there was not much call for sophistry in the tribunals of the Frankish counts. Dialectic meant formal logic, the study of the classes of proposition, the laws of evidence and the rules of induction. With the textbooks available, an introduction by Porphyry and two books of Aristotle with commentaries by Boethius, the subject could not have been treated very thoroughly. It came into its own in the twelfth century, when contact with the Arabs made more of Aristotle's treatises available.

The subjects of the *quadrivium* were similarly taught from classical textbooks. Geometry was taught from Euclid. The clumsy Roman system of numerals was still in use for arithmetic; the Indian system with the addition of the Arabic zero, which made calculation much easier, was used by the Byzantines but was not to penetrate to the west for some two centuries more. The Greeks also had some knowledge of Arabic algebra. Arithmetic consisted of multiplication and division, the use of the abacus, chronology, especially as it related to such problems as the date of Easter, and led up to the allegorical and mystical interpretation of numbers. The textbooks were Bede's. Music, as part of the curriculum, had nothing to do with singing or playing instruments. It was the study of such questions as the relation of the notes of the scale to numbers, the mathematical basis of harmony, and led up to mystical ideas about the music of the spheres. Astronomy, in the absence of algebra and instruments of observation, was a similar mixture of arithmetic and mysticism. In addition to all this there were encyclopaedic works used for instruction in what we would call general knowledge, which included all sorts of diverse titbits of information. The whole course was intended to equip the students to study the scriptures and the classical commentaries on them; theology was the only recognised higher study.

Opposite: The Ardennes Cross, a ninth-century processional cross made of gold and copper gilt on a wooden core, decorated with filigree work, gems, and rock crystal.

E
A
M

TNSUIR

In practice, between the year 500 and time of Alcuin the subjects of the *quadrivium* were generally not studied; between his time and about 1000 they were treated briefly and factually. Even though some idea of the basic categories and operations of logic was invaluable for understanding the classical theologians, whose intellectual outlook was that of Greek philosophy, dialectic was often omitted from the *trivium*, leaving merely grammar and rhetoric to be studied as preliminaries to scripture. This was a purely literary education, and its effects are clear. Even the theology of the Carolingians was written in a literary way. This literary emphasis served to justify the reading of pagan classical authors, with the excuse that they were models of good style.

Alcuin's teaching was largely oral and informal, which left its mark on the textbooks he wrote for the *trivium*: they are presented as dialogues. The one on grammar, which re-works the classical authors mentioned above, was written in the form of dialogues between Alcuin and two boys at the palace school, one a Saxon, the other a Frank, who had just 'burst into the thicket of grammar', and needed to be instructed in the mysteries of number, gender, case and tense. In those on dialectic and rhetoric, the main speakers are Alcuin and Charlemagne. Alcuin wrote no comprehensive treatises on the *quadrivium*, but two short works have survived: *On the Full Moon and the Moon's Course* and *On Leap Year*. They are essentially chronological.

Alcuin's textbooks continued in use throughout the ninth century, the grammar being particularly popular. His example was probably just as important to his successors as what he actually produced. Much of the best Carolingian work in the educational field was done when he and Charlemagne were both dead, and the empire was beginning to break up. The later Carolingian work was in the same tradition of remodelling classical sources to fit them for use in a Christian context. The only original thinker was John Scotus Erigena (c. 810–75), who was head of the palace school under Charles the Bald. Both his surnames mean 'the Irishman'. He knew Greek, translated several theological works from it, wrote a highly original treatise on the problem of predestination and another on 'natural theology', and attempted to give an account of the physical structure of the universe in Christian terms. Several centuries later his books were condemned as heretical, more because they had been taken by the losing side in a theological quarrel than for their actual content.

Erigena was an isolated figure, a 'voice crying in the wilderness'. Raban Maur was much more typical of later Carolingian scholarship. Born at Mainz in 784, he received the tonsure at Fulda, and completed his studies under Alcuin at Tours. Alcuin nicknamed him Maurus, after the favourite pupil of St Benedict. Returning to Fulda he became head of the school, then abbot, and died in 847 as archbishop of Mainz (after being dispossessed of his abbey and spending five years in forced retirement when he took an impolitic stand in a struggle over the imperial succession). To his contemporaries he was known as the 'foremost instructor of Germany', an honorific which sums up his work

Opposite: An illuminated initial from the Corbie Psalter, produced in northern France c.800. The interlace ornament is a feature of earlier Anglo-Saxon and Irish designs, but the figures have the flexibility of Carolingian style. At the top is the figure of St John the Evangelist with his symbol, the eagle; at the bottom is St Matthew with his symbol, the angel.

well enough. His three best-known treatises are *On the Education of the Clergy*, *On Number*, and *On the Universe*. The first is significant mainly because it shows that the most prominent ninth-century teacher had still not abandoned Alcuin's hope that all seven of the liberal arts would take their place in the curriculum. It has eight chapters, one for each subject of the *trivium* and *quadrivium* and an extra one for the 'books of the philosophers'. *On Number* deals with the subject in an intensely mystical way, and treats number as an essential part of universal order and of human reason.

Number has existed since the world began: take away number and all is enveloped in blind ignorance: nor could we differ from the animals without it, for they know not how to reckon.

The heaven is by nature subtle and fiery and distant everywhere from the earth its centre by equal spaces.

The section on astronomy gives an account of the universe based on the neo-platonists, which was becoming conventional. It is also highly mystical.

The point of this sort of writing about the physical world was not to give empirical accounts or expound scientific hypotheses, but to fit the ideas about the universe which had been inherited from classical writers into a Christian scheme of things, and to explain them as manifestations of God's will.

Raban Maur's most important treatise, *On the Universe*, with its thoroughness, ambitious aims, dependence on classical models and touch of pedantry, is very representative of Carolingian scholarship. It is a product of the encyclo-paedic tradition that went back to Isidore of Seville and beyond, to the classical etymologist Vegetius. It contains a mass of information on the most disparate topics – the nature of God, the six ages of man, the canon of the gospels, domestic animals, atoms, the heavens, the weather, ports, sewers, baths, prisons, windows, poets, philosophers, the pagan gods, racial names, warfare, tools, utensils, the art of building. The facts are often taken over wholesale from earlier sources, with their etymologies, which Maur thought were the key to wisdom. These linguistic conjectures are often fanciful, what a modern philologist would dismiss as 'folk etymologies'. Nevertheless, Maur took them seriously. His entry on the plough, for instance, does not explain why it is a useful agricultural tool or why it should increase fertility, but names some of its parts and attempts to give a rational explanation of the words and their origin. In an analogous way, his remarks on the structure of the universe accept classical opinion, but strive to find an explanation for the place of natural phenomena in the divine scheme of things. To the existing etymo-logical gloss he added a theological one. In doing this, he uses the fourfold interpretation of the scriptural commentators, who held that each verse of the Bible could contain as many as four quite separate meanings, literal, historical, allegorical and mystical. Maur treats facts in the same way.

This is not great literature, but the product of an orderly, well-informed and unoriginal mind. The achievements of later medieval thinkers and writers would be inconceivable if scholars like Raban Maur had not done their part in

Raban Maur presents his book to Gregory IV, from his work *De Laudibus Sanctae Crucis*, 831–40. (Österreichische Nationalbibliothek, Cod. 652 f 2v.)

uemenſ ſubſolani &a... ...nauiouſ in iga ...erra
cardinaliſ qui&nothur uocatur· Plage meridiane exhumili flanſ
humiduſcaliduſ atqueſulmineuſ generanſ largaſnubeſ &pluuiaſ
loe tirſimaſ ſoluenſ &iam floreſ· Euroaſter caliduſ uentuſ adex
triſ intonat auſtri temperatur· Euſdnotuſ uentuſ caliduſ aſi
niſtriſ auſtri inſpirat· Guattuor uentarum cardinaliſ Zephiruſ
qui&faboniuſ dicit· aboccidente interiore flat

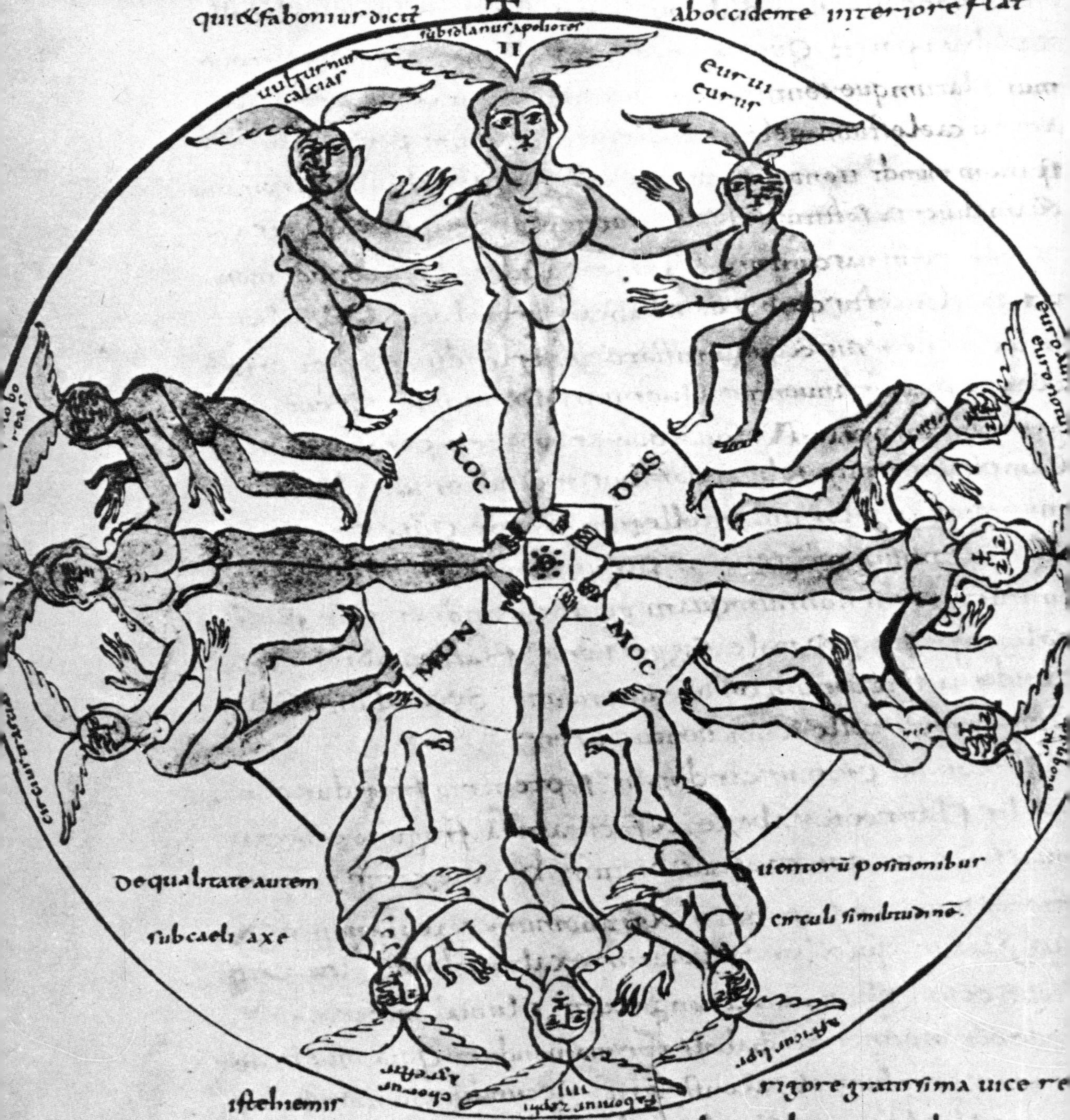

uulturnuſ
calciar

ſubſolanuſ apolioreſ
II

euruſ
euruſ

euroauſter
euronotouſ

KOC   ƧПΛ

ИOИ   MOC

circumtracuſ

Deaqualitate autem   uentoruü poſitionibuſ
ſub caeli axe   circuli ſimilitudnē·

africuſ lipſ

zephirus ſubſolanuſ
choruſ   fauoniuſ zephir

iſtehiemir   rigore gratiſſima uice re
cat floreſ producit· Afrı Heur qui dicitur lipſ ex zephiri dextr
latere intonant hicgenerat tempeſtateſ &pluuiaſ &facit nubiſ
... ...

keeping Latin literature and the tradition of classical learning alive. The efforts of Carolingian scholars to rework this tradition may seem odd to us, but their ability to do so indicates a fluent command of the material, a basic competence without which the later, more original work would have been impossible. They are rather like Moses, unable to enter the territories they open up for others (and would probably not have objected to the comparison).

After the collapse of the Carolingian empire, the monasteries were the main guardians of culture in western Europe. The attempt to educate the mass of the clergy was abandoned for a while, but the number of men learned enough to pass on their skills and understanding to others had immeasurably increased. The twelfth-century renaissance did not need pope or king for patron: it was the work of an international fraternity of writers, teachers and thinkers, ultimately the product of the Carolingian educational movement. Just as important, the number of books available had been increased, and this is directly attributable to Alcuin and his colleagues. The capitularies that Charlemagne enacted on the subject of education were probably the first of their kind in Europe, and they were an important factor in creating a climate of respect for book learning, and making schools a respectable object of patronage, but the copying of manuscripts that Charlemagne's court scholars set in train was probably even more important for the history of western culture.

Some of the copying was done originally in the palace writing office, where many copies of the documents that were the basis of Charlemagne's programme of church reform – the collection of canon laws that Hadrian had given him, the authentic Benedictine rule and above all the Bible – were produced. These books obviously had a wide circulation. Many prominent churchmen acquired the habit of asking their colleagues for copies of fine or rare books in their libraries – Alcuin was a great collector. A great many works copied in this way were the books of classical Latin authors: poets, lawyers, theologians. If it had not been for this sudden passion for collecting books, many fine Latin authors of the second rank would be completely unknown to us. Under the Roman empire, most books were written on papyrus, a fragile, highly inflammable material which was very liable to decay and which became unavailable with the decline of the Mediterranean trade in the sixth century (see p. 78). Important works, such as Virgil, the Bible and the legal codes, had always been written on the more expensive parchment, but the writing offices of the Carolingian monasteries came just in time to preserve many books which existed only in papyrus copies.

Parchment was very expensive; a whole sheepskin made only one folio, four pages, and the business of preparing the skins for writing was messy, complicated and time-consuming. A great many Carolingian manuscripts are 'palimpsests', meaning that one text is superimposed on another. Owing to the shortage of parchment, many older books were washed down, and used to copy texts that the monks thought were more valuable. Luckily, the original texts can sometimes be reconstructed by infra-red techniques. The monks of

Opposite: The wheel of the winds depicted in a ninth-century copy of *De Natura Rerum* by Isidore of Seville. (Bibliothèque Municipale, Leon, Ms 422 f 5v.)

Bobbio, an Irish foundation in Switzerland, were particular offenders in this respect. They washed down a great many books in Gothic, an early Germanic language of great interest to historical linguists of which few written examples survive, and a great deal of minor Latin poetry, to replace them with commentaries on scripture.

As it was scarce and expensive, the writing material had to be used economically. A fine, clear hand was evolved which was small, yet easy to read. The Romans had used several different forms of hand-writing: rustic capitals, uncial and half-uncial, and cursive. Rustic capitals were essentially the same as the lettering used in inscriptions, and are the model for the capitals in modern typefaces; all the letters were of the same height, but rather narrower and closer together than when they were cut in stone, which gave a cramped effect. This hand was used particularly for the law codes. Christian writings tended to be in uncials, a fine hand in which the letters were separate as in rustic capitals, but more rounded, which made it more elegant and easier to write. Both these hands were written without punctuation, except that sometimes the first letter of a paragraph was illuminated, and the space between the words was the same as that between letters, which made them difficult to read. There was also a cursive hand, which was developed for legal and business records, where speed of writing was important. It was adapted to the irregular surface of papyrus (which was made of reeds laid edge to edge, each alternate layer running at right angles to the ones above and below). The connection between the cursive hand and the law lasted until the barbarian kingdoms; the Merovingian notaries evolved a particularly ugly and illegible form of it.

Many different scripts were developed from the various classical models available, in Ireland, Italy, France and Spain. The Irish bookhand was particularly attractive, but it was neither easy to write nor economical of parchment. The monks of Corbie in Picardy worked out a script based on cursive which was beautiful, compact and very legible. A four-line system of heights was used for the letters, which were joined by ligatures, and spaces were left between words. Our modern cursive hands all ultimately derive from these innovations, and the lower case letters of typefaces are also derived from a Carolingian model, the famous Carolingian miniscule, so called because of its small size.

Alcuin, always alive to the potential of new ideas, introduced the miniscule to the palace school and writing-office, where it was used for making copies of the texts that Charlemagne wanted to see widely distributed. These made it familiar throughout the empire, and it rapidly passed into general use. Despite the advantages of the new script, copying entire manuscripts by hand in an unheated monastic cell was an arduous and trying job. Many monastic scribes have left us touching records of their feelings in marginal notes: 'I am cold'; 'Oh my hand'; 'Bad parchment'; 'It takes only three fingers to hold the pen, but the whole body must work with them.' It is to the numerous copies made by the men who jotted down these complaints that we owe the survival of the

Opposite: A page from the Corbie Psalter *c.*800 showing the clear and compact script devised by the monks of the abbey of Corbie in north France.

contur batus.
die dñe clamabo &
ad dm meum depre
cabor.

uae utilitas insangu
ine meo dum descen
do incorruptionem.
Nunquid confitebitur
tibi puluis aut adnun
tiabit ueritate tuã.
Audiuit dñs & miser
tus est mei. dñs fac
tus est adiutor meus.
Conuertisti planctum
meum ingaudiũ mihi
conscidisti saccũ meũ
& circũdedisti me
laetitia.

Vt cantet tibi gloria
mea & non conpungar
dñe ds meus inaeter

NED
speraui non con
fundar inaeter
nũ iniustitia tua
libera me.

Inclina ad me au
rem tuã accelera
ut eruas me.

Esto mihi indm
protectorem & indo
mũ refugii ut saluum
me facias.

uo for titudo mea
& refugium me
& propter noi
deduces me & enu
duces me delaqueo
hoc quem absconder

bulk of Latin literature. It is a huge debt. Virgil, Terence and Livy have survived in parchment manuscripts of the classical period, but we know the works of Caesar, Lucretius, Juvenal, Tacitus, Martial and both the Plinys only though Carolingian copies. (The fifteenth-century humanists imagined that the miniscule was the original Roman script, and called it 'antique letters'.) This preservation of the classics is the positive aspect of the lack of originality of Carolingian scholars, who saw their function as safeguarding and handing on the masterpieces of the past. It goes a long way towards proving the value of Charlemagne's apparently grandiose schemes.

Right: Carolingian miniscule in the Loisel Gospel Book (845–82). Alcuin introduced the miniscule into the palace school and it soon became used throughout the empire. For a comparison with the illegible Merovingian style of writing see the illustration on page 15.

BEATISSIMO PAPAE DAMASO
HIERONIMUS

Nouum opus me facere cogis ex ueteri, ut post exemplaria scrip
turarum toto orbe dispersa, quasi quidam arbiter sedeam,
et quia inter se uariant quae sint illa quae cum greca consenti
ant ueritate decernam. Pius labor, sed periculosa praesump
tio, iudicare de ceteris ipsum ab omnibus iudicandum, senis mutare
relinguam, et canescentem mundum ad initia retrahere paruu
lorum. Quis enim doctus pariter uel indoctus cum in manus uo
lumen adsumpserit, et a saliua quam semel inbibit uiderit discre
pare quod lectitat, non statim erumpat in uocem me falsarium
me clamans esse sacrilegum, quia audeam aliquid in ueteribus
libris addere mutare corrigere? Aduersus quam inuidiam du
plex causa me consolatur. Quod et tu qui summus sacerdos es
fieri iubes, et uerum non esse quod uariat etiam maledicorum
testimonio conprobatur. Si enim latinis exemplaribus fides est
adhibenda respondeant quibus tot sunt exemplaria pene quod
codices, sin autem ueritas est quaerenda de pluribus. Cur non
ad grecam originem reuertentes ea quae uel a uitiosis inter
pretibus male edita uel a presumptoribus inperitis emendata
peruersius uel a librariis dormitantibus aut addita sunt aut
mutata corrigimus? Neque uero ego de ueteri disputo testamento,
quod a lxx senioribus in grecam linguam uersum tertio gradu
ad nos usque peruenit. Non quaero quid aquila quid simmachus
sapiant. Quare theodotion inter nouos et ueteres medius incedat,
sit illa uera interpraetatio quam apostoli probauerunt. De nouo

14
The Carolingian Arts

There is often a close correlation between economic expansion and cultural activity. It is as if nations under certain circumstances generate energy so abundantly that it overflows from purposeful, productive activities into the arts. Or, to put it more prosaically, only affluence creates the necessary leisure and patronage for the arts to flourish. The Greek tragedies of the fifth century BC might never have been written if it had not been for the prosperity that the export trade in olive oil and the opening of the silver mines of Laurion brought to Athens; the patrons of the Dutch and Flemish painters of the sixteenth and seventeenth centuries were burghers grown rich in the spice trade of the Indies; and the period of greatest continuous achievement in the English novel, 1790–1870, coincides almost exactly with the time when England was the world's leading manufacturing nation.

The Carolingian empire enjoyed no such abundance, and the conditions for a widespread revival of the arts simply did not exist. The bulk of the population always suffered from scarcity, even in years when there was no famine, and it was only on the monastic and royal estates – better managed than those of the great magnates – that the regular surpluses necessary for the support of non-productive activities such as the arts were achieved. In these conditions, it is surprising that there was any artistic activity at all, and in practice, apart from the decorative efforts of swordsmiths or jewellers, there was no secular, private art. The barbarian raiders of the ninth century destroyed a great deal of Carolingian art, and time and neglect, as always, have accounted for a great deal more, but enough has survived for it to be clear that almost all Carolingian art was a direct response to royal or ecclesiastical needs (which of course were often synonymous). In view of this, it is perhaps surprising, and rather distasteful, that the public, self-consciously devout art of the period should reveal the same instinct for display, for conspicuous consumption as a proof of social position and power, that was the defining characteristic of the noble way of life.

The Carolingians did not produce many large monuments, and the only piece of sculpture in the round that can confidently be assigned to the period is

Opposite: Mary and the Apostles at the Ascension, part of an ivory relief from the palace school, early ninth century.

the ninth-century bronze equestrian statue in the Louvre, which was once thought to be a portrait of Charlemagne. There is very little evidence of a tradition of stone relief carving, as there was in contemporary Northumbria (where it seems that a long tradition of working in wood was adapted to the more difficult material). Even the official art of the Carolingian empire concentrated on the production of small objects, most of which ostensibly had a purpose and were not simply vehicles of artistic expression: chests and ivory reliquaries, fine church books, magnificent ornamental covers for them. A shortage of skilled craftsmen and the difficulty of assembling large numbers of labourers prevented much building in stone. Stone churches were built at some of the great religious centres, such as St Denis and Fulda; a few great magnates built stone halls; and several of the royal villas were rebuilt in stone under Charlemagne. Most buildings, including churches, were of wood and wattle and daub with thatched roofs, and have not survived. Indeed, many stone buildings of the period have been destroyed, or incorporated into later buildings on the same site, and are known only indirectly and partially.

The greatest Carolingian building was Charlemagne's new palace at Aix. It was probably under construction between 789–94. When it was completed, Charlemagne began to curtail his journeyings about his territories, and Aix became much more of a fixed centre of government than there had been in the earlier part of the reign or under his predecessors. Several of the palace departments took up permanent quarters there. The change was partly due to age and the fact that Charlemagne's sons were old enough to act as deputies in reality as well as in name, but it is also a result of the imperial ideology – the Christian empire needed a Christian imperial city, and Aix was to be the new Rome.

Part of the palace chapel has survived, and the ground-plan and appearance of the whole palace have been reconstructed from contemporary descriptions, and archaeological discoveries. It was in fact a complex of buildings; the royal hall, the palace proper, was linked to the palace chapel, and the layout gave equal emphasis to the two buildings. Although Charlemagne's ecclesiastical courtiers, Alcuin in particular, were very careful not to infringe the responsibilities of the pope and the primacy of Rome, there was a sense in which the chapel of Aix was intended to be the religious centre of the empire. The integration of the chapel into the palace complex expressed the importance of religion in Charlemagne's plans for his people.

The city's French name, Aix-la-Chapelle, is a reminder of the importance of the new buildings in the life of the community there. Charlemagne's forefathers had had a royal villa, or at least a hunting lodge, at Aix for some time, but it appears that by the time work began on the palace the earlier building had been allowed to fall into disrepair, and Aix was an ordinary agricultural hamlet. The site was a good one, however, fertile and well drained; it had been occupied since Celtic times. There were warm sulphur springs, which had been dedicated to Granus, a Celtic god of light and healing whom the Romans identified with Apollo. They rededicated the shrine to the latter. The Roman

Opposite: An ivory liturgical comb known as 'Heribert's comb' from the second half of the ninth century. On either side of the Crucifixion scene are pierced motifs symbolising the Tree of Life, a frequent theme of Byzantine ivory reliquaries.

Sixth Legion had a fort there, and piped the warm springs into the barracks bathhouse. 'Aix' is a corruption of the first part of the Roman name of the place, Aquisgranus, which means the warm spring of Granus.

The main palace building, the royal hall, was two storeys high. It was designed by Einhard, after Roman models. His correspondence with a pupil shows that he knew the manual by Vitruvius, a Roman engineer and architect of the first century BC, which was the standard classical handbook. The ground floor housed the kitchens and other service rooms, and the quarters of the palace staff and servants, while the upper storey was divided into a reception hall, one hundred and fifty feet by sixty in size, and a throne room at one end. The external walls were of dressed stone, and the internal facing of the walls and some of the floors were of marble, brought from Italy. Using marble was a deliberate attempt at creating an impression of magnificence; wall paintings, rich tapestries, and ornaments including solid gold and silver tables helped to attain the same end. The royal hall was surrounded by smaller wooden buildings, which included the emperor's private rooms, his wardrobe and library, the treasury, the armoury and the writing office. Charlemagne did not intend to be uncomfortable. His rooms were heated, something which was unusual enough at the time to be mentioned in writing, and he used the Roman springs for his bathhouse and swimming-pool. Remains of the Roman system may have been visible, and given Einhard the idea, but the legionaries' bathhouse was nothing like as sumptuous as Charlemagne's. Marble steps led up to his, and the swimming-pool could hold a hundred people. The hall eventually declined to the status of the town guildhall, and with its associated buildings was destroyed by fire in the thirteenth century. No trace of the domestic buildings remains.

The palace was built on top of a rise, and linked to the chapel at the bottom by a covered colonnade. The central core of the chapel was incorporated into the later cathedral. Halfway along the colonnade was a gatehouse, the upper part of which was used for the sittings of the palace tribunal. The chapel, built by Odo of Metz, was modelled on a fine Greco-Roman church at Ravenna, St Vitale, which had been built for the Emperor Justinian and was consecrated in 547. Charlemagne knew Ravenna, having been there several times to see his vassal Duke Eric of Friuli. It is possible that it is Ravenna, the late imperial capital, which inspired the magnificence of Aix, rather than Rome. Rome was essentially a pagan city, while at Ravenna a wealth of oriental colour was applied to subjects which were Christian, and therefore easier to assimilate.

The chapel was sixteen-sided in plan, with a chancel at the east end and a central, higher, octagonal core. The external walls were of well-cut, well-fitted stone, pierced by two rows of arched windows. Marble columns, the gift of Pope Hadrian, with Corinthian capitals of local stone, supported the central octagonal cupola, which was lit by rectangular windows with inlaid marble surrounds. Originally the cupola was topped with a golden apple, and had brass grilles, each with a different design, as balustrades. The vault of the

Opposite: Charlemagne's stone throne in the tribune of the Octagon at Aix (Aachen). It contained relics.

Above: A sixth-century mosaic of Christ between two angels on the basilica of San Vitale, Ravenna, which was the model for Charlemagne's palace chapel.

Left: Aachen Cathedral showing the incorporation of Charlemagne's chapel into the later building.

The doors to the Octagon with ornate bronze handles in the form of lions' heads.

Right: Bronze lion's head from the wolf portal of the chapel.

dome was ornamented with a mosaic showing the twenty-four elders of the apocalypse laying down their crowns before Christ, a symbol of the divine government of the universe. As the worshipper's eye declined from the figure of the heavenly ruler, it fell on Charlemagne's throne, positioned in the most conspicuous place in the octagon, as a symbolic reminder of the divine grace by which the emperor ruled. The chapel was as magnificent as the royal hall. Einhard writes that Charlemagne adorned it 'with gold and silver lamps, and with rails and doors of solid brass. . . . He provided it with a great number of sacred vessels of gold and silver and with such a quantity of clerical robes that not even the doorkeepers [the lowest of the seven holy orders] had to wear their everyday clothes when they participated in divine service.' This richness of ornament must have impressed the Franks considerably, as must the building itself, and considering how little tradition there was in the Frankish empire of building in stone, it was a remarkable achievement. However, the design of the octagon is heavier, less fluent and much less subtle than in the original at Ravenna. In St Vitale the piers which support the cupola are drawn out into deep niches, which modulates the transition between the central space and the ambulatories around it, giving a hint of mystery and emphasising the inner sanctum. In Odo's church the niches are flattened, and become simple openings between short, sturdy piers, thus losing the subtlety with which the builders of St Vitale handled space.

Italy also provided the models for new stone churches at such great monastic centres as St Denis and Fulda where churches were begun in 760 and 802. They were imitations of basilican churches in Rome, particularly St Peter's (as it then was, not the baroque structure which stands today). The basilican plan was the usual one, and the palace church does not seem to have been much imitated.

The wall paintings in the royal hall recorded Charlemagne's Spanish campaigns. It is a great pity they have not survived, and that no detailed description has come down to us, for they would surely have shown the official version of the disaster of Roncesvalles. In fact, no wall paintings at all of the Carolingian period have survived north of the Alps, but from contemporary descriptions we know that it was a very common form of art, particularly in monasteries and bishops' palaces. Written references to the subject matter show that any reticence about the pagan gods of Greece and Rome had disappeared (the gods of recently conquered Saxony were of course a different matter). Other subjects were taken from pagan mythology; for instance allegorical personifications such as Earth, usually represented as a woman. The bishop's palace at St Denis had a painting of the seasons as women; St Gall had the great pagan conquerors, Cyrus, Alexander, Hannibal and so on, opposite Constantine, Theodosius, Charles Martel, Pepin the Short and Charlemagne. Classical pagan subjects must have been very familiar to the monks; Apollo as the healing god, or laurel-wreathed bacchantes, often slipped into the borders of liturgical books.

Manuscript illumination gives some idea of what the wall paintings might

Opposite: Part of the bronze balustrade of the chapel, designed in the Frankish or Lombard tradition.

St John from the Coronation Gospel Book, said to have been found on Charlemagne's knees when his tomb was opened. The manuscript was produced by the palace school in the early ninth century. The leaf motif round the border is the classical acanthus.

have been like in style. There was a great demand for decorated manuscripts, especially for copies of books used in divine service, gospel books (which contain the prescribed texts to be read during the church's year) and psalters (collections of psalms with a rudimentary musical notation). In general there is not much illumination in manuscripts of the classical period, except sometimes in Christian texts written in uncials, where the first letter of a paragraph was often decorated as a form of punctuation. Illumination becomes usual and elaborate only when parchment replaced papyrus, and books immediately became costly objects. A fine manuscript was reckoned part of the treasure of the church which owned it, and to a large extent this was because of the cost of the materials, not the infinite skill and pains that had gone into copying and decorating. Labour was the only commodity that was plentiful in Carolingian France, and it was accordingly held of very little account. Fine gold ornaments were reckoned at the same value as an equivalent weight of dust or ingots, and would be melted down at need to meet financial demands with no thought of the craftsmanship that had gone into making them. The artistry of a Carolingian manuscript was just the proper way of treating such an expensive collection of sheepskins.

During Charlemagne's reign, the centres of Irish monasticism on the continent – the abbeys of St Gall, Echternach and Bobbio above all – continued to produce manuscripts in the Irish style. The designs of borders and illuminated initials are abstract and geometrical; figures, where they occur, are stiff and formal. They are fine manuscripts, but as Celtic as the famous *Book of Kells*, and had very little to do with the mainstream of Carolingian illumination, which was affected by Celtic style only in detail – the elaboration of an initial, a geometrical theme for the border of a page. The distinctively Carolingian style evolved mainly from Byzantine models, which the Franks encountered among refugees from iconoclasm in Italy. As the monks became more confident and practised, a more lively and naturalistic approach appeared, resembling the antique originals of Byzantine design.

There were several main schools of Carolingian illumination. The earliest, the Palatine or Aix school, flourished during Charlemagne's reign and was closely connected with the court at Aix, hence its name. Its products are strongly Byzantine in style. The evangelists, a favourite theme of illuminators, are represented in white togas, modelled by careful shading. As a concession to western practice, some manuscripts add their animal symbols, which were not in general use in Byzantium. The manuscript known as the Coronation Gospel Book has the classical acanthus on its borders, quite possibly directly inspired by a classical monument seen in Italy. This was the volume that Otto III was said to have found on the knees of Charlemagne's corpse when his tomb was opened in 1001; the German kings took their coronation oath upon it.

The manuscripts of a school which seems to have been based in Trier are known as the Ada group, because of a dedication in one example supposedly addressed to a sister of Charlemagne. In fact the manuscripts of this school do all seem to have been made for royal patrons, and use extremely lavish materials. One example is written in gold on purple parchment. The style of the earlier Ada manuscripts shows more Celtic influence in the borders and initials, but the figures are strongly Byzantine. The evangelists of this group are like effigies, surrounded by a stylised architectural frame and surmounted by their symbols. The colouring, however, is rich and humanistic.

Under Alcuin, who introduced the miniscule there, a school of illumination flourished at the two abbeys of Tours. The style mingles Irish geometric designs with the animal forms popular among Merovingian illuminators, which were a common theme in early Germanic art; they appear on buckles, brooches and other ornaments long before the Germans began to use the alphabet. Under Alcuin's successor, the lay abbot Vivian, the Tours school developed a more typically Carolingian style. A fine example, the Bamberg Bible, uses continuous strip narrative. Details in the background of some of the scenes suggest that the artists knew antique models. Narrative scenes of course occur in classical reliefs, such as those depicting Trajan's campaigns on his triumphal column, but it is a form that one associates particularly with medieval art. Every schoolchild is familiar with the vigorous propaganda of the Bayeux tapestry, the style of which derives from the tradition of illuminated manuscripts.

The Utrecht psalter, a product of a group known more or less arbitrarily as the Reims school, is a fine example of this technique. The words of the psalms are illustrated by bands of small scenes, which alternate with each few lines of text. Oddly, the text is written in rustic capitals: it is as if the scribes felt that the

Opposite: The Octagon in the royal chapel, Aix, built around 789–94. Marble columns support richly decorated capitals in the classical style, and the vaulting is divided into triangles, as in Roman architecture. Charlemagne's throne can be seen through the opening in the bronze parapet.

This illustration to psalm 103 (CII) in the Utrecht Psalter represents heaven: Christ is surrounded by nine angels, the sun and moon looking on; below stands the Psalmist receiving his heavenly crown from the angel and escaping the pit of hell; on the right is Moses with the children of Israel.

older, more cumbersome script was more suitable for solemn uses than the efficient miniscule. As in all the manuscripts of the Reims school, the drawing is lively and naturalistic; the fluent handling of figures in particular is in striking contrast to the style of the palace and Ada manuscripts.

Books of all these schools were widely distributed, and the schools of the later ninth century are generally eclectic, adopting themes and techniques from examples of various styles. The covers of Carolingian manuscripts often reveal the status of the books as art objects; gold and ivory were favourite materials. Significantly, the ivories in particular are usually more remarkable for workmanship than design. While the latter tends to be derivative, the execution is often very fine; figures are beautifully modelled, borders are complex, and the designs are often undercut to add delicacy. It is an art of decoration. Portable altars were another favourite vehicle for the Carolingian love of lavishness. Later examples often have gold, silver, coloured enamels and figures in relief on the same surface.

It was possibly in choral singing that the Carolingians made their most important contribution. There was a splendid instrument to hand in the cathedral and monastic choirs. The latter especially were naturally inclined to experiment with more elaborate music, for with the encouragement of the strict Benedictine observance divine service was usually celebrated several times a day. The particular achievement was to unite the oriental tradition of church music with the more articulate Greco-Roman ideas about music. (Unfortunately nothing whatsoever is known about contemporary secular music.)

Classical philosophers had discussed harmony and the octave, and a system of fifteen modes (scales) had been established, but cult music (like cult itself) tended to be local, and was little influenced by sensible abstractions. In the early church, forms of worship were naturally more elaborate in the east, beyond the imperial frontier, where Christianity was not persecuted and worshippers could assemble openly. With the end of the persecutions, the church music that had been developed passed to the west via Byzantium. The antiphonal element, the use of alternating responses often sung by two choirs, comes from the synagogue. The church of Seleukia-Ctesiphon segregated the congregation (as orthodox synagogues do today), reserving a separate part of the church for the women. The women sang one verse, the men sang the response, and both choirs then sang a refrain.

The melodies of early church music also seem to have been very like Jewish ritual music, with a great deal of ululation and lengthy formulae on for example the alleluia. Gregory the Great set out to prune and redirect the style of church singing, and the result is still known as Gregorian chant. Under Pepin, this style of singing was deliberately introduced into the Frankish church. Rural priests and their altar boys were said to 'sing' the mass, but this probably meant no more than giving a voiced sound to the words, intoning them in the way that the creed is still recited in Anglican churches today. A body of people

Opposite: The four evangelists from the Aachen Gospels of the early ninth century. The evangelists are placed with their symbols in the four corners of the world, an expression of St Augustine's idea that though the gospels are independent texts, they derive from the same source and truth. (Aachen Cathedral Treasury, f 14v.)

cannot recite in a speaking voice, or the result will be a confused and inaudible murmur, and even the voice of a single priest or cantor projects much better if he intones. Pepin asked Pope Stephen to send him priests to teach his clergy 'Roman singing', the new style of chant using intervals, as simplified by Gregory. Charlemagne diffused it as part of his programme for clerical education, and the Frankish monks and clergy adopted it enthusiastically and developed it. Many of the graduals now known as Gregorian are probably Carolingian in origin.

As part of the general passion of the Carolingian church for uniformity, the monastic choirmasters made great progress in the developments of an exact musical notation. The Byzantines, who simplified the fifteen classical modes to eight, also developed an aide-memoire system of musical notation. It was based on the prosodic signs used in poetry. This system was introduced to France at the same time as Roman chant. The adoption of the eight Byzantine modes meant that exact intervals could be established for western chant, but they could not be recorded with the Byzantine notation, which only showed whether a note rose or fell and whether a syllable was long or short. The Carolingian monks introduced the stave above the words in their 'antiphoners' to indicate the intervals, developed different symbols to show the duration of notes, and added clef signs to simplify the recording of different parts. This notation made it possible to write down a melody exactly, and the modern musical notation derives from it.

Left: One side of the carved ivory binding of the Lorsch Gospels, produced by the palace school c.810. The Virgin with the infant Jesus is enthroned between John the Baptist (*left*) and the high priest Zacharias. Below is the Nativity and the angel appearing to the shepherds.

Right: Fragment of a sandstone head from Lorsch c.800. Despite its condition it shows a mastery of antique form nearly matching that of contemporary ivory carving.

Louis the Pious depicted on the reliquary of Charlemagne made to contain his arms by order of Frederick Barbarossa in 1165, when Charlemagne was canonised.

15
The Decline of the Carolingian Empire

If the inscription on his tomb is correct, Charlemagne was fifty-six at the time of his coronation, in his prime by modern standards. He remained active right up to his death, when he was officially seventy, and his passion for physical exercise, with what for a Frankish noble was a moderate appetite for food and drink, must have had a lot to do with the length of his life. Charlemagne took literally the Bible's figure of three score years and ten as the natural span of a man's life – the average life expectancy of his subjects may well have been as low as half that – and it seems that when he reached sixty he was very conscious of only having ten years left.

After receiving the imperial title, Charlemagne spent much more time in his magnificent new palace of Aix than he had previously done in any of his villas. His progresses through the realm were curtailed. and he tended to allow his sons and magnates to lead the army on its campaigns – most of which by that time were minor border wars, defensive in intention, rather than full scale wars of conquest. His three legitimate sons were now grown men, well able to act as his deputies, trained to rule by his most intimate councillors. Prince Charles, the eldest and the favourite, was normally with him, and knew the east Frankish vassals, the backbone of Frankish power, better than his brothers. There is very little evidence about his potential as a statesman, but it is clear that as a military commander he was at least competent. Pepin had been created king of Italy while an infant; he now ruled the country personally as his father's viceroy, and he too had inherited something of the Arnulfing strategic ability. Louis had been made king of Aquitaine while equally young, and had grown up in an environment very different from that of Charlemagne's court. Many of the leading families of Aquitaine thought of themselves as Romans, not Franks, and were jealous of the position of the Frankish nobles. Louis was very much influenced by them, and consequently out of sympathy with the east Frankish magnates. Like most of the Arnulfings, he was pious, but his kind of piety tended to make him deferential, rather than simply protective, towards the church. He seems to have had neither generalship nor statecraft, and it is said he really wanted to be a monk.

This relief of Charlemagne's palace chapel, from his tomb in Aachen Cathedral, shows the gold apple on top of the chapel which was struck by lightning in the Emperor's last years, supposedly an omen of his death.

In February 806 Charlemagne enacted a formal act of settlement at his villa of Thionville, to come into effect after his death. It was a 'division of the kingdom', on the lines of those drawn up by Charles Martel and Pepin the Short, and the Merovingian kings before them. The emperor was to keep his titles and power until his death; none of his sons was associated with him as emperor. On Charlemagne's death, the empire was to be divided more or less equally between his sons. Pepin and Louis were to keep Italy and Aquitaine respectively; Pepin was also to have Bavaria, Rhaetia, and part of Alemannia; Louis would gain Gascony, Septimania, Provence and part of Burgundy. Charles was to have the central Frankish lands, Austrasia, Neustria, Hesse and Franconia, and also Saxony, Frisia, part of Thuringia, part of Burgundy, part of Alemannia and one province of Bavaria. If any of the brothers died without a recognised heir, further divisions were specified; if there was a son whom the people wanted as their king, he was to be allowed to succeed. No mention was made of the title of emperor, and the only specifically imperial responsibility that was dealt with, the protectorate of the Holy See, was to be shared equally; access routes to Rome were stipulated. The brothers were enjoined to defend their own frontiers, to help each other in need, and to 'keep charity' with each other.

Charlemagne made his nobles swear to uphold the act of Thionville, and sent out missi to take new oaths of fidelity including a reference to the provisions of the act; a copy was sent to Pope Leo for him to recognise and sign. It was obviously the Emperor's intention to impress on his subjects that the act was to be a permanent settlement, which raises the question why, after so many years during which he had been dedicated to the idea of a unitary empire, had founded his whole policy on that idea and had fought a minor war with Byzantium to exact recognition of his imperial title, Charlemagne was so readily prepared to see both the title and political centralisation discarded after his death. The Act of Thionville treats the Frankish empire not as a state but as the property of the ruler, in the old Germanic fashion. Charlemagne's descendants imitated him in this respect, if not in others, and the whole empire was very soon to be divided among minor rulers as France had so often been under the Merovingians.

Obviously, the force of tradition was strong, and even Charlemagne could not lightly set aside the traditions of his family; what would become of the Carolingian right to rule if there were legitimate Carolingians who did not do so? Equally obviously, it would have been difficult – and unnecessary – to dislodge Louis and Pepin from the real power they already enjoyed in their respective kingdoms. After all, the two countries concerned had been given Carolingian kings because they were genuinely distinct entities. But if Charlemagne had wanted to perpetuate the unity that the empire enjoyed under his own rule, it would not have been difficult for him to find a constitutional expedient to satisfy the legitimate expectations of all his sons and respect the political realities.

One of the most obvious solutions to the succession problem would have been to associate one of his sons with him as emperor during his lifetime – the obvious choice would have been Prince Charles – and to have let the other two continue to hold their kingdoms after his death but as sub-kings under the new emperor. Association was the method that had been used at Rome, and there were more recent precedents as well; Charlemagne himself and his brother Carloman had been anointed kings during their father's lifetime. Charlemagne did not choose to do this, and the territorial division prescribed by the Act of Thionville did not even give Prince Charles a clear preeminence over his brothers. It is probable that Charlemagne did not regard the title of emperor as heritable in the same way as that of a king, but thought that a ruler should obtain it by his own efforts, as he had done. This is the most likely explanation for his willingness to see it lapse, for a time at least, with his own death. As for the empire itself, he probably saw its unity as spiritual and what we should call cultural, rather than political. The term 'kingdom of the Franks' had after all remained in use long after the emergence of Austrasia and Neustria as separate kingdoms, and Charlemagne may have felt that the idea of a united empire, reinforced by that of the Christian people, would retain its reality in a similar way, no matter what the political divisions. Through the accident that only one of the three princes survived their father, the empire did in fact continue to have a sole ruler, but the precedent of the Act of Thionville was not forgotten. Charlemagne was the only one of his line with enough prestige to have introduced a system of primogeniture; he chose not to do so, and is ultimately to blame for the civil wars between his descendants that were to bring so much misery and hardship to the people of his empire in the century after his death.

Almost as soon as the Act of Thionville was promulgated, and the future of the empire apparently settled, Charlemagne was afflicted with a series of misfortunes. These setbacks, illness, old age and the thought of his approaching death seem to have made the Emperor melancholy, and he became depressed about the empire. Raban Maur gives an account, which he claims to have heard from Einhard, of a dream of Charlemagne's that suggests these fears. The Emperor dreamed that a man came to him with a present from God, a sword symbolising rulership. On the blade were engraved four words, which were interpreted to mean that the plenty and power of Charlemagne's reign would diminish, that the third generation would be unjust and oppressive, and that Charlemagne's line would then end.

Whether or not this rather too neat dream was actually reported by Einhard, his *Life of Charlemagne* refers repeatedly to the omens that were thought to foretell the Emperor's death. The Rhine bridge collapsed, as did the colonnade that linked the chapel and the royal hall at Aix; lightning struck the golden apple that topped the cupola of the palace chapel; the Emperor's triple crown broke; earth tremors were felt in the palace; the Emperor was plagued by the creaking of beams in whatever house he was in; and in 807 there was an eclipse of the sun and a transit of Mercury. One is reminded of the lines in *Hamlet*:

> In the most high and palmy state of Rome,
> A little ere the mightiest Julius fell,
> The graves stood tenantless and the sheeted dead
> Did squeak and gibber in the Roman streets.

Einhard and Shakespeare share a conception of authority which puts a ruler so far above the common run of men that his end, like a natural disaster, is prefigured by portents.

The harvest of 806 was one of the worst for years. By the spring of 807 there was widespread famine, and bands of starving peasants, having eaten the grain they should have sown that spring, were roaming the countryside, looting or begging indifferently. For the first time, the nobles stayed away in large numbers from the annual assembly and did not lead their troops to the spring muster; they summoned them, but kept them at home to guard the barns and storehouses from the marauders. In the winter of 807–8, thousands succumbed in their weakened state to an epidemic of what was probably pneumonia. The spring of 808 brought a Danish raid on the Obodrites, a client Slav people who lived near Hamburg on the empire's eastern frontier. This was the first serious occurrence of what was to become, with the dynastic civil wars, the worst menace to peace in the ninth century.

The Danish army under King Godfrid drove the Obodrite Duke Thrasko southwards out of his duchy, killed one of his subordinate chieftains, and took much booty. Prince Charles led an army which stopped the Danes without being able to force them to give battle, and Charlemagne and Godfrid made peace. The truce did not last. Thrasko antagonised Godfrid, who had him murdered, burnt his Baltic capital and considered himself at war with the Franks again. In 810 he led a large army on a seaborne raid to Frisia, ravaged the country, and boasted that he would march to Aix, dethrone Charlemagne, chase the Franks back across the Rhine and stamp out Christianity. This was the first time since the Saxon raids that helped to provoke Charlemagne's wars of conquest that the Frankish heartland had been invaded in any strength.

Charlemagne attempted to summon a full levy of the host, the first since 807, but his subjects were still suffering from the effects of the famine and the epidemic, and again many nobles and freemen stayed away. A resentment of the continual demands for military service and supplies, brewing for several years, began to be widely expressed; the Franks were growing war-weary. For the first time Charlemagne was irresolute, and could not decide whether to pursue the Danes through Frisia or to strike directly into Denmark, thus forcing Godfrid to call off the raid to protect his kingdom. When Godfrid, without waiting for Charlemagne to decide, opted for caution and returned to Denmark anyway, Charlemagne slowly began to march through Saxony after him. On the journey the pet elephant, Abbul Abbas, died, and this was taken as another omen. Soon after Godfrid's fleet reached Denmark, he was murdered, and civil war broke out over the succession. Instead of seizing the opportunity to smash the Danes, as he might have done ten years before, Charlemagne disbanded his army now that the immediate danger was over and went back to Aix. (Godfrid's eventual successor in fact sued for peace in 811.)

The Emperor was depressed, and apparently even considering abdication. On the journey back, he was thrown by his horse (according to one story the animal shied at a ball of fire that streaked across the sky, which, needless to say, was interpreted as an omen). Charlemagne was so weakened by age and worries that he could not get to his feet unaided; he was carried back to Aix on a litter.

Altogether it was a bad year. An epidemic had killed thousands of horses and cattle, and the peasants had begun to react hysterically, suspecting poisoning and witchcraft. The Frankish freemen, the backbone of the army, were finding it difficult to honour their military obligations without sinking into dependence on their lords, and discontent with the hardness of the times was general. In addition, Charlemagne suffered several personal blows. His sister Gisela and his eldest daughter Rohtrud, of both of whom he was very fond, died early in the summer; his son Pepin, king of Italy and a good general, died in July.

In 811, the Emperor shook off his depression, accepted that he had not very long to live, and made a will. Two thirds of his hoard was divided between the principal cities of the empire. The third that Charlemagne reserved for his own use until his death, including his personal ornaments and ceremonial robes, was to be divided between his sons and the metropolitan churches. The library was to be sold, and the proceeds given as alms to the poor. (There could be no clearer indication that Charlemagne thought of his treasure as personal, and not in any sense as a public treasury.) In December 811 he suffered another personal blow; his eldest and ablest son, Prince Charles, the only one of his legitimate heirs who had grown up at his side, and who was increasingly acting as his deputy, died suddenly, apparently of a stroke.

The deaths of Charles and Pepin and Charlemagne's increasing infirmity made a decision on the succession pressing. Greek ambassadors arrived in 813 to recognise Charlemagne as emperor, and the Frankish nobles used this opportunity – conscripting Einhard as their spokesman – to press the Emperor for a formal settlement. Charlemagne summoned Louis from Aquitaine to Aix, and crowned him with his own hands in the palace chapel after making him a homily on Christian rulership. The nobles acclaimed Louis, in imitation of the ceremony in St Peter's in 800, and a thanksgiving mass and banquet followed. Before the assembly dispersed, Pepin's young son Bernard was crowned king of Italy. Louis was then packed off to Aquitaine.

Charlemagne spent the whole of October hunting. In January 814 he caught a chill after a bath, developed pleurisy and died on the twenty-eighth after receiving the sacraments. His last words, according to the ever-pious Einhard, were: 'Into thy hands, O Lord, I commend my spirit.' He was buried in his chapel, beneath a white marble sarcophagus with a dubiously relevant bas-relief on the side; Pluto, assisted by Minerva, raising Proserpine. Louis had a monument erected. The exact spot of the grave is now unknown, and the monument was destroyed by the Norsemen who sacked Aix in 881. The inscription, however, has been recorded, and its bald statement of the facts is charming in its simplicity, in an age which had a fondness for exaggerated rhetoric:

Beneath this tomb rests the body of Charles the great and orthodox emperor who nobly extended the kingdom of the Franks and ruled prosperously for forty-seven years. He died seventy years old in the year AD 814.

In 1165 the Emperor Frederick Barbarossa, who saw Charlemagne as one of his precursors, removed his bones from the tomb and placed them in a golden reliquary. At the same time he proclaimed Charlemagne's canonisation. Despite Charlemagne's unwavering confidence that he enjoyed God's special favour, this last accolade might have surprised even him.

One could date the end of the Carolingian empire as late as 997, on the death of Louis v, or as early as 887, when the ineffectual, dropsical Charles the Fat was deposed by his own nobles and replaced by a king not of Carolingian stock. The precise date is really rather a metaphysical point, like trying to fix a year in which we could say the middle ages ended and the modern period began. There were really very few factors that contributed to the decline of the Carolingian dynasty and their empire, and most of them appeared in the reign of Louis the Pious. His successors were merely less able to cope with them.

The two main destructive forces in the empire after Charlemagne's death were the civil wars fought between his descendants, often brother against brother, over the division of the Frankish lands, and the pressure from external enemies: Saracens, Slavs, later Magyars, but in particular the Norsemen. The break-up of the empire into smaller kingdoms meant that all the resources of the lands under Carolingian rule could never be concentrated against a particular invasion; cooperation between even two Frankish kingdoms was rare. Furthermore, constant struggles for succession and civil wars tended to dissipate the resources of the kings. In order to secure the support of the magnates in their dynastic squabbles, the later Carolingian rulers alienated many of the royal estates, the main source of royal revenue, that Charlemagne had built up. At the same time, the honours, the estates that the great magnates held in payment of office, tended to become heritable, thus limiting royal patronage even further. It had never been easy for a Frankish king to dispossess his vassals, and during the ninth century even the assumption that he could disappeared. With the lands, the military, fiscal, judicial and administrative powers of the counts passed from father to son. This devolution of power from the king to the nobles was accompanied by a localisation of defence. The Frankish host, though formidable, could rarely be kept in the field for more than six months in any one season, and took time to muster and provision. It was incapable of

Opposite: The Crucifixion depicted on a ninth-century book cover from the Museo Archeologico, Cividale del Friuli. St John and the Virgin Mary stand either side of two soldiers; one holds the sponge soaked in vinegar, the other the spear.

Overleaf: The golden altar of Sant'Ambrogio in Milan dates from *c.*840. In the centre is the figure of Christ in majesty surrounded by biblical scenes. The rear of the altar is decorated with scenes from the life of St Ambrose and portraits of both the artist Vuolvinius and of Archbishop Angilbert II, who commissioned the altar.

responding effectively to a tip-and-run raid, and the raiders had often sailed off or ridden away, leaving another district devastated, by the time the army arrived. Increasingly defence became the responsibility of local magnates, strong enough to maintain standing garrisons in fortified strongpoints and to levy the local host on their own initiative. Thus even control over military matters slipped out of the kings' hands.

Louis the Pious was not a success as emperor. His partisans among historians speak highly of his piety, his church reforms and his respect for the papacy – the activities and qualities which earned him his surname. Unfortunately in his zeal for religion he neglected defence and internal order. His desire to be represented on his seals and so forth with the cross instead of a sword revealed rather more than he meant it to. Pepin the Short and Charlemagne were favourite sons of the church because their military prowess, their ruthlessness, created the conditions of order and security in which the church could thrive. From the church's point of view, a ruler's primary responsibility was to keep the peace; this Louis failed to do. Even his indulgence towards Rome, his relaxation of the irksome Frankish controls on the papacy, did not benefit him in the long run. He lived to see a pope support a rebellion against him. Finally, Louis' character was not that of a statesman. He was weak, impetuous and vacillating. Had he been capable of resolution, many of his troubles might have been avoided.

On his accession as emperor, Louis' first major act was to reform the palace at Aix. The chroniclers represented this as a moral purge, and Louis was certainly quite genuinely shocked at the loose living of his father's court. He arrived at Aix escorted by armed retainers whom he used to tighten up the security of the palace, and by Benedict of Aniane, a noted clerical reformer, whose presence as Louis' main religious adviser set the moral tone of the palace. The princesses, Charlemagne's daughters, notorious for their liaisons, were packed off to nunneries. This was obviously a fairly reliable way of reforming their lives, but it was also the traditional Frankish way of dealing with political enemies, actual or potential, and the princesses had enjoyed some influence at their father's court. Louis obviously did not feel secure among his father's advisers and associates, and throughout his reign relied mainly on those provincial magnates and clerics he had brought with him from Aquitaine. Nevertheless, on the surface Louis' rule resembled that of Charlemagne; capitularies were issued, missi were sent out, the empire was ruled, whether effectively or not, as one. A number of the old emperor's men, among them several of Arnulfing stock, clung particularly firmly to the idea of unitary rule and the imperial ideology, and worked hard to influence Louis. Their stock with the emperor fluctuated in line with his policy.

During the early years of Louis' reign, their influence dominated his councils. Possibly at their instigation Louis dropped the titles of king of the Franks and king of the Lombards from the protocols to his decrees, styling himself only emperor and augustus, a sign of the hold that the idea of empire

Opposite: The second cover of the Lindau Gospels, made of gold and precious stones by the school of goldsmiths at the court of Charles the Bald in the second half of the ninth century. It is related in style to the Sant'Ambrogio altar but the design is more lively.

had already taken on men's minds; a sign also of Louis failure to grasp that his power derived from the Frankish lands and the Frankish host. His imperialist councillors often similarly lacked political insight. Bishop Agobard of Lyons made the attractive but politically naive demand that the different systems of customary law in the empire should be replaced by one, the code of the Salian Franks. When Agobard succeeded on Benedict of Aniane's death to the direction of Louis' ecclesiastical reforms, he lost his master a great deal of support by trying to limit the practice of lay patronage of churches. Lay patronage was both damaging and uncanonical, but Agobard merely succeeded in antagonising many nobles without improving matters much. In the end, Agobard put his rather narrow ideas of piety above his loyalty to Louis, and fell out with him over the latter's tolerance of the Jews. Louis seems to have encouraged them partly because of their mercantile contacts with the east and with Muslim Spain, and partly because of a respect for their considerable culture, Arabic as well as Hebrew. However, the scandal caused by the conversion of his personal confessor to Judaism provided excellent ammunition for his political enemies.

Louis held reforming synods – one of which enacted no less than one hundred and forty-five canons and recommendations – and made extensive grants of land to the church to compensate for Charlemagne's confiscations. (The grants of course came out of royal estates.) He also behaved indulgently to the papacy. Leo III did not take an oath of loyalty when Louis succeeded; his successor, Stephen IV, did not delay his coronation in 816 to await imperial confirmation; nor did Stephen's successor, Pascal I, in 817. Louis let all these infringements of the Franco-papal concordat pass without protest. In 817, he reaffirmed the alliance, confirmed the pope in all his territories, renounced imperial jurisdiction in Rome and promised not to meddle in imperial elections. Louis' impulse to show that the pope was not a Frankish court bishop was commendable, but its effect was to allow Rome to emerge as a rival centre of moral authority to Aix within the empire.

Also in 817, Louis made an act of succession. Its terms reveal, again, the influence of the imperialist group of councillors. In sharp contrast to the Act of Thionville, Louis' eldest son, Lothar, was straightaway associated with his father as emperor, and was to be sole emperor on Louis' death. Louis' other sons, Pepin and Louis, had not yet reached fifteen, the Frankish age of majority. Pepin was to continue to rule his father's old kingdom of Aquitaine, given him in 814, and on his majority was also to have Gascony, the march of Toulouse, and some counties in north-west France. Louis was to be the king of Bavaria, and Bernard, Louis' nephew, was formally confirmed as king of Italy. The emperor was to allow the sub-kings to appoint their own officials and dispose of benefices, and to raise their own revenues; they were to make him the customary annual 'gifts' and to defer to him on matters of general policy; all the rulers were enjoined to cooperate in defence.

For some reason King Bernard was discontented with this settlement, though

Opposite: Emperor Lothar I, son of Louis the Pious, from the Lothar Psalter, 840–50. (British Museum, Add. 37768 f 4r.)

it is not clear what more he could expect to gain, and rebelled. When his army met Louis', he lost his nerve and submitted; Louis had him sentenced to death, but then in a show of magnaminity commuted the sentence to blinding. Bernard died in 818 of the torment inflicted, as the emperor probably expected him to. This was the first time that a descendant of Charlemagne's had died on the order of another. Louis appears to have lost his nerve at this point, and had Charlemagne's illegitimate sons, Drogo, Hugh and Thierry, removed from the court to monasteries. In 822 Louis was persuaded by his clerics to do public penance at Attigny for the harshness with which he had repressed the rebellion; his nobles were horrified by what they saw as a gratuitous display of weakness.

Not long after Bernard's rebellion, Louis' wife Irmengard died, and he married Judith, a beautiful, forceful and accomplished Alemannian princess of the Welf (Guelph) family. In 823 she bore him a son, Charles, later surnamed the Bald. For the rest of his reign, all Louis' efforts were directed to upsetting the ordinance of 817 to provide Charles with a portion equal to that of his half-brothers. The political manoeuverings are a little obscure. Louis began to summon the imperialist councillors, including his father's bastards, back to Aix, possibly to give countenance to his divisive policies, or perhaps just to keep them away from Lothar, who naturally had a high idea of the prerogatives of the emperor and was perhaps a more obvious rallying-point for the imperialist group. Judith, however, seems to have been a more important influence on Louis than any of his councillors. Certainly Agobard's resentment of her ascendancy with Louis contributed to the breach between him and his master.

Louis' efforts at neutralising the opposition were not entirely successful. Several of the imperialist group began attending Lothar's court instead of Louis'. During the years after 823, complaints against Louis' rule multiplied. Frankish arms suffered several reverses on the frontiers; there were complaints that the army was being kept too long in the field each year; and the great vassals were beginning to take advantage of the ill-feeling between the emperor and his sons to oppress the people. In addition, there was a series of bad harvests, which always tended to produce disorder. In 829, Louis showed unusual resolution by making a pre-emptive move; he retired Lothar to Italy, dropped his name from the imperial decrees, and endowed Charles with a compact block of territory based on the Welf family lands in Alemannia (at this stage Charles was not created king). Councillors who objected were banished. In 830, Lothar, Pepin of Aquitaine and Louis of Bavaria combined forces, and marched against Louis in an attempt to force him to abdicate. They failed, but succeeded in having Lothar's name restored to the protocols, exacting promises of good government and forcing Judith into a nunnery.

Louis refused to accept the situation, and managed to restore his power at assemblies held in October 830 and February 831, without fighting a battle. The conspirators of 830 were declared traitors; Lothar was sent back to Italy, and forbidden to return without permission; his name was again dropped; his supporters on the council were exiled; and Judith was brought back from her nunnery. In a new act of partition, Lothar, Italy and the imperial title were not mentioned, the empire was to be divided on the death of Louis the Pious between young Charles, Louis the Bavarian and Pepin (both Louis and Pepin were to receive more territory than they had been allocated in 817). If, by concentrating his displeasure on Lothar, Louis had hoped to detach Pepin and Louis of Bavaria from Lothar's party, he failed. Both of them were too nervous of what the emperor might still intend to do at their expense for young Charles. At the end of 831, Pepin was in revolt, and in 832 Louis of Bavaria led an abortive invasion of Alemannia, The emperor declared Pepin deposed and Charles king of Aquitaine, but was unable to enforce his decision; the vassals in Aquitaine split between the two claimants and proceeded to exploit the confusion to their own advantage.

In 883 Lothar, Pepin and Louis the Bavarian concocted a general rebellion. This time Pope Gregory IV gave them his support, on the grounds that the rebellion was in the interests of the peace and unity of the empire. This confusion of loyalty did not help the cause of Louis the Pious, and the reflection that he himself was probably largely to blame for it probably did not help his peace of mind. When the two armies met at Colmar, Louis tried to avoid bloodshed by negotiation; his vassals, convinced he was afraid to fight, slipped away to join the rebels and Louis was forced to surrender. Lothar dictated a harsh settlement, which before long lost him the support of his brothers. Charles was dispossessed and locked up; the emperor himself was also kept a prisoner, and pressure was put on him to become a monk in penitence; Judith was exiled to Italy, under Lothar's eye. Louis the Bavarian and Pepin both gained territory. In 834, Louis the Bavarian, Pepin and several powerful magnates released Charles and Louis the Pious. Lothar was unable to prevent Louis making his peace with his other sons, his magnates and the church. From 834 until his death in 840, Louis was recognised, outside Italy, as emperor; in 835 he was recrowned, with great pomp, at Metz.

In 837 the emperor attempted to enact a fresh partition in Charles's favour, which led to fighting between him and Louis the Bavarian, in 838–9. Pepin of Aquitaine died in 838, the year that Charles came of age and was crowned, and Louis again attempted to secure Aquitaine for his youngest son. Some of the vassals, however, recognised Pepin's son as Pepin II, and neither party gained control of the kingdom. In the year of Louis the Pious's death, he was reconciled to Lothar, and they made yet one more partition. Louis the Bavarian was to be restricted to the rule of his home duchy, with the title of king, and Lothar and Charles were to divide the rest. Lothar was to keep Italy, and to have in addition the lands to the east of the Rhone, Meuse and Saone; Charles was to have the lands to the west of those rivers. This partition was quite unenforceable. Charles could not control Pepin's partisans in Aquitaine, and Louis of Bavaria commanded too much loyalty in the German-speaking lands to be displaced. (He was to become known as Louis the German.) Three more years of civil war followed, despite the increasing boldness of Slavs, Bretons, Bulgars

CUM SEDEAT KAROLUS MAGNO CORONATUS HONORE
EST IOSIAE SIMILIS PARQUE THEODOSIO

and Norsemen, until the rival claims were settled at the Peace of Verdun.

Lothar insisted, as soon as his father died, on his right to the imperial succession, with all the prerogatives that had been attached to it in his father's original settlement of 817. In this he had the support of several councillors and learned churchmen, including the scholar Raban Maur. Louis the German took Lothar's disregard for the original settlement as a precedent for claiming more territory than he had been allowed by the ordinance of 840. Lothar led his army against Louis the German and Charles the Bald in turn, but did not commit it to a pitched battle against either of them, fearing that the other would fall upon him with a fresh army. Thus he let the initiative slip away, and in 841 Charles and Louis joined forces. Lothar persuaded Pepin of Aquitaine to support him; in June they were defeated in a hard-fought battle near Fontenay by the combined hosts of Louis and Charles.

Lothar was reluctant to accept defeat. He intrigued with his brothers' vassals, and went so far as to attempt to stir up the pagan diehards in Saxony, and to plot with one army of Norse pirates. He was gambling with the security of the Frankish lands to achieve his own supremacy within them. In 842 Louis and Charles pledged common cause against Lothar in the famous Oath of Strasbourg. A document recording it has survived, and is of interest for several reasons. Firstly, after Charles and Louis had sworn to support each other 'in charity and justice' and not to make separate agreements with Lothar, a representative of each host swore not to support the brother who should break the oath; the oath that the armies swore was to supersede, if necessary, even that of vassalage. Secondly, the document gives the text of the oath in the vernaculars of each kingdom, German and French; the version in French is the oldest document in that language. The phrase 'for the love of God and for the Christian people' occurs in the German version as: '*In godes minea and in thes christianes folches*'. In French it is: '*Pro deo amur et pro christiano poblo.*' Romantic historians call this the birth of the French and German nations, in which they are being a little hasty.

Charles and Louis went on to put down the Saxon revolt and defeat Pepin II. They were not strong enough to engage Lothar in battle, but they forced him to withdraw to Lyons. They could not depose and exproptiate Lothar as they had wished, but they made him realise that his hopes of supremacy were futile and he would have to accept another settlement. Possibly the civil war would have gone on if it had not been for a particularly serious threat from the Norsemen, who had sacked Nantes and fortified a base at the mouth of the Loire from which they were ravaging the countryside. By the Peace of Verdun, in a partition adjudicated by one hundred and twenty commissioners, Lothar was given Italy, the Carolingian homelands around Aix and the Rhine mouth, and a corridor between them. Charles the Bald took the lands to the west of the corridor and Louis the German those to the east. The division, unlike most of those which Louis the Pious had attempted, was realistic; the commissioners very sensibly adjudged to each brother the lands his soldiers actually held when

Opposite: Charles the Bald, youngest and favourite son of Louis the Pious. The portrait is from the Psalter of Charles the Bald, produced between 842 and 869, possibly at Saint-Denis. (Bibliothèque Nationale, Lat. 1152 f 3v.)

A reliquary presented to the abbey of Conques by Pepin II,
king of Aquitaine, in the middle of the ninth century.

the fighting stopped. Lothar's corridor was without natural frontiers or linguistic or cultural identity. It was not to survive as a separate state, but its creation helped to confirm the growing sense that west and east Frankland were separate entities. There was no longer a single imperial authority. In theory, unitary rule returned in 885 under Charles the Bald, but by that time the emperor's power was negligible. The period between the Peace of Verdun and the death of Charles the Bald forty-five years later was the effective disappearance of Carolingian imperial power.

Lothar I used the title of emperor until his death in 855, and was recognised as such by his brothers after the Peace of Verdun. However, neither of them recognised Lothar as their overlord. The only genuinely imperial function to which Lothar succeeded was the protectorate of the Holy See, and while the obligation remained, Louis the Pious had given away most of the rights that had accompanied it. Lothar and his son Louis II tried to reassert Carolingian

Seals of Lothar I (*left*) and Charles the Bald.

control and had some success, but during their reigns only one pope-elect bothered to wait for imperial confirmation before having himself crowned. Throughout the period the kingdom of Italy suffered from a series of raids from Saracens who had established themselves at Bari. In 846 they raided Rome and profaned St Peter's. Louis II, who acted as his father's viceroy in Italy, retook Benevento, attempted to resolve the disputes over the succession to the southern Italian dukedoms so that they could concentrate on defence against the Saracens, and attacked Bari itself but failed to take it. Leo IV, who became pope in 847, was as energetic in local defence as any Italian lay ruler; he built a wall around the part of Rome that lay on the right bank of the Tiber, which enabled the city militia to keep off a Saracen fleet in 849. In 850, Louis II was crowned emperor.

Other parts of the empire also suffered from raiders. Arles was plundered in 850, Frisia was raided continuously in the years 845–52. Lothar I secured peace there only by conceding a duchy at the mouths of the Rhine, Meuse and

Overleaf: Pope Leo IV stands on the far left in this ninth-century fresco of the Ascension from San Clemente Lower Church, Rome. He was so confident of his fortifications to protect Rome that he brought back some of the treasures taken in the Saracen raid of 846.

Scheldt to the Danish leader Rurik. Charles the Bald's west Frankish kingdom was particularly hard hit. Three different Danish armies had fortified bases on river islands; one sacked Tours in 853 from an island in the Loire, and another, from the Gironde, sacked Bordeaux in 855. The third, which had seized a base in the Seine, withstood a seige in 852, were bought off and left the island in 853, whereupon they went marauding through the district, sacked Nantes in 854 and reoccupied their island in the following year. The east Franks were more fortunate. The Slavs on the eastern borders had to be subdued from time to time, but Louis the German's kingdom was only raided by Norsemen three times in thirty years. Charles the Bald did not only have Norsemen to contend with; in 845 he had to acknowledge Pepin II as king of Aquitaine, in 846 he conceded independence to the Bretons, and in 851 he ceded the Breton march that Charlemagne's faithful Roland had created.

On the death of Lothar I his lands were divided between his sons Louis II, who kept Italy and the imperial title, Lothar II who was given Frisia and 'middle France', and Charles, still a minor, and an epileptic, who was to rule Provence and the Rhone counties. There were now six kings of Carolingian stock ruling within the frontiers of Charlemagne's empire. Aix was no longer the imperial capital, and the kingdoms which had been created out of Lothar I's northern corridor were ill-defined, vulnerable, and a constant temptation to Louis the German and Charles the Bald, both of whom might hope to annex them. 'Middle France' had so little identity that it became known as *Lotharii regni* (Lothar's kingdom), corrupted to Lotharingia and eventually to the modern 'Lorraine'.

Charles the Bald was not immediately at leisure to covet his neighbours' kingdoms. In 857 he lost the province of Maine to the Bretons; between 856 and 859 various Norse armies burnt Paris, Bayeux, Chartres, Tours, Blois, Noyon and Amiens, and ravaged the region of the Scheldt mouth. The only reverse the Norsemen suffered was in Septimania and Provence, where they were defeated by the efforts of the local magnate. In 858 Charles met Lothar of Lorraine at St Quentin to attempt to concert defence against the Norse pirates; they decided to turn the Norsemen's own tactic of fortifying river islands against them, starting with that of Oissel near Rouen, to deny them the Seine. However, Charles had little time that summer to attend to defence, for he was nearly ousted from the throne. Louis the German, at the invitation of the Burgundians and Pepin II's supporters, invaded Charles's lands in an attempt to obtain the throne. Charles's vassals saw no point in wasting in the support of their king resources which could be used against the Norsemen, and Charles was unable to raise enough of an army to give battle. Louis the German summoned a synod of west Frankish clergy, hoping to persuade them to offer him the crown. Hincmar, archbishop of Reims, remained loyal to Charles, and rallied both clergy and laymen against Louis, who recrossed the Rhine early in 860, his prestige damaged. Peace was made later that year by the efforts of Lothar II.

Opposite: Lothar I on his throne with two guards, from the Gospel Book of Lothar, school of Tours, 849–51. (Bibliothèque Nationale, Lat.266 f IV.)

This crystal bearing the inscription of Lothar II is covered with scenes from the life of St Susanna. The liveliness of the figures is reminiscent of the Utrecht Psalter. The crystal was made in Lorraine, c. 860.

In the same year, Lothar II's own difficulties moved to the centre of the Frankish political stage. His wife Theutberga was childless, and as he had had children by his mistress Waldrada before his marriage to Theutberga, he believed the latter to be sterile. In his desire for an heir, he declared that he had in fact married Waldrada before the ceremony with Theutberga, which was therefore invalid, and summoned two synods in an attempt to have his child-less marriage annulled. The archbishops of Trier and Cologne refused to comply, but did forbid further relations with Theutberga (which must have been rather a galling outcome). Hincmar of Reims defended the marriage; he had sound moral and canonical grounds for doing so, but it also happened to suit the ambitions of his master Charles, who had an interest in Lothar's dying without having produced an heir to Lorraine. Theutberga fled to Charles, and got him to support her in a petition to Pope Nicholas I; Lothar in turn obtained a promise of support from Louis in exchange for a promise of the succession to Alsace.

In 862 Lothar bullied a third council into granting an annulment, married Waldrada and proclaimed her queen. Pope Nicholas immediately dispatched two bishops as his legates to hold a great synod and inquire into the findings of the one summoned by Lothar. When they upheld the earlier verdict, Nicholas quashed their findings, deprived both men of their sees, and held a Lateran synod which forbade further relations with Waldrada. The pope remained firm even when Louis marched on Rome with an army, and when Lothar submitted in 864 the primacy of Rome and the supremacy of the pope over a Frankish king in a matter of canon law had been vindicated. Charles and Louis agreed to partition Lotharingia on Lothar's death, and confirmed their agree-ment in 867. On Lothar's death in 868, Charles in fact tried to seize the king-dom for himself but withdrew when Louis threatened him; the agreement was implemented. Pope Hadrian II protested that Louis II, Lothar II's brother and the emperor, had a better right to succeed, but he was ignored. (Louis and Charles had already divided the lands of Charles of Provence in 863, Louis taking the main share.)

At about this time Charles the Bald finally realised that existing military arrangements were simply not coping with the Norse threat. He began to issue a series of miscellaneous edicts dealing with fortifications, refugees and local defence. The main defensive strategy was to be to deny the rivers to the Norsemen, by blocking them with bridges or barrages or fortifying islands. It was not immediately successful. The Norsemen of the Loire burnt Poitiers and Orleans in 865, and killed two counts the following year. Those of the Seine got past the barriers in 865, and looted in the region of St Denis. In 866, after an inconclusive campaign, Charles bribed them to go away. An east Frankish nobleman called Hugh was then made duke of the whole region between the Seine and the Loire, the main theatre of the Norse raids. He was given the military command of·the region – the title duke still retained much of its original connotation of the command of a district – the revenues of many of

the royal estates in the area, and was created lay abbot of Tours and Noir-moutier. Next to the king himself, Duke Hugh was the most powerful man in west France. Even with a quasi-royal command of the resources of the region, however, Hugh had difficulty in containing the raiders. Charles was forced to conclude a disadvantageous peace with the Bretons to leave Hugh's hands free.

Louis II died in 875, also without leaving a male heir. In the closing years of his reign he had contained the Saracens and driven them back; by 867 they held only Bari and Taranto. The Byzantines lent him a squadron for his attack on Bari, which had been their Mediterranean headquarters, in 871. When it fell, the Emperor Basil I expected the city to be given up to him. In the quarrel that ensued when Louis II decided to keep it, Basil denied him the style of emperor on the grounds that he did not rule all the Frankish lands. Louis countered with the intriguing argument that 'we may be said to rule those territories which are held by the same flesh and blood as us'.

On the news of the emperor's death, Charles set out for Italy. He accepted the imperial crown from Pope John VIII in Rome on Christmas day 875, but when he had taken new oaths of fidelity as emperor and annexed Louis' lands in Provence he did nothing for the defence of Italy or the Holy See. When Louis the German died in 876, Charles tried to occupy the lands on the left bank of the Rhine, but was driven off by Louis the Young, son of Louis the German, who divided the kingdom with his two brothers. Carloman received Bavaria and the Slav marches, Charles (the Fat), Rhaetia and Suabia, Louis the Young took Franconia and Saxony. All three brothers used the title of king. In 877 Charles the Bald did go to Italy, but turned back without fighting the Saracens when he heard that Carloman was on the march and that lay abbot Hugh was at the head of a revolt. Before leaving for Italy, Charles had conceded to the assembly of nobles that if any vassal died before he returned, his son Louis the Stammerer, who was to act as viceroy in his absence, would not force the vassal's heir to give up his father's benefice but would leave him in possession until the emperor's return. This is the first open recognition by a Carolingian ruler that succession to benefices had become hereditary.

On his return from Italy Charles died and was succeeded by Louis the Stammerer. Louis swapped Italy, or rather his claim to it, for Carloman's share of Lorraine. In Italy the Saracens were in the ascendant again, and the southern Italian dukedoms were incapable of combining in their own defence. Pope John VIII, in an attempt to imitate the successful alliances concluded by his predecessors Stephen II and Stephen IV, travelled to France to ask for Louis the Stammerer's help. When that was not forthcoming, Pope John offered the Italian crown – which was not really in his gift – to Duke Boso of Provence, who considered the offer, but faced with opposition from the Italian nobles, declined in his turn. In 879 Louis the Stammerer died. A faction among his nobles offered the crown to Louis the Young, but Duke Hugh, Duke Boso and Count Bernard of Aquitaine, the three most powerful magnates of the king-dom, proclaimed Louis the Stammerer's sons, Louis III and Carloman, kings,

Opposite: This silver buckle of West Frankish workmanship was found in a Norwegian grave with ninth-century coins, so was probably among the treasures looted from France by the Norsemen.

The reconstructed prow of a Viking ship found at
Oseberg, Norway. The prow is decorated with
carved lines of interlaced animal forms ending in a
serpent's head. The mobility of the Viking fleets
was the chief factor in their success, for by the
time the local defenders had been summoned,
the Norsemen had sailed miles away.

and bought off Louis the Young with Lorraine. The two young kings partitioned their territory, Louis III taking the north and west, Carloman, Burgundy and Aquitaine.

In the year of Louis the Stammerer's death a host of Norsemen landed in Flanders, sacked several towns and established a base in Ghent. In 880 they withstood a seige, and burnt Arras and Cambrai, while a second Norse army defeated the Saxons in the field and sacked Hamburg, and a third took Nymwegen, set up camp there, and resisted Louis III's attempts to blockade them. In 881 the army at Ghent were defeated in battle by Louis III, but not crushed; they merely marched eastwards, sacking Maastricht, Liège, Cologne, Bonn, Stavelot, Malmedy, Prüm, Trier, and, finally, the town, palace and chapel of Aix. Louis III did manage to drive off the Norsemen of the Loire, however; they transferred their attentions to England for a while.

Duke Boso of Provence, presumably attempting to exploit the confusion caused by the new Norse incursions, had himself elected king of Aquitaine. This was the first time that a non-Carolingian had attempted to carve himself a kingdom out of the crumbling empire. It is significant that this should have happened in Aquitaine, where people had always been resentful of Frankish domination and conscious of their cultural distinctness. The Carolingian rulers could not fail to realise how great a threat Boso's pretensions were, and for once set aside their differences to deal with him. Obviously Louis II's ideas about the unity of lands ruled by a single stock still had some reality in the minds of the Carolingian kings. It is a pity that they could not cooperate as effectively to achieve peace and security as they did to defend dynastic prestige. An army led jointly by Louis III, Carloman, and Charles the Fat, which included a contingent sent by Louis the Young, defeated Boso in 882 and reduced him to a small territory around Vienne. Before the matter was settled, Louis III died in an accident and was succeeded by Carloman. The territories of which Boso was deprived were shared between Carloman and Charles the Fat.

The latter was emerging as the most prominent Carolingian ruler. Pope John VIII, still hard pressed by the Saracens, had invited Charles to help him in 879. Charles went to Italy and had himself accepted as king, but without reference to the pope and without staying to help him. In desperation Pope John turned to the Byzantines; nothing could show more clearly that all the gains from the Frankish alliance had been dissipated. The Byzantines were in no position to help, and in 881 Pope John offered Charles the imperial title in exchange for help. Charles accepted the title but again did nothing for the security of the Holy See. In 882 Louis the Young died, and Charles the Fat was more interested in consolidating his succession to Louis' throne and in dealing with the Norse threat to his new kingdom than in Italy; in that year too, Pope John was assassinated.

Charles managed to pacify one faction of the Norse army of the Rhine in 882 by granting Godfrid, one of the Danish leaders, a duchy in Frisia in exchange for his baptism and homage (the duchy did not last long; in 885

The seal of Charles the Fat.

Overleaf: A Viking ship carved on a picture stone from Norway.

Godfrid was involved in a defeated rising in Lotharingia, and stripped of his lands). The rest of the army continued its marauding, sacking Deventer and Duisberg. When the count of Lotharingia and the bishop of Hamburg organised resistance, the army moved to the Scheldt and sacked Reims (one band chased the aged prelate Hincmar, who escaped them but died soon after). Hugh and Carloman had some minor successes, but could not bring the main body of the Norsemen to battle, or prevent them quartering in Amiens for the winter of 883–4. In the campaigning season of 884, Carloman's vassals refused to continue the apparently interminable struggle, and the king, unable to raise an army, was forced to buy the Norsemen off. Later that year he died.

In 885 he was succeeded by Charles the Fat, now the only ruling Carolingian, who in name ruled all the lands of Charlemagne's empire and since 881 had enjoyed the title of emperor. In practice his authority was shadowy. In Italy he was unable to control the magnates or protect Rome. After attempting to curb Guy, duke of Spoleto, by confiscations that he was unable to have enforced, Charles was forced to rescind the orders, thus recognising Guy as *de facto* an independent ruler. Pope Stephen V (885–91), finally despairing of the Franks, managed to persuade the southern Italian cities to cooperate, and to conclude a common alliance with Byzantium. In the German-speaking lands of the empire, the counts and dukes fought out their disputes without reference to their nominal overlord.

In west France, the only real power was that of Duke Hugh. It was unfortunate for Charles that the climax of the Danish raids, a great seige of Paris, occurred in the year of his accession. Its progress made it quite clear that the Franks could no longer count on their kings for defence. The Danish army moved from Amiens to Louvain, and from there to the Seine, without the Franks being able to stop them. They laid seige to Paris, which was defended by Bishop Gozelin, who died during the siege, and the count of Paris, Eudes (Odo). Charles the Fat came to help, but his aid consisted of offering the Norsemen a large bribe, the emperor's usual expedient, and free passage upstream to Burgundy. The citizens of Paris, elated at their own success on the city walls and indignant at Charles's weakness, refused to honour his promise, and the Danes were forced to drag their boats overland around the city to the upper reaches of the river. Charles, in a pique, withdrew, and left the Norsemen to harry Burgundy unmolested.

After his ignominious conduct at the siege of Paris, Charles the Fat's flimsy prestige in west France declined even further. Count Odo took the glory of the successful defence of Paris; Charles created him duke of Paris, and conferred on him all the lands and powers of the late Duke Hugh. In 887, on the death of Boso of Vienne, his son Louis did homage to the emperor, but it was a meaningless gesture. By that time Charles the Fat's vassals were treating him with open contempt, and later in 887 the emperor was deposed. He died in January the following year and with his death disappeared the nominal unity of the Carolingian lands.

Opposite: The ciborium presented by Emperor Arnulf to St Emmeran at the end of the ninth century. The work dates from the middle of the century. The pediments supporting the roof are decorated with emblems referring to the life of Christ. Sculptured leaves and precious stones ornament the whole ciborium, which was a sort of canopy placed over the altar. It is a splendid example of the magnificence of Carolingian church treasures.

There was only one Carolingian with a lawful claim to the throne of west France, Charles, posthumous son of Louis the Stammerer. Unfortunately he was only seven years old, which hardly fitted him to give the Franks the vigorous military leadership they needed against the Norsemen. The west Franks preferred Duke Odo of Paris, who combined military prowess, reputation, and a solid power base in the counties between the Seine and the Loire. Fulk, archbishop of Reims, initially wanted Guy of Spoleto for king, possibly because his lands and vassals were far enough away to make it difficult for him to dominate French politics. When Guy was denied the throne, he conspired with Count Baldwin II of Flanders (who was of Arnulfing descent) and a number of bishops to encourage Arnulf, the illegitimate son of Carloman of Bavaria, to claim it. Had it not been for his illegitimacy, Arnulf might have been in a position to try for the imperial throne; he was experienced in government and diplomacy, having ruled his father's Slav marches, and a successful field commander. As it was, on Charles the Fat's deposition he was elected king of Germany, and for the moment did not wish to become involved in unnecessary adventures. Arnulf and Odo met, and recognised each other in their respective kingdoms.

There were once again six separate kingdoms within the frontiers of Charlemagne's empire, but now only two of the rulers was of Carolingian stock. (Louis of Provence was an Arnulfing on his mother's side.) Odo's line were to gain permanent rule in France in 987, on the accession of Hugh Capet. Boso's son Louis seized Provence and made himself king. Rudolf of Burgundy, a Welf, claimed Lorraine. The crown of Italy was disputed between Guy of Spoleto, who was eventually successful, and the marquesses ('marchgraves', barons of the march) of Friuli. Both families were the descendants of Frankish counts planted there at the time of the conquest of Lombardy; as the Carolingian empire broke up, the new rulers were not on the whole survivors of pre-Carolingian dynasties, but the offspring of Frankish vassals who had been long enough established in their new homes to build up lands and support.

Rome continued to hope for a restoration of the Carolingian empire; a revival, that is, not only of the imperial title, but of a Carolingian power strong enough to deliver Italy from 'bad Christians and menacing pagans'. With this in mind, Pope Stephen V overcame his objections to Arnulf's illegitimacy and began to try to persuade him to come to Italy, restore Carolingian rule, and accept the imperial title. Arnulf, plagued by Norsemen and Slavs and afraid of rebellion, did not come. In 891 the pope crowned Guy of Spoleto, who began to style himself emperor and to issue capitularies in the Carolingian manner. The other Frankish kings ignored him. In 893, Arnulf fought an inconclusive campaign in Italy; in 894 Guy died and Arnulf returned. He marched to Rome and was crowned emperor there, but could not crush the armies led by Guy's son and widow. Marching on Spoleto, he was stricken with paralysis and had to be carried back to Germany on a litter. He did not recover, and died in 899.

Arnulf's six year old son, Louis the Child, was elected to succeed him, as

REX·REGVM·DOMINVS·MVNDVM·DICIONE·GVBERNANS
IMPERITAC·SCEPTRVM·REGNANS·QI·IVRE·PERENNI
INMORTAL·TENES·CVM·CRIMINA·MVLTA·PARENTVM
LAXAST·INCRVCE·IVSTITIAE·CVM·FRENA·LOCARAS
OMNIBVS·ERGO·TVIS·SERVI·SVPER·ASTRA·BEATAM
SPERARE·HINC·VITA·IESV·C·TO CHRISTE·DEDISTI
DONIQVE·EST·MODO·CRISTE·DE·S·PATRIS·Q·TVIQE
NVNC·NOMEN·DORITE·IAM·CVNCTA·STVPEBANT
SAECVLA·DVDV·MEN·CE·QOD·GESTAT·AMICA
SVMMI·XPICOLAE·DV·GNATRITE·GERENDVM·HOC
PER·IVSTA·THRONVM·DVD·QOD·TOLLERE·LEGE
ATQ·DECET·TOTVM·AVGVSTV·NVTV·EXCOLAT·ORBEM
NAM·HOC·REGNVS·TANTRANDO·CARDINE·PRODIT
ORBS·SCIX·TVTGAEAMC·SVLTV·CAESARIS·ORET
AVGVSTOP·VREFERBAT·AL·HINC·LAVDE·CORONAM
NAM·OPTIMA·DEXTRAM·VIRTV·DIVINA·PARET·ARTE
STIPS·IES·VTVADE·TQTRIVMPVM·POSCIMVS·OMNES
IAM·ALMVM·IVSTQ·IVSTITIAE·QVOD·REGNET·VBIQE
HAEC·SILI·CE·ARATATQVELIGATVG·IRET·AMICO
DVM·AFFERT·LORICA·PLACITVS·SIC·IPSA·PARATVM
OPTEMVSN·OSSEMPER·AMICVMSQ·EMPIE·CHRISTVS
RETVTATQ·RQ·NVLLVS·IACVLO·PREMITAST·FVR
FAS·VELIN·ILLO·PROTERAT·HOSTIS·CRIMINE·DIRO
DEFENSOR·ARTISSEDERTRVM·ONSTRATAMANDVM
IVS·ORNAT·VLANEAT·CAESARIS·OBTINET·HAVSTVM
OMEN·FITQ·EAM·IVM·IMPERIVM·MANET·ORBE
EN·REGNAG·RA·IVMONNE·PRAEVV·MVNERA·DONANT
ET·PERSAD·ATISICQVE·EIVS·SOBOLIS·LATVS·AMBIT
GENS·PLEB·LETAPROP·VCINNAMPIE·DONAT
MVSAMVIG·ATENE·S·DVNEAT·SCITSCVT·VETAMARE
SPEME·CV·LSCEPTRATENENDO·HIDEI·DATVBIQ
REM·HAVST·VDONEC·SAECLAS·DEPELLIT·ABARTE
QAE·FORMO·SEIVRATENEBVNT·TELA·NE·FASSINT
ET·SEDARE·QECE·EREAS·DANDA·PROTERVIAM
QVAM·EST·S·OLIDVS·PORMAN·TECITAVGVSTOVILE
TRANSFOR·MATQ·TIBI·CRISTI·CVMCLARA·TRIBVTA
IVRE·COLE·NDIDVM·MOREQ·TROPAEA·RANS·DAT
QVAE·HOC·S·INTNOMENVBIQMEANS·DEVOTVABORE
NEMPE·TON·ATVRGETQVE·PROBE·PRAETVS·DIVAMARI
SIT·TREMO·ESTQVEBONAE·DIVINO·MVNERE·FAMAE
PROFICIT·INDE·ORBEM·QD·DVM·FRETVS·ILLICITAQ
SIC·ABICI·ET·PORTVMCRVCE·DAT·LAESVM·SEQITVRQ
HVNC·TIBI·ENIM·INDODATVMOS·EMPER·CASTAEPIVS
CAESAR·LA·GEMODOVISVTVCASTRA·INIMICIAST
TERRES·S·P·EMQ·ETIMORAT·INIMICA·FVGANS·DAT
TV·PIVS·ET·GRATNIMIVMPRONVMROGATHAECGENS
ADVENIAM·IREANIMVS·NOBISADIVSSA·PARENTIS
CONSCRIP·SIDVDVMNAMCRISTILAVDELIBELLVM
VERSIBVS·ET·PROSATIBIQEMNVNCINDVPERATOR
OFFERO·SANCTE·LIBENSCVIVSPRAECEDIT·IMAGO
STANSARMATAFIDEVICTOREMMONSTRATVBIQVE

king of Lotharingia and Germany. (Arnulf's illegitimate son Zwentibold attempted to hold Lotharingia as a separate kingdom, but was soon crushed.) During his reign Germany and Italy suffered from the depredations of the Magyar horsemen. The Magyars had settled in the middle Danube plains, and, using the conquered Slav population as serfs, devoted themselves to breeding horses, for which the area was very suitable, and raiding. The Germans mounted several full-scale expeditions against the Magyars without breaking their power, and by the time Louis the Child died in 911 the country was exhausted; the south and east in particular had been laid waste. Defence had become a purely local matter, and the safety of the villagers depended on the ability of the local seigneur to maintain a stockade where they could take refuge, and a handful of soldiers to man it. The pre-Carolingian territorial units, based on affinities of dialect, custom and law, and often with well-defined boundaries that had been maintained throughout the imperial period, now re-emerged in Germany. The so-called 'national duchies' were Saxony, Franconia, Suabia and Bavaria; Lorraine, the remnants of *Lotharii regni*, emerged as another duchy.

When King Odo died, the faction among the nobles led by Archbishop Fulk of Reims, who had opposed his election in the first place, dressed up their opposition to Odo's line as a legitimist, pro-Carolingian policy, and managed to have Charles the Simple accepted as king (he had been crowned, more or less surreptitiously, when Odo was in Aquitaine in 893). The main event of Charles the Simple's reign was the concession of a Danelaw along the lower reaches of the Seine. This was fairly realistic. The Norsemen dominated the area, and had settled in some numbers. Expelling them had proved impossible, in the weakened state of the country, while their presence might hopefully act as a buffer against any new Norse invasions. The result was of course the duchy of Normandy.

Charles the Simple was imprisoned in 923 by Duke Raoul (Radulf) of Burgundy, who had himself crowned on Charles's death in 929. On the death of Raoul in 936, Charles's son, known as d'Outremer because of his long exile in England, succeeded to the throne as Louis IV, and ruled until 954; he was succeeded in turn by Charles's grandson Lothair, 954–86, and his great-grandson Louis V, 986–97. The power of these late Carolingians was hardly greater than that of the Merovingians that their ancestors, the Arnulfing mayors of the palace, had kept as puppets; the reality of royal power evaporated with the royal lands and revenues, and had to be painfully built up again by the Capetians after 997.

The pressures that destroyed the Carolingian empire are easily identified; the raids, particularly those of the Norsemen, and the dynastic civil wars. That said, one might wonder why these factors were enough to undermine Charlemagne's creation. The Norse invasions were the last phase, the final spasm, of the centuries-long Germanic migrations of which the Franks themselves were

Opposite: Another nonbiblical illustration in the First Bible is the delightful contemporary scene where Abbot Vivian, accompanied by the monks of Saint-Martin, presents the Bible to Charles the Bald. (Bibliothèque Nationale Lat. 1 f 386v.)

a part. The Norsemen made themselves feared throughout Europe, but rarely settled in large numbers. The vernacular of some remote parts of England, and the place names for example of Normandy, show traces of Old Norse, but the movement of population was nowhere large enough to replace the local speech by a Scandinavian dialect. It is strange that the Franks, so recently the foremost military power in Europe, should have been so helpless before a few piratical bands.

The superficial reasons for the failures in defence are the inability to adapt tactically to the new kind of mobility represented by the Viking fleets, the steady decline in resources available to the kings, and the distraction of effort entailed by the civil wars. But underlying all this, cannot one see a simpler, more radical, and perhaps less discreditable failure? – a loss of the impetus, the surge of national energy, that Charlemagne had had the insight and the charisma to harness? One must never forget the precarious economic base of Frankish society. Even in a good year, the better part of the peasants' exiguous surpluses were swallowed up in the pursuits of the ruling classes – organised religion, war, luxury and display. There must have come a point where the nobles could no longer accumulate the resources to finance aggression. In at least one particular respect, the dependence of Carolingian power on expansion can be isolated; the question of benefices and their provision. The only way a Frankish ruler had of rewarding his followers was by the grant of lands. If he alienated his own estates, he was reducing his only direct and secure source of revenue, and literally giving away his own power. Charlemagne was very conscious of the dilemma, and solved – or postponed – it by utilising his conquests. The estates of conquered kings, or additional estates carved out of the defeated country, swelled his revenues and created a pool of surplus lands from which grants could be made. As soon as Frankish expansion ceased, it was again difficult for Carolingian kings to satisfy the expectations of their vassals and at the same time to protect their revenues. Territorial expansion was thus a self-sustaining process, as long as it continued; once it stopped, centrifugal forces set in.

The Carolingian empire is not to be compared with the empires of antiquity, with Egypt, Persia, Macedon or Rome. If one is generous, and dates it from the conquest of Lombardy to the deposition of Charles the Fat, it lasted barely a century. One could insist on a shorter period, say between Charlemagne's imperial coronation and the death of Louis the Pious, the period of clear ascendancy and central rule, which is a mere forty years. Even the higher estimate leaves us with an empire that lasted many fewer years than some of the gaps in the king lists of the Egyptian temples. One is entitled to ask whether the Carolingian empire left a lasting heritage, or whether it was just a footnote to the centuries of migration.

Charlemagne's empire was not the ancestor of the modern European nation states. True, some of the territories that emerged when the empire broke up look very like modern France, Germany and Italy, at least in embryo, but the

Carolingians cannot take the credit for the re-emergence of geographical, linguistic and cultural realities that had been temporarily suppressed under Frankish domination. Other post-Carolingian states – Provence and Burgundy, for instance – had existed long before the rise of the Franks, and the one undoubtedly Carolingian creation, Lorraine, has not had a happy history; it has been a cause of war in the three worst conflicts Europe has ever seen, the Thirty Years' War and the two world wars. Charlemagne must also take some of the blame for the example he set to the later medieval German emperors, who by their insistence on embroiling themselves in Italy delayed the unification of both countries.

Nevertheless, Charlemagne's conquests did make a contribution to the political geography of later Europe. One might almost say they began it. The correspondence, after the lapse of a millenium, between the extent of Charlemagne's lands and what one thinks of as western Europe, is quite striking. The Franks never attempted to conquer the British Isles, Scandinavia, or Poland, and they did not complete the conquest of Spain or Italy, but the core of the lands that we include in our idea of the European west were united, and politically speaking have only ever been united, in Charlemagne's empire. Some of the details of continuity are remarkable. Czechoslovakia, converted to Christianity by Catholic missionaries under the protection of Frankish soldiers, was firmly orientated towards the west until 1948, while its neighbour Bulgaria, evangelised from Byzantium, has always been an eastern country. Its inhabitants speak of 'going to Europe' in the way that the Greeks do. It might be objected that the Roman empire included, in area, just as much of modern Europe. Of course it did, but its centre of gravity was Mediterranean, as that of the Macedonian empire had been eastern Mediterranean and that of the Persians had been between the two rivers. The Carolingian empire was the first world power to have a *European* centre of gravity; Aix, its capital, where the Rhine, the highway from the North Sea ports to the Alps and the road across the north European plain all meet, had been a Roman frontier town.

The catalyst that made Frankish rule something more than a semi-barbarian eruption was the close alliance with the church. Charlemagne's conquests defined the sphere of Latin Christianity, the intellectual, moral, cultural tradition that is the essential common element in the ways of life of the different European nations. The monastic schools and writing-offices survived, and flourished, during the breakdown of public order in the ninth and tenth centuries; their role in the preservation and diffusion of Latin culture has already been discussed. The clerical tradition in public government, established at Charlemagne's court though perhaps of earlier origin, survived too, and contributed something hard to define to the texture of medieval life. The limits of the diffusion of these defining elements of European culture are essentially the furthest marches of Charlemagne's armies.

Latin Christianity did not only flourish under Charlemagne's protection, it formed, through the idea of the Christian empire, the nature of his rule. The distinctively European version of theocratic kingship, in which the king rules by God's grace, or, in the extreme version of the theory, as of divine right, is directly attributable to Charlemagne and his court, and unthinkable without their ideological efforts. On a lesser but analogous plane, the remarkable consistency throughout Europe in the institutions of the nobility is ultimately due to Charlemagne's dissemination of the model of the Frankish count, who combined territorial, fiscal, civil, judicial administrative and military power, a mix of responsibilities which survives as late as the nineteenth-century landowning English JP. It is not currently fashionable to admire the feudal nobility or absolute monarchs; it is not necessary to admire them to see that they were essential stages in European development, and to recognise the extent of the Carolingian contribution to the ideas of kingship and nobility.

German historians of the nineteenth century liked to call Charlemagne 'the Father of Europe'. It is not inappropriate. Charlemagne came to the throne among the ruins of Rome, in the lull before the last eddies of the Germanic migrations; his creation of an empire was the first event of the middle ages.

Select Bibliography

GENERAL WORKS

F. H. Bazeuml *Medieval Civilization in Germany 800–1272* (London 1969)
J. Boussard *The World of Charlemagne* (London 1968)
W. Braunfels (Editor) *Karl der Grosse* 5 vols. (Düsseldorf 1965/8)
D. Bullough *The Age of Charlemagne* (London and New York 1965)
J. Calmette *Karl der Grosse* (Vienna 1948)
Cambridge Medieval History vols. 1, 2 & 3 (Cambridge and New York 1911–22)
S. Epperlein *Karl der Grosse* (Berlin 1971)
L. Halphen *Les Barbares* (Collection 'Peuples et Civilisations'; Paris 1940)
L. Halphen *Charlemagne and l'Empire Carolingien* (Paris 1947)
H. A. Lamb *Charlemagne* (London 1962)
A. E. Thompson *The Early Germans* (Oxford 1965)
J. M. Wallace Hadrill *The Barbarian West 400–1000* (London 1952)

BACKGROUND READING

M. Bloch *Feudal Society* (London and Chicago 1961)
F. W. Buckler *Harun'il Rashid and Charles the Great* (Cambridge Mass. 1931)
Cambridge Economic History 2 vols. (Cambridge and New York 1942 & 1952)
H. Fichtenau *The Carolingian Empire* (London and New York 1954)
A. Fliche and V. Martin *Histoire de l'Eglise* vols. 5 & 6 (Paris 1934)
J. de Ghellinck *Littérature laterie du moyen âge* vol. 1 (Paris 1932)
A. Grabar and C. Nordenfalk *Early Medieval Painting from the Fourth to Eleventh Century* (Geneva and New York 1957)
J. Hubert, J. Porcher, and W. F. Volbach *Carolingian Art* (London 1970)
M. L. W. Laistner *The Intellectual Heritage of the Early Middle Ages* (Oxford and New York 1957)
R. Latouche *The Birth of the Western Economy: Economic Aspects of the Dark Ages* (London and New York 1961)
W. Levison *England and the Continent in the Eighth Century* (Oxford 1956)
E. Patzelt *Die Karolingische Renaissance* (Vienna 1924, reprinted 1965)
J. W. Thompson *Economic and Social History of the Middle Ages 300–1300* (New York 1959)
L. Wallach *Alcuin and Charlemagne: Studies in Carolingian History and Literature* (New York 1959)

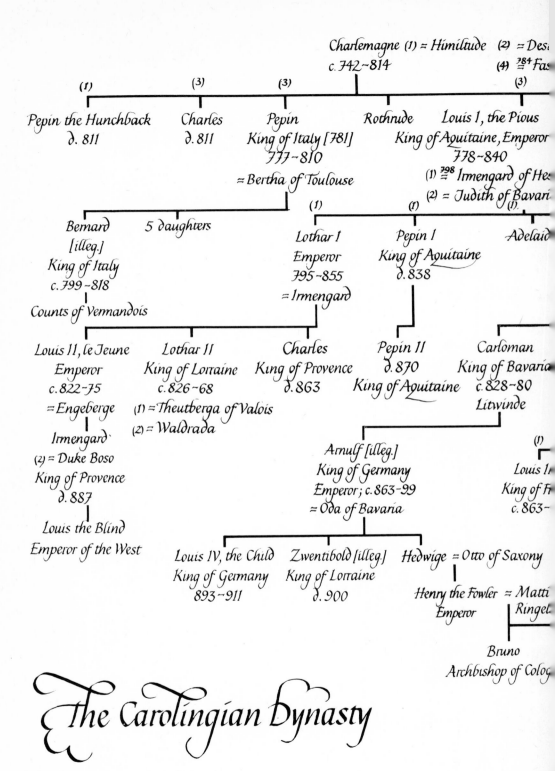

Charlemagne (1) ≈ Himiltude   (2) ≈ Des...
c. 742~814   (4) ²⁸⁴ Fas...

(1)	(3)	(3)		(3)

Pepin the Hunchback
d. 811

Charles
d. 811

Pepin
King of Italy [781]
777~810
≈ Bertha of Toulouse

Rothrude

Louis 1, the Pious
King of Aquitaine, Emperor
778~840
(1) ⁷⁹⁸ Irmengard of Hes...
(2) ≈ Judith of Bavari...

Bernard
[illeg.]
King of Italy
c. 799~818

Counts of Vermandois

5 daughters

(1)
Lothar I
Emperor
795~855
≈ Irmengard

(1)
Pepin I
King of Aquitaine
d. 838

(1).
Adelaid...

Louis II, le Jeune
Emperor
c. 822~75
≈ Engeberge

Irmengard
(2) ≈ Duke Boso
King of Provence
d. 887

Louis the Blind
Emperor of the West

Lothar II
King of Lorraine
c. 826~68
(1) ≈ Theutberga of Valois
(2) ≈ Waldrada

Charles
King of Provence
d. 863

Pepin II
d. 870
King of Aquitaine

Carloman
King of Bavaria
c. 828~80
Litwinde

Arnulf [illeg.]
King of Germany
Emperor; c. 863~99
≈ Oda of Bavaria

(1)
Louis 1...
King of Fr...
c. 863~

Louis IV, the Child
King of Germany
893~911

Zwentibold [illeg.]
King of Lorraine
d. 900

Hedwige ≈ Otto of Saxony

Henry the Fowler ≈ Matti
Emperor   Ringel...

Bruno
Archbishop of Colog...

The Carolingian Dynasty

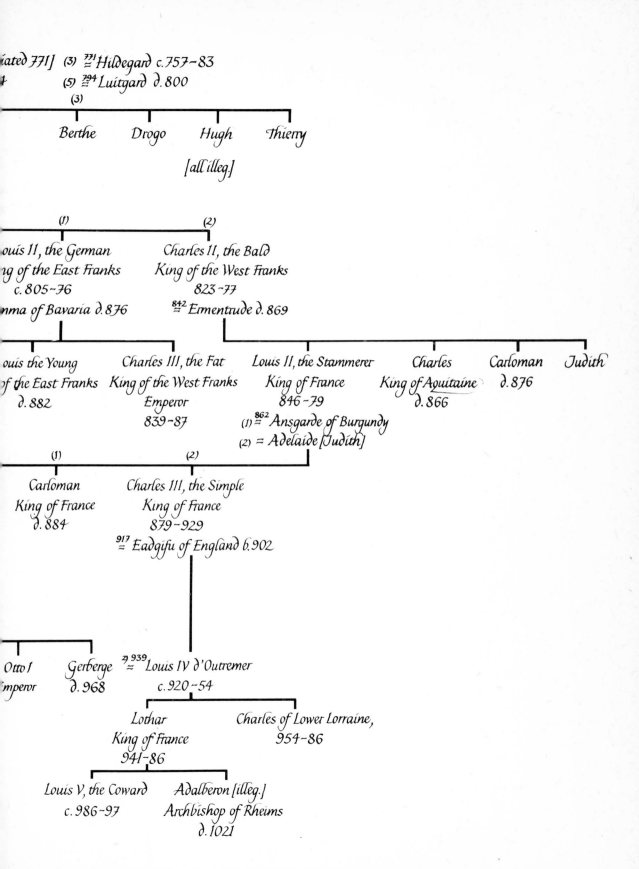

…ated 771] (3) ⁷⁷¹= Hildegard c.757–83

(5) ⁷⁹⁴= Luitgard d.800

(3)

Berthe   **Drogo**   **Hugh**   **Thierry**

[all illeg.]

(1)   (2)

…ouis II, the German   **Charles II, the Bald**
…g of the East Franks   **King of the West Franks**
c.805–76   823–77
…mma of Bavaria d.876   ⁸⁴²= Ermentrude d.869

…ouis the Young **Charles III, the Fat** **Louis II, the Stammerer** **Charles** **Carloman** **Judith**
…f the East Franks **King of the West Franks** **King of France** **King of Aquitaine** d.876
d.882   **Emperor**   846–79   d.866
    839–87   (1)⁸⁶²= Ansgarde of Burgundy
        (2) = Adelaide [Judith]

(1)   (2)

Carloman   **Charles III, the Simple**
King of France   **King of France**
d.884   879–929
     ⁹¹⁷= Eadgifu of England b.902

Otto I **Gerberge** ^{2) 939}= **Louis IV d'Outremer**
…mperor d.968   c.920–54

Lothar   **Charles of Lower Lorraine,**
King of France   954–86
941–86

Louis V, the Coward **Adalberon [illeg.]**
c.986–97   **Archbishop of Rheims**
    d.1021

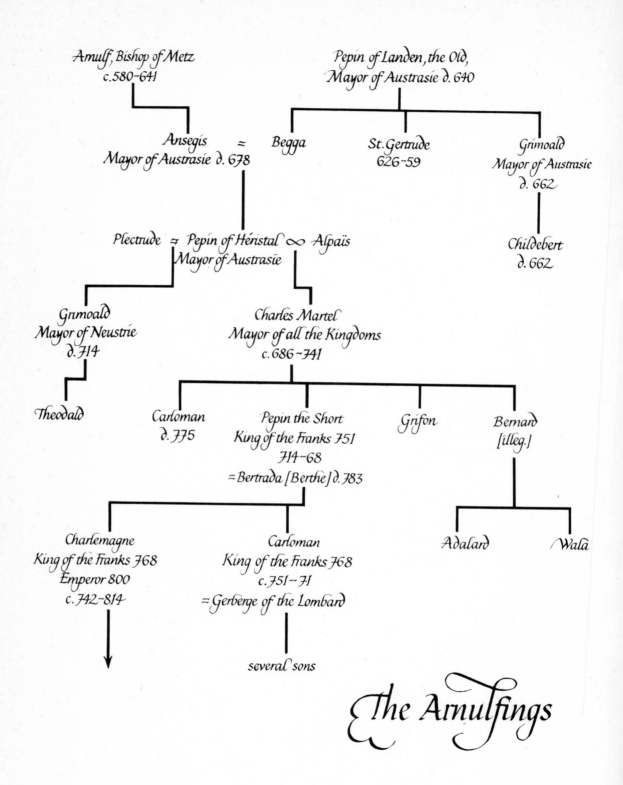

Arnulf, Bishop of Metz
c.580–641

Pepin of Landen, the Old,
Mayor of Austrasie d. 640

Ansegis
Mayor of Austrasie d. 678 ≈ Begga

St. Gertrude
626–59

Grimoald
Mayor of Austrasie
d. 662

Childebert
d. 662

Plectrude ≈ Pepin of Héristal ∞ Alpaïs
Mayor of Austrasie

Grimoald
Mayor of Neustrie
d. 714

Charles Martel
Mayor of all the Kingdoms
c. 686–741

Theodald

Carloman
d. 775

Pepin the Short
King of the Franks 751
714–68
= Bertrada [Berthe] d. 783

Grifon

Bernard
[illeg.]

Charlemagne
King of the Franks 768
Emperor 800
c. 742–814

Carloman
King of the Franks 768
c. 751–71
= Gerberge of the Lombard

Adalard

Wala

several sons

𝔈he Arnulfings

Index